BRIGHTON AND ITS COACHES

A HISTORY OF THE

LONDON AND BRIGHTON ROAD

WITH SOME ACCOUNT OF THE PROVINCIAL COACHES

THAT HAVE RUN FROM BRIGHTON

BY

WILLIAM C. A. BLEW, M.A.

(EDITOR OF VYNER'S "NOTITIA VENATICA" AND RADCLIFFE'S "NOBLE SCIENCE
OF FOX-HUNTING")

WITH TWENTY ILLUSTRATIONS FROM ORIGINAL WATER-COLOUR

DRAWINGS BY J. & G. TEMPLE

All Coloured by Hand

LONDON

JOHN C. NIMMO

14, KING WILLIAM STREET, STRAND

MDCCCXCIV

PREFACE

FIFTY-TWO years have passed since the opening of the London and Brighton Railway caused the break-up of what was perhaps the best-found, the most popular, and the busiest coach-road out of London. He, there-fore, who can remember even the last flicker of the expiring embers of the "Coaching Era" must have exceeded that uncertain period of life known as middle age; while, if we would hear from living lips of the golden age of Brighton stage-coaching, as it was from, say, 1825, we must listen to an octogenarian. But these old-world coachmen, alas! are growing fewer in number; and their memories, once so amply stored with reminiscences which would now be priceless, from the standpoint of the coaching historian, are not quite so retentive as they once were. Moreover, these ancient artists are difficult to find; and even they cannot convey one back to the earliest days of the Brighton road—that is to say, to the middle of the last century. In venturing to put forth, therefore, some account of the Brighton road, so far as it has been possible to glean its history, I do not claim to do any more than give the dry bones of stage-coaching. It has been my good fortune to converse with more than one of those who drove on the Brighton road in its best days, and their sayings and experiences are incorporated in the following pages: they are, I venture to hope, that little leaven which may go some way towards leavening a whole lump of dry facts.

Still, it were useless to shut one's eyes to the fact
that the table or, more correctly speaking, the box-
seat talk is absent; nor can I say anything of coaching of old from personal experience, my earliest
recollection of the Brighton road dating from about
1857, when, as a small boy, I was taken on Clark's
Age, which ran through Kingston, Dorking, and
Horsham. Somewhat earlier I had travelled on a
white coach with green wheels, which ran, I think,
between Dover and Ramsgate ; and these two journeys
awoke in me a love for stage-coaching, which at the
present time shows no signs of abatement, even though
the road is not in many respects what it was ; but
1 am one of the many who have known nothing
better.

"Nimrod," the late Mr. Birch Reynardson, the late
Captain Haworth, Lord W. Lennox, Captain Malet,
Mr. Stanley Harris ("An Old Stager"), Colonel Corbett, and the contributors to the Badminton Library,
have given us much that is of interest in connection
with stage-coaching ; but these gentlemen have one
and all confined themselves almost entirely to writing
about the history of their own time ; and, so far as
I know, the present is the first attempt to sketch,
in however incomplete a fashion, the history of
any coach-road from the earliest times to the period
of its decay. In so saying, I am not unmindful of
the chapter on "The Coaching Era" in Mr. J. G.
Bishop's interesting work on "Brighton in the Olden
Time," which embraces some of the main features of
the history of the road ; but, as it forms one chapter
only of the book, it was obviously impossible to deal
with the subject *in extenso*. I have apologised above
for having little else to set before the reader than the
dry bones of stage-coach history ; but the provision of
this scanty fare is less my fault than my misfortune,

for it has already been explained that many of those
who could have thrown light upon the coaching of old
have now crumbled to dust like the "machines" they
once drove; my material, therefore, has been almost
exclusively drawn from old newspapers and magazines.
The files of all the Sussex papers have been carefully
searched page by page, from the date of their establishment down to the time when it was no longer in the
power of their respective editors to give coaching news.
The *Times*, *Morning Post*, *Public Advertiser*, *Morning
Chronicle*, and other journals, mentioned in the Index,
have been laid under contribution; and so have the
Gentleman's Magazine, the *Annual Register*, and the
Sporting Magazine, together with as many other books
likely to give information as I have been able to discover. In the British Museum I was able to find the
files of the Sussex papers from 1825 only; but the
proprietors of the *Sussex Advertiser* very kindly permitted me to have access to their back numbers; Mr.
Crunden of Brighton was good enough to lend me the
two first volumes of the *Brighton Herald*; Mr. J. G.
Bishop, its proprietor, with equal kindness, allowed me
to ransack the remaining volumes; and Mr. Towner, of
the *Brighton Gazette*, permitted me to search the files
of that journal. I must also acknowledge the assistance
I have received in searching and compiling the Index
from my friend Mr. Edward Penton. To these gentlemen my best thanks are gratefully rendered.

There has been some little doubt as to the best
arrangement of the book. It would probably have
been more readable had all minor details been dis-
carded, and had the more important matters been
treated with a free hand under such headings as "Old
Coaches," "New Coaches," "Fast Coaches," "Slow
Coaches," "Accidents," "Mails," &c., without regard
to chronological order. But there was a desire to

draw up a record of the Brighton road from the earliest times; to show, if possible, how the business of stage-coaching grew; how coaches became more numerous; when they were accelerated; and with what difficulties in the direction of bad weather, accidents, informations, &c., the callings of coach proprietor and coachman were beset. In case the verdict should be that I have come to the ground between two stools, that I have missed the succinctness of a bare chronological record without having succeeded in writing a story to which any interest attaches, I can only plead that a bushel or so of newspaper extracts is not the easiest material out of which to weave a narrative. I have not attempted anything in the shape of an itinerary. As in one form and another the places of interest on the road between London and Brighton have been fully described, the sole object has been to give, as far as possible, a history of the coaches which ran in and out of Brighton. If in another two centuries balloons or some other mode of travel shall have superseded railroads, he who sits down to write a history of trains will search the papers in vain for anecdotes of the engine-drivers and passenger-guards who occupy to-day the position that the Snows, the Hines, and the Millises did sixty years ago.

The twenty illustrations from water-colour drawings by James and George Temple represent the principal points of interest on the Brighton road.

W. C. A. B.

LONDON.
October 1893.

CONTENTS

CHAPTER I.

Modes of spelling—Pepys's Diary—Brighton, her streets and
carriages—Navigation—Descriptions of Brighton—"Merry
Doctor Brighton"—First visit of the Prince of Wales (Ge rge
IV.)—The Pavilion—"Princely Affability"—Mrs. Fitzherbert, her lineage—"Lass of Richmond Hill"—The Prince
and Mrs. Fitzherbert — The Prince marries Caroline of
Brunswick—Sir John Lade—Lady Lade—Sir John Lade's
coachmanship—Colonel Mellish—Sir John Lade and Lord
Cholmondeley—The Marchioness of Conyngham—Absence
of George IV. from Brighton- Smoaker Miles and the Prince
—The Brighton barber.

CHAPTER II.

Badness of Sussex roads—Visit of the Emperor Charles VI.
to Petworth—Horace Walpole—Dr. John Burton's "*Iter
Sussecience*"— Long legged animals in Sussex — Tubb &
Davis's machine—Road-mending—Broad wheels advocated
— Acts of Parliament relating to turnpikes — New roads
— Lewes route to London — Horsham route to London
—Cuckfield route to London—New road by Hickstead—
Protest of inhabitants of Reigate against new road—The
White Hart, Reigate, and George the Fourth's rooms.

CHAPTER III.

The broad-wheeled waggon—Overloaded coaches—Mr. Gammon's
proposed legislation against overloading coaches—Act of

xi

CHAPTER V.

PAGE

coach—Coaches and the carriage of letters—Thames frozen
over in 1814—Mr. Whitbread and his sleigh—Coaching
arrangements in 1814—Green peas at four guineas a pint—
" Imperial condescension "—The Emperor Alexander and
the church congregation.

CHAPTER VII.

French oats at eighteen shillings per quarter—Careless driving
by coachman of the Comet—Coaches for 1815—John Gully's
set-to with "The Chicken"—Hine's light coach—Coach
proprietors and tolls — A test action — Tandem matches
between London and Brighton—A Sussex parson makes
a bet—A trotting-match—Juvenile mendicants—A fast
coach—Breakage of three whips in a journey, and death
of fifteen horses in a week—Pace of the modern Comet—
Collision between the Phœnix and the Dart—Coaches in
1817—French Government and English mail-coaches—A
hint to coachmen—Robbery from a van—Coaches in 1817
—The New Times—A hinged horse-shoe—Death of Mr.
John Palmer—The mail-coach system—A safety-coach—Its
weight—Accident to the Coburg coach—The "Trivector"—
Coaches in 1819.

CHAPTER VIII.

Mr. Milton and his safety-coach—" Accommodation " and " Post "
coaches — Procession of mails on King's birthday — Mr.
Waterhouse's greys—Coaches in 1820—Two Defiances—
New derivation of *safety* coach—Subscription for Whitchurch, coach proprietor—Snowstorm in 1821—Accident
to Snow's coach—" Running with a fury " between London
and Brighton—William Hine's Alert coach—William Genn's
new coach—Breakdown of a safety coach, and capsize of
Brighton mail—Coaches for 1821—Number of coaches on
Brighton road in 1822—Coach advertisement—The common
informer—Price's Islington coach—Coaches from George
and Blue Boar, and Boar and Castle (London)—Summer
coaches—Subscription for booking-clerk—Horse sales at
Rymill's and Maitan's repositories — Accommodation at
George and Blue Boar—Coaches from London to all parts—
Post-horses at Barnet.

CHAPTER IX.

CHAPTER X.

CHAPTER XI.

CHAPTER XIV.

CHAPTER XV.

CHAPTER XVI.

The broad-wheeled waggon—A period of advance—No history of driving—An old Act of Parliament—The carrier period —Improvement in driving must have taken place between 1780 and 1800 — Who invented pole-hook and bars — Leaders drawing from wheelers' traces—The possibly original bar — The coupling rein — Holding reins — Treatises on riding—"Nimrod's" Essays on driving—Driving clubs—Amateurs—The short wheel-rein—Driving with a full hand —Use of the whip—Ancient whips—A day's stock of whip-points—Catching or folding a whip—"Nimrod's" directions for hitting a wheeler—The old coachman and his whip—Expert use of whip not common in "Nimrod's" time—The "flea biting the lobster"—Hitting a leader—Exaggerated stories of—Old and new school of coachmen compared—Collisions—A skilful coachman presuming upon his skill v. a careful muff—Coaching and coach-horses in

PAGE

LIST OF ILLUSTRATIONS.

FROM ORIGINAL WATER-COLOUR DRAWINGS BY J. & G. TEMPLE.
ALL COLOURED BY HAND.

BRIGHTON AND ITS COACHES

CHAPTER I.

BRIGHTON OF OLD.

THE ancient town of Brighthelmstone, now almost a marine suburb of London, is said to derive its name from a Saxon bishop of Selsea, named Brighthelm, who lived there in the time of the Heptarchy. The name of the place has been spelt in a variety of ways; but, in the days of the pack-horse and stage-waggon, people were in no greater hurry to get through their words than they were to reach the end of their journey; probably, therefore, a long name was not objected to in the good old days. But, as the time drew near for men to again impair the stability of a waggon by cutting out one of its "g's," and literally to curtail the programme by snipping off the two final letters of the word, Brighthelmstone came to be called Brighton ; but I believe the identity of the person to whom we owe the contraction has never been ascertained. While, however, the place was described as Brighthelmstone until well into this century in a good many guide-books, road-books, and maps, the *Sussex Advertiser*, the London *Morning Advertiser*, and other newspapers adopted the form Brighton so long ago as 1786, and possibly earlier than that; but then, as well as at a later date, both forms of spelling may be found in the same copy of

A

a newspaper. The editor of the *Gentleman's Magazine*, too, adopted the abbreviated form, for which he was pulled up by a contributor to the second part of the fifty-seventh volume (1787). "Many of your English readers," objected the critic, "will know that you meant Brighthelmstone. Several of them may not know where this new home for our ancient town is. Foreigners will want to know where Brighton is, and they will go north, Yorkshire being the only county according to our maps and indexes in which there is a place so designated." I have tried to find this Yorkshire Brighton, but have not succeeded in so doing; it does not appear in any of the editions of Cary or Paterson.

In his Diary, Samuel Pepys makes casual mention of the fact, under date 17th September 1666, that Captain Balls' ship, the *Success*, called off Brighthelmstone, and that the captain wrote thence to Sir W. Coventry news concerning the French fleet; though what period of time elapsed between the writing and the receipt of the letter we are not told. The excitement consequent upon the Fire of London had kept the cheery old gossip from bestowing the usual amount of attention upon the niceties of his toilet, as on the above-mentioned day (17th September 1666) he wrote, "Up betimes, and shaved myself after a week's growth;" and, having duly admired his changed appearance, Pepys felt constrained to reduce his feelings into writing : "Lord ! how ugly I was yesterday, and how fine to-day !"

May not modern Brighton say the same of herself? When the town consisted of no more than five principal streets—East, Black Lion, Ship, Middle, and West Streets, with North Street receiving the tops of them—she was probably more or less ugly; yet how fine she is to-day—fine in her air, her sea "front," her visitors (some of them), her equipages, and in some of her buildings; while, as we are going to talk about public conveyances, let us add that Brighton is fine in her hackney carriages; for, with the possible exceptions of her near neighbour, Worthing, and the more distant Edinburgh, I know of no place which has equally good vehicles on its ranks.

For at least as long as we know anything about the means of access to Brighton, the place has always been a popular resort; and no wonder. It is the nearest place to London at which one can obtain a glimpse of blue water—the sea of Southend is not as the sea at Brighton—and inhale the glorious sea-air, the finest tonic in the world, according to my way of thinking.

For these, amongst other reasons, Brighton was in favour in the long distant days, when the principal streets above mentioned were "bounded," as Dr. Relhan tells us, "on the west by a large cornfield, on the east by a fine lawn, called the Steine, which runs winding up into the hills for some miles." In Sir W. Burrell's MSS., we are told that in Queen Elizabeth's time there was a bye-law to the effect that "for every sow found unwrung on the Steine where the nets lye," the owner should forfeit one and eightpence for ever, *toties quoties*. The Steine, by the way, is said to have been the camping-ground of Julius Cæsar. Now that large cornfields have to be sought for farther off, and the fine lawn has practically vanished, Brighton delights to call herself the "Queen of watering-places."

In still earlier times, we read, lawless banditti used to infest the coast of Sussex between Brighton and Portsmouth; they would land, break into houses, and then put off to sea again, taking their plunder with them; while in the papers of 1780, and later, are plenty of accounts of collisions between smugglers and the Preventive Service men. Prior to 1761, however, Brighton was a fashionable resort for people to drink salt-water and bathe in the sea; while one old writer,

in trying to account for the fact that sea-bathing dis-
agreed with some of the visitors, attributes it to the
omission on their part to drink the sea-water before
immersing themselves in it. This gentleman must
surely have subscribed to the doctrine that he who
drives fat oxen should himself be fat.

Though Brighton lacks, and always has lacked, a
harbour, the place would appear to have been in early
times a nursery for mariners, as Dr. Relhan informs us
that boys of twelve years old could earn a good living,
and learned navigation at the Free School. Here is
a hint for the School Boards of seaport towns! In
turning over the files of the *Sussex Advertiser* between the years 1788 and 1793, I came across several
advertisements for masters of schools; and in nearly
all of them the ability to teach navigation is either
required, or stated to be an advantage.

A gentleman who spent a month at Brighton in the
summer of 1765, describes the place as being "fifty-
seven miles from London, a small, ill-built town on the
sea-coast, then greatly resorted to in the summer-time
by persons labouring under various disorders, for the
benefit of bathing and drinking sea-water." But,
according to the same authority, it was also visited by
the "gay and polite, on account of the company which
frequented it at that season."

So far back, however, as 1765, Brighton had taken
an upward step. It had previously been described as
"a miserable fishing-village;" but when the above-
mentioned sojourner penned his account for the thirty-
sixth volume of the *Gentleman's Magazine* (1766), it
must have been changing its character. "Until the
last few years," he wrote, "the place was no better
than a mere fishing-town, inhabited by fishermen and
sailors." The men fished, the women making and mend-
ing nets; for as yet boat-letting and mild co-operative

yachting, as exemplified by Mr. Collins's *Skylarks*, had
not been invented, nor had Brighton's simple inhabitants learned that laying themselves out for the
visitors' gold was a more remunerative and less labo-
rious means of gaining a livelihood than going down
to the sea in ships to dredge oysters—they were then
from fivepence to sevenpence a dozen—in the spring ;
catching mackerel or herrings, or setting lobster-pots.

And how, it may be asked, did Brighton come into
notice, and grow, in a comparatively short period, into
a fashionable resort ? Dr. Russell was one of Brighton's
earliest, as well as one of its best friends. He found
himself amongst the fishermen in the middle of the
last century, and was so taken with the place that he
wrote it up, and did for Brighton very much what
Roger Swizzle and Sebastian Mello did for Handley
Cross. Since the time of these most useful puffs,
Brighton has not, to use a common phrase, "looked
back ;" and Dr. Russell, for whom a spacious white
house was built at the southern part of the Steyne, and
who gave his name to a street and a square, fully deserved to have his name and fame handed down to
posterity. Brighton was popular, it would seem, when
the choice lay between the stage-waggon, a vehicle
in which people of quality never travelled, and the
travelling carriage as a means of transit. A journey
by a two-day stage-coach was not too great a price
to pay for a sojourn at the seaside ; Brighton was
sought after in the days of slow coaches and fast
coaches ; while how popular she now is no one needs
to be told. "It is quiet without dulness, busy without
noise, and fashionable without a Court," was the description given of it by Mr. Edward Cobby [1] in 1800.

---

[1] Compiler of the Brighthelmstone Directory for 1800. This rare
book is reprinted in Mr. Bishop's "Brighton in the Olden Time."

Thackeray, as every one knows, christened the place
"Merry Doctor Brighton," a sentiment which would
not seem to be perfectly original.   On the title-page
of a curious little book, called "A Description of
Brighthelmstone and the Adjacent Country; or, The
New Guide for Ladies and Gentlemen," relating to
that place of health and amusement, are the lines :—

> "Of purest air and healing waves we tell,
> Where Welcome Maid Hygeia loves to dwell."

The book was published long ago, and on page 17 the
anonymous author writes: "The inhabitants are remarkable for a strength of constitution; and they are
naturally of alert, active, and sprightly disposition."
It is observed by Dr. Johnson that a fine air must
co-operate with health of body and serenity of mind
"to expand the human features to the fulness of
perfection;" and in a letter to the author of this
pamphlet, the writer said that the "deservedly celebrated Dr. Goldsmith" remarked, upon observing the
health and spirits so strongly expressed in the features
of the inhabitants of Brighthelmstone, that he conceived the following sentiment, which he soon after
introduced in the "Vicar of Wakefield": "As some
men gaze with admiration at the colours of a tulip
or the wing of a butterfly, so I was by nature an
admirer of happy human faces."

Altogether, then, Brighton owes much to the writings
of her early visitors; but had the mayor and corporation
put up a memorial lamp-post in every street—had they
spent the whole of the money bequeathed to them by
Davis, the "Leviathan," in perpetuating the memory
of Brighton's greatest patron—and had they in every
possible way extolled the House of Hanover, they would
never pay in full the debt they owe to George IV.
When Prince of Wales, he decided to make it his

seaside residence ; and from the moment that he carried
out his intention, the fortune of Brighton was made.

The Prince appears to have visited Brighton for the
first time on September 7, 1783, when the townsfolk
were naturally anxious of according a fitting reception
to His Royal Highness. As a part of the ceremony,
they arranged that a salute should be fired from the
battery at the bottom of East Street. The salute went
off very well ; and so, alas ! did one, if not both, of the
arms of the gunner to whom was intrusted the management of the guns. The Prince, who came to know of
the accident which had been unintentionally caused by
the town's loyalty, at once gave an indication of his
kindly nature—it would be unjust to deny him *that*—
by making the remaining days of the mutilated gunner
as comfortable as possible. Brighton, however, was
rather unlucky in connection with her guns, for in
Mr. J. G. Bishop's "Brighton Pavilion and its Royal
Associations," we are told that in the previous year
(1782), when the Princess Amelia visited Brighton
while on a visit to Lord and Lady Pelham, at Stanmer,
the master-gunner, while firing the salute, had one of his
hands so badly shattered that it had to be amputated.

According to Mr. Bishop's book, the Prince had gone
to Brighton to see his uncle, the Duke of Cumberland ;
according to others, it was, after all, by the merest chance
that the Prince went to Brighton at all. Some of
his friends, they say, proposed an expedition thither,
and he joined them, more for the sake of something
to do than for any other reason. At the same time,
so far as a member of the Royal Family can be said
to be house-hunting, the Prince of Wales was certainly
engaged in this occupation. George III., who, if not
without his virtues as a king, does not appear to
have been a great success as a father, managed to
occupy all the royal residences himself, leaving the

junior members of his family to house themselves as
best they could. The Prince of Wales, being at once
struck with Brighton, determined to live there, and at
once entered into negotiations with Mr. Kemp to rent
of him a pretty cottage which stood in what are now the
Pavilion grounds; but this was occupied for a short
time only. His next work was a dwelling on a small
scale, surrounded by small grounds; then alterations
and additions were made; and, in 1784, the hideous
Pavilion was begun; surrounding land and premises
were subsequently leased, and in 1801 the Pavilion and
its adjuncts were bought "out and out." Another
four years saw the completion of the Prince's stables—
now the Dome—which were very complete, and far in
advance, it is said, of anything of the kind then in
existence.

It would possibly have been well for the Prince had
he borne in mind the dictum of Horace Walpole, that
a man should never lay the first stone till he has settled
his children, buried his wife, and hoarded thrice the
amount of the estimate: there is no royal road to
building operations; and the Prince's experience was
that of others. When the Prince of Wales had once
comfortably established himself in his new home, he
proceeded to enjoy himself after his own fashion; and
what that fashion was, we pretty well know. So much
has been written about the Prince's life at Brighton
and elsewhere, that there is no need to go over the
ground again; it will suffice, therefore, to relate an
incident mentioned in the *Sussex Advertiser* of the 20th
of March 1819. It is headed "Princely Affability,"
and it appears that one night when the Prince was in
a merry mood, a phrase which certainly admits of two
meanings, he took it into his head that he would have
supper in the kitchen at the Pavilion. Whenever
royalty steps beyond its own apartments, whether to

open a new building, to depart from a railway station, or to visit a pictur egallery, it appears to be absolutely necessary that a scarlet cloth should be laid down; and so it was in the kitchen, whose "pavement" was forthwith covered; a "splendid" repast was provided, and the good-humoured Prince sat down with a select party of his friends, and spent a joyous hour. "The whole of the servants," we are told, especially the female part, were delighted with this mark of condescension, though whether the great Mr. Weltjé, the Prince's cook, looked upon the intrusion in the same light, is another matter, with which we need not concern ourselves.

Subterranean passages are doubtless great conveniences, even in the prosaic form of subways at underground railway stations; and it has been said that the Brighton Pavilion had two. One of them is reported to have led to the stables, where there was an apartment containing sundry garments and wigs, to enable the Prince and his light-hearted companions to disguise themselves before setting out on their nocturnal rambles—they were fond of hearing the chimes at midnight. The other subterranean passage led to the house of Mrs. Fitzherbert, on the west side of the Steyne—it is now, by the irony of fate, the Young Men's Christian Association, and seems to remind one of the somewhat unchristian manner in which that unhappy and long-suffering lady was treated by her royal husband.

Mrs. Fitzherbert, it may not be out of place to note, came of a good old sporting family. She was born at Tonge Castle, Hants, in 1757; was the daughter of Mr. William Smythe, a Hampshire squire; and was niece of Sir Edward Smythe of Acton Burnell, Salop, whose kinsman, the Sir Edward Smythe of a later date, was master of foxhounds in Shropshire about the year 1815. Her first husband was Mr. Weld of Lulworth

Castle, Dorsetshire; and Mr. Weld, curiously enough, was a great friend of George III., who rarely failed to visit him when staying at Weymouth, to which place he was as much attached as was George IV. to Brighton. At Lulworth it was, then, that the King first saw the girl who was destined to be his future daughter-in-law. Mr. Weld was an ancestor of the gentleman of that name, who subsequently owned the famous cutter *Lulworth*. To Mr. Weld, jun., Mrs. Fitzherbert was married when no more than eighteen years old, and she was a widow before a twelvemonth had passed. Two years later she married Mr. Fitzherbert, of Swinnerton, Staffordshire; but in 1781 she was once more a widow; and, having the comfortable income of £2000 a year, went to live at Richmond, and she has often been called the original "Lass of Richmond Hill;" but, unfortunately, the Richmond Hill of the song is in Yorkshire, and not in Surrey.

It was at Richmond that the Prince, who had gone thither to dine with some of his set at the Star and Garter, first saw Mrs. Fitzherbert, and at once fell in love with her on account of her great beauty, notwithstanding the fact that he was at this time deeply smitten with "Perdita" Robinson, the actress. Mrs. Fitzherbert, however, quite appreciating the force of the Royal Marriage Act, would have nothing to say to her royal adorer, and desired him not to come to her house. Thereupon the Prince is reported to have behaved rather like a maniac. Of self-control he had not a particle. Lord Malmesbury suggested to him a royal alliance, but he indignantly scouted the idea; and after having indulged in the feminine luxury of "a good cry" in the presence of Charles James Fox, assured Lord Malmesbury that he would go abroad, and live as a private person, as soon as he had married Mary Fitzherbert.

To win her hand the Prince had recourse, so the story
goes, to all manner of absurd ruses. One day some of
his emissaries came to the lady's house with the intelligence that George had stabbed himself, and that
she alone could save him. She consented to go on the
condition that some lady of repute went with her. The
Duchess of Devonshire's services were accepted, and away
went the deputation to Carlton House, where Mrs. Fitzherbert's feelings were worked upon, and she consented
to become the affianced wife of the Prince. All that
followed belongs to history rather than to stage-coaching. so it must suffice to say, it is now admitted that
the marriage took place on the 21st December 1785
in Mrs. Fitzherbert's drawing-room ; the officiating
clergyman being Mr. Burt of Twickenham, who many
years afterwards acknowledged, when at the point of
death, that he had performed the marriage ceremony,
and had received the sum of £500 for so doing. In
the Hon. Charles Langdale's Memoirs of Mrs. Fitzherbert, it is stated that the marriage certificate, a letter
written by Mr. Burt, and a memorandum by Mrs. Fitzherbert attached to the letter, together with other
important papers, were lodged at the banking-house
of Messrs. Coutts. Nevertheless, the Prince was mean
enough to allow Fox to state in the House of Commons
that no marriage had taken place ; and when Fox discovered that he had been made a tool of, he promptly
cut the Prince, to whom he declined to speak for
upwards of a year.

In 1795, as the only way out of the difficulties which
had overtaken him, and in which Mrs. Fitzherbert
shared, the Prince married Caroline of Brunswick,
who subsequently made the declaration : " I never
committed adultery in my life, unless it was with Mrs.
Fitzherbert's husband." In about a couple of years
the pair separated, and the Prince once more became

"Mrs. Fitzherbert's husband." After the death of
George IV., his successor acted in the kindly manner
characteristic of the British sailor, and handed over to
Mrs. Fitzherbert every scrap of paper bearing upon the
connection which had subsisted between herself and
his brother, and showed his faith in the theory that
they had been married by asking Mrs. Fitzherbert to
wear widow's weeds for the dead king. Furthermore,
he offered to make her a peeress, a compliment she
declined, stating that she had never brought disgrace
upon the name of Fitzherbert, and she would not
abandon the name then. Through the intervention of
the Duke of York an annuity of £5000 a year was
secured to her, upon which she lived at Brighton,
mixing in the best society, and being respected by all
to the time of her death, which happened in 1837;
and some of Brighton's present *habitués* can, I have
been told, remember this elegant lady and her well-
appointed carriage. By the poor she was a good deal
missed, as she was foremost in the cause of charity,
and her decease was much regretted by persons of all
grades.

All this is perhaps a digression from the main object
of the book ; yet Mrs. Fitzherbert was so much bound
up with the fortunes of Brighton during a good deal
of the period of which this work treats, that it seems
permissible to mention part of this lady's life.

If, however, the Prince was an unfaithful husband
and an indifferent father to his only daughter, he was,
as I have before remarked, a good friend to Brighton.
He was the first to make it a really fashionable resort ;
and whither went "the first gentleman in Europe,"
others were sure to follow. His perch phaeton, drawn
sometimes by four, and sometimes by six horses, was
a familiar sight in Brighton's streets ; and he rarely
failed to drive, or be driven, to the races.

The Prince's informal Master of the Horse, who, for the consideration of £400 a year, also appears to have acted in the capacity of driving-tutor and gentleman-coachman, was that curious character, but excellent waggoner, Sir John Lade, who had to wife a certain Letitia, described as being one of the most abandoned women about the Court. This person was born in Luckner's Lane, in the not very aristocratic region of St. Giles's, and was for some years the *chère amie* of John Ram, the highwayman, better known as "Sixteen-String Jack," who was hanged at Tyburn. His "relict" next passed into the possession of the Duke of York, and was subsequently married to Sir John Lade.

In the course of her early life she had necessarily picked up a great collection of "filthy conjunctions and dissolute nouns," not to mention adjectives and expletives adapted to every occasion; in fact, in strong language her ladyship was more than a match for any of the Prince's party, than which higher praise can scarcely be awarded her. The Prince himself acknowledged her superiority in this line; and when he heard any one giving vent to language more than ordinarily blasphemous, he was accustomed to say: "Why! he swears almost as well as Letitia Lade."

One of the exhibitions of coachmanship with which Sir John Lade used to astonish Brighton was to start at a gallop from Castle Square, go up Market Street, passing to the west of Pear Tree House, now, I think, forming a portion of Messrs. Hannington's premises, by the Knibb Pump, which at that period projected into the road at the bottom of the dunes. Then the route lay into what was called Brighton Place, round the corner into Market Street, and so into Castle Square again.

Another of the Prince's intimates was Colonel Mellish, who, having come into a huge fortune on attaining his

majority, addressed himself to the task of running
through it in the least possible time. When seventeen
years old he obtained a commission in the 18th Light
Dragoons, but subsequently exchanged into the 10th
Hussars, of which regiment the Prince of Wales was
colonel; and at that time he was guilty of such
reckless extravagance as to fairly surprise the Prince
himself, who was only too ready to give Mellish
permanent leave of absence, lest by his example he
should bring half the officers in the corps to beggary.
Like Sir John Lade, Colonel Mellish was an excellent
coachman, and he knew it; for when he drove on to
Lewes race-course on the 25th July 1806, the day set
for the decision of the match between his horse Sancho
and Lord Darlington's Pavilion, he remarked to the
royal party as he took off his white hat to the Prince:
"If Sancho is beat to-day, I hope some of you will
take me for a coachman." On this occasion Colonel
Mellish drove four greys, while the Prince, who sat
on the barouche seat of his carriage, had six greys,
driven by Sir John Lade. Buckle, whose colours
were white jacket with crimson sleeves, rode Sancho,
Pavilion being ridden by the younger Chifney, in a
light orange jacket with gold stripes. Sancho broke
down close to home; Pavilion won easily, and the
sun of Colonel Mellish set soon afterwards.

Prior to this, however, Sir John Lade had made a
bet that he would carry Lord Cholmondeley twice
round the Steyne within a given time. His Lordship
was a stalwart man, and news of the wager having
been noised abroad, there was an enormous concourse
of people "to see the dwarf carry the giant." Both
came to the scratch at the time appointed, and Lord
Cholmondeley approached his bearer to get on his
back. "Not so fast, please," said Sir John; "please
to strip first; I did not say I would carry your clothes;

my wager was that I would carry you, so strip and
we'll begin." Lord Cholmondeley naturally protested
against this stipulation ; but the Baronet remained
obdurate—he declined to carry his Lordship's clothes ;
and the story goes that, as he declined to strip, the bet
was decided in favour of Sir John Lade.

"Public opinion in England, under the inspiration
of the Whigs," wrote that well-informed chronicler,
Captain Gronow, "raised a cry of indignation against
the Prince. It was imagined, I presume, that a royal
personage should be born without heart or feeling;
that he should have been able to live only for the good
of the state, and for the convenience of his creditors.
. . . It is well known that the Prince eventually became
so unpopular as to exclude himself as much as possible
from public gaze. His intimate companions after the
trial of Queen Caroline were Lords Conyngham and
Fife. . . . These gentlemen generally dined with him,
the dinner being the artistic product of that gastronomic
savant, Wattier. . . . When he became George IV., no
change took place in the *personnels* at these banquets,
excepting that with the fruits and flowers of the table
was introduced the beautiful Marchioness of Conyngham, whose brilliant wit, according to the estimation of
his Majesty, surpassed that of any other of his friends,
male or female.

Some of the leaders of Brighton society are said to
have in some way snubbed the Marchioness of Conyngham, and this, they hint, was the reason of the King
turning his back on his once beloved Brighton. He
found London and Windsor agree with him very well,
and visited the Pavilion no more after about 1824.

The grief of the Brighton reporter at this period
knew no bounds. For weeks and weeks at a stretch
he began his column of local news by lamenting the
continued absence of " our beloved King," "our amiable

monarch," " our liberal benefactor," &c., &c.   In one
week he would announce there was a rumour that the
Pavilion would be again inhabited; in the next he
grieved that the hope of the Brightonians had not been
realised.   Then the local correspondent would express
misgivings lest the continued absence of the King
should have a prejudicial effect upon the society and
trade of Brighton.

When, however, the intelligence reached his ears
that the housemaids had been seen applying some
polishing cream to the Pavilion furniture, an operation
which was supposed to point to the speedy return of
royalty; and when a couple of painters were discovered
at work, and a member of the King's household came
down from town, the local man's cup of joy was well-
nigh full—until it became his duty to say that the
messenger had merely come down to pack and remove
a portion of the royal wardrobe.

Nevertheless, although George IV. never visited
Brighton again, he had given it what most places and
undertakings stand in need of—a good start.   As a
matter of fact, Brighton got on very well without its
" beloved benefactor," and continued, as in 1766, to
be the resort of, amongst others, " the idle and dissi-
pated."

To go back, however, for a moment to an earlier
time, baths, bathing-men, and bathing-women appear
to have sprung into existence as soon as there was the
slightest demand for them.   By 1770 even the fishermen were able to find tenants for such rooms as they
could spare; while a baker who took some empty premises never had a room to let during the summers of
1790 and 1791.

But the mention of bathing-men reminds me that
there was one, a certain Smoaker Miles, who attained
to the dignity of " a character."   The Prince, it would

appear, had a private bathing-machine at the bottom of East Street, and when His Royal Highness bathed, Smoaker Miles kept watch to see that no harm came to him. One day, however, the Prince swam out sea-wards farther than Miles thought was compatible with safety, so he loudly vociferated, "Mr. Prince, Mr. Prince, come back, Mr. Prince." "Mr. Prince," however, when he had once got clear of the leading-strings with which his old-fashioned father had en-circled him, was accustomed to having his own way, and heeded not the entreaties of Smoaker Miles. The bathing-man, however, felt that he had a duty to perform, and so, swimming out to the Prince, he, according to an ancient chronicler, caught him by the "lugg"—a man in bathing costume is not easily handled—and, to use a homely phrase, "towed him ashore." In no measured terms did the Prince expos-tulate, but Smoaker Miles was equal to the occasion, and excused himself for his prompt action by declaring to his patron that "your father, the King, shall not hang me for allowing his son to drown." Miles had no doubt been at sea, and knew the value of discipline.

Smoaker Miles seems altogether to have been a man who lacked not the spirit of repartee, for on another occasion, whilst loafing about waiting for business, he was asked by two dandies, then lately arrived from London, where they could best procure asses' milk, which they had been recommended to take for the benefit of their health? The old bathing-man is re-ported to have looked them up and down, and to have answered their question with the curt reply, " Suck each other." About the year 1790 the Prince of Wales had a racehorse called Smoaker, and he was doubtless thus named after the eccentric Smoaker Miles.

Towards the close of the last century Brighton boasted another "character," a barber; and from the length of

B

his advertisements we may conclude that so long ago
as 1798 the number of possible patrons was sufficient
to make it worth his while to announce himself, which
he did in these words :—

To the inhabitants of the town of Brighton, also to the Nobility
and Gentry of either sex, who may resort to that fashionable watering-
place the coming season, for the pleasure or benefit of Bathing.

This is intended to inform the world that a native of London,
Mr. GEORGE FERDINAND AUGUSTUS CHARLEMORE, has had the honour
of carrying arms in the Middlesex Militia, and was particularly
distinguished in the course of the last Campaign, when he had the
good fortune to be employed in some eminent services at Dover
Castle, the advanced fortress of His Majesty's British dominions. He
combines the intrepidity of *Alexander* with the caution of *Fabius :*
his principles patriotic ; equal to *Cæsar* as a man, nor inferior to
Brutus as the friend to liberty ; amorous as *Anthony*, and like
him, too, an irresistible person. Incorrupt as *Aristides ;* patient as
Socrates ; eloquent as *Cicero*. In manners and address what *Chesterfield* was, *he is*. Although a stranger to *Locke*, and unacquainted
with *Newton*, he is familiar with the Seven Wise Masters.

This extraordinary young man, since the conclusion of the war,
received his discharge from the service of his country—not enriched
by plunder, rapine, or extortion. Poor as *Fabricius* he retires, and
now practises the improvement of those heads *without* which nothing
can improve *within*.

** He is avowedly the first Hair-dresser, Shaver, and Wig-
Maker of the present Age ; and humbly solicits that encouragement
and support his transcendent abilities and exalted virtues so justly
demand.

P.S.—He condescends to shave the poor almost *gratis*, viz., for
a PENNY each.

Chapter II

IN the previous chapter a hasty outline has been given
of old Brighton and its surroundings. Before going
on, however, with the history of stage-coaches between
London and Brighton, it may be convenient to say a few
words in connection with a couple of matters the understanding of which may make plainer what is hereafter
written. These matters are the roads and routes between
London and Brighton ; and secondly, some of the legislation which governed mail and stage coaches.

The Sussex roads would seem to have enjoyed an un-
enviable notoriety for badness from a very early period.
When the Emperor Charles VI. came to England (having
claimed the title of King of Spain) in 1703, and went to
visit the Duke of Somerset, whose seat was at Petworth,
it is on record that his coach was capsized a dozen
times ere he arrived within measurable distance of his
destination. Whether the Emperor—he had been no
stranger to hardships—mildly protested against the
risk and discomfort to which he was subject, or
whether his attendants became alarmed for the monarch's safety, does not appear ; but, at any rate, during
the latter part of the journey, the services of some
sturdy Sussex labourers were secured, and they, by
planting their shoulders against the vehicle, kept it
right side uppermost until it drew up at the portals
of Petworth House, to the great delight, no doubt, of
the royal passenger. Horace Walpole, too, has told
us how he despised the Sussex roads.

19

Dr. John Burton, who, in his "*Iter Sussexiense,*" gave an account of the Sussex roads, as he found them in 1751, is equally uncomplimentary. " I fell immediately upon all that was most bad, upon a land desolate and muddy, whether inhabited by men or beasts a stranger could not easily distinguish, and upon roads which were, to explain concisely what is most abominable, Sussexian. No one would imagine them to be intended for the people and the public, but rather the by-ways of individuals, or, more truly, the tracks of cattle-drivers; for everywhere the usual footmarks of oxen appeared, and we too, who were on horseback, going on zig-zag almost like oxen at plough, advanced as if we were turning back, while we followed out all the twists of the road. Not even now, though in summer time, is the wintry state of the roads got rid of; for the wet even now in this mud is sometimes splashed upwards all of a sudden, to the annoyance of travellers. Our horses could not keep their legs on account of these slippery and rough parts of the road; but sliding and tumbling on their way, and almost on their haunches, with all their haste got on but slowly. . . . Why is it that the oxen, the swine, the women (note the doctor's table of precedence!), and all other animals are so long-legged in Sussex? May it be from the difficulty of pulling the feet out of so much mud by the strength of the ankle, that the muscles get stretched, as it were, and the bones lengthened?"

Sussex roads, therefore, had an evil reputation in bygone times; but the doctor perhaps forgot that not in Sussex only, but in all clay countries, the soil does its own puddling.

As the early van and coach proprietors lived at Lewes, and worked to Brighton, their conveyances, of course, travelled to London from Brighton through

Lewes, for as yet there was no independent Brighton coach or other conveyance. That convenience did not arise much, if at all, before 1780, when Tubb and Davis's machine went through Steyning.

As coach and van traffic continued to expand, attention was more and more directed to the state of the roads ; but while several laudable experiments were made in the art of road-mending, a good many surveyors, and others, were of opinion that their labour would be all in vain so long as vehicles were allowed to have narrow wheels. Consequently they agitated for a Bill to render broad wheels compulsory, advocating a width which would cause the wheel not only to discharge its own functions with regard to the vehicle, but to act as a roller to the roads as well. When, however, we read that about sixteen hundred Acts of Parliament, having to do with turnpikes, were passed between 1761 and 1810, it is clear that the subject of highways received no little attention.

In addition to the making and repairing of the roads, however, it was soon noticed that much time and distance might be saved by levelling, or at least reducing, hills, and making new thoroughfares to cut off corners ; and, so far as the Brighton roads are concerned, these improvements were early suggested, or rather they pressed themselves upon the notice of the then not very large coaching world. The road by Falmer, on the way to Lewes, was a difficulty ; while to drive to London *viâ* Cuckfield, or Henfield and Horsham, involved the climbing of sundry steep hills, and the travelling of a somewhat circular route into the bargain.

In the following pages the coaches are described as going to London by three chief routes, and it may save trouble if these are specified at the outset.

I. Through LEWES.—By this route the distance from

Brighton to London was 58 miles; and horses were
changed at Lewes (8 miles), Uckfield (8 miles), East
Grinstead (13 miles), Godstone (10 miles), and Croydon (9 miles), from which place to London is 10 miles,
so that the coaches going by this road used six teams.

II. Through HORSHAM.—This road was one mile
shorter than *viâ* Lewes, viz. 57 miles. The Brighton
horses ran through Poynings to Henfield (10 miles);
the second team went to Horsham (10 miles); the
team from Horsham did 13 miles to Dorking, whence
to Epsom was but nine miles; but the Epsom horses
had fifteen miles to cover before they reached London.

III. Through CUCKFIELD.—This was the shortest
and by far the most fashionable of the three routes.
The post-chaises, private carriages, and most of the
coaches travelled by this road. Leaving Brighton, the
first team worked to Cuckfield (14 miles), whence the
fresh horses ran to Crawley (10 miles). The next
change was Reigate (9 miles), from which place there
was an eleven miles run to Sutton, where the London
horses were taken on for their ten miles' journey.

In course of time, however, this route became subject
to material alterations. On reaching Pyecombe, the
way to Cuckfield was straight on to Clayton Hill; but
the road-making operations at Pyecombe, which had
their origin in more effectually opening out Henfield,
led also to the making of the road to Hickstead, through
what the old newspapers were accustomed to call the
"well-wooded vale of Newtimber," and by this road,
which was opened in 1813, Clayton Hill, and of course
Cuckfield, were avoided; but some coaches still continued to run through Cuckfield and Reigate. Eventually came the proposition to make a new cutting to
the eastward to meet the Horley road, whereupon the

THE WHITE HEIFER GATE.

inhabitants of Reigate, unwilling to be deprived of the custom which coaching and posting brought them, protested against the proposed innovation. They argued that, as the Prince of Wales always travelled through Reigate, all the King's subjects should do likewise. Maps were produced; distances were quoted; and the Reigate folk proved to their own complete satisfaction that the best and quickest way to London was through their town : figures proved anything and everything. The White Hart, then as now, was the chief hotel in the place; and under the guidance of Mr. Girton, the present proprietor, who ministers to the wants of travellers by the modern " Magnet " coach, reminiscences of the Brighton road are still to be seen there in the shape of the rooms the Prince used to occupy when he halted on his travels between the Brighton Pavilion and Carlton House.

The Reigate protest was not, however, strong enough to check the march of improvement. In spite of opposition, the new road was made ; and, though Reigate was no longer the shortest way to London, it would not have been expedient for every coach to have travelled by the same route ; so as the coaches increased in numbers they took different roads. Some went the quickest way, some by Cuckfield, some by Balcombe, and others by Reigate ; while the entry into London was also made by a variety of ways. Then there were one or two coaches which at different dates ran through Ditchling and Lindfield.

CHAPTER III.

STAGE-COACH LEGISLATION.

WE are a good deal in the dark as to the precise pattern of the early coaches. The forerunner of the stage-coach was, of course, the broad-wheeled waggon drawn by six or eight horses, which were controlled by a man who rode a stout cob. In course of time came vehicles which, whatever their construction, were known as coaches. Some of these carried no outside passengers at all, as the advertisements tell us. On other vehicles, however, the coachmen were accustomed to crowd as many passengers as they could find room for. There would not at first appear to have been any regular seats for them, as they sat on the luggage on the roof, and hung on as best they could. The coaches were high, and, when fully loaded, very top-heavy; while, as the roads were bad, upsets were of everyday occurrence; and so many of the King's subjects were either killed or injured that the papers took notice of it, and were for ever pointing out the risks to which coach-passengers were exposed. In Mr. Gammon the advocates for safety found a champion for their cause. The late Mrs. Giaccometti Prodgers was not more resolved to compel cabmen to walk in the paths of rectitude than was Mr. Gammon to cause to be passed a Bill having for its object the limiting of the number of passengers to be carried on the roof of a coach. At last he obtained permission to bring in a Bill; and, according to the Journal of the House of Commons for the 19th of May 1788, the Bill was read a first time and ordered to be printed.

This measure was stringent enough in all conscience, as it not only limited the passengers to a number which would have prevented any coach from paying its way ; but it also provided that any coachman who infringed the enactment might be forthwith arrested, with or without a warrant, at the instance of any person or persons who saw the offence committed. These propositions naturally called forth a protest from the coaching interest, the outcome being a petition that they might be heard by counsel against the Bill, which was considerably modified before it became law. In the same year, however (1788), the Act was passed. It was the 28th George III. c. 57, and was called an Act "for limiting the number of persons to be carried on the outside of stage-coaches or other carriages." It was an enactment which put money into the pocket of the common informer—a sneaking sort of rascal, who, nevertheless, performed some service for the good of the community.

The preamble of the above Act stated that "great mischiefs frequently arise and bad accidents happen by reason of an improper number of persons being allowed to go as passengers on the roofs or boxes of coaches, chaises, and other carriages of the like sort travelling for hire." In the hope of ensuring greater safety for travellers, the Act decreed that on and after the first of November 1788, no more than six persons should "at one and the same time ride or go upon the roof, or more than two persons besides the driver on the box." For every person in excess of the proper number, the coachman was, on conviction, liable to a penalty of forty shillings ; while, if the offending coachman happened to be also the proprietor of the coach, the maximum penalty was four pounds. In

default of payment, the offenders were to go to prison,
" without bail or mainprise," for a month, unless the
penalty were sooner paid. If the coachman could not
be found, the proprietor could be proceeded against;
and by way of stimulating a general interest in the
enforcement of this Act, it was decreed that half of
the penalty should go to the informer, and the other
half to the surveyor of highways for the parish or place
where the offence was committed.

Two years later it was admitted that the above
Act had " proved insufficient to answer the good purposes thereby intended." It was, as a daily newspaper
pointed out, transgressed every hour; and one correspondent to a Brighton paper went so far as to say
that the evil of overloading coaches would never be
checked until a fine of twenty pounds was inflicted
upon each of the persons who mounted the coach after
the proper number were seated.

The failure of Mr. Gammon to pass his original Bill
brought forth the following verses in the columns of
the *Public Advertiser* :—

ON STAGE COACHES.

Whene'er a loaded Stage drives by
    With more than it *should* draw,
We view the *outside* group, and cry,
    " That's contrary to Law."

But all the folks who clamour thus
    Are totally mistaken,
For *Gammon's* Bill did never *pass*,
    So Coachmen *save their Bacon*."

In order more effectually to accomplish the end the
Legislature had in view, the 30th George III. c. 36
was passed, to take effect on the 29th September 1790.
The new provisions were that—(1.) On a coach drawn
by three or more horses, the maximum number of out-

side passengers should be one on the box and four on
the roof. (2.) If the coach were drawn by less (sic)
than three horses, one on the box and three on the roof ;
but (3.) One on the box and four on the roof might be
carried by a pair-horse coach which did not travel
more than twenty-five miles from the General Post-
Office.

Instead of leaving it to chance and the common
informer whether the offenders were proceeded against
or not, the framers of this new Act conceived the idea
of making the "pikemen" the officers of the law, so
the statute provided that the coachman who carried
more than his proper number of passengers should pay
to the collector of tolls at *every turnpike gate* through
which the vehicle passed a sum of five shillings for
every passenger in excess of the proper number.

A simple way of evading this Act would have been
to set down the excess number of passengers before
reaching a gate, and to take them up afterwards ; but
the penalty for so doing was imprisonment without
the option of a fine.

Another section made it compulsory that, with the
exception of the mails, every coach should have upon
the outside of each door the name of the proprietor,
painted in large and legible characters. Under some old
Act having a clause of similar import, a rather amusing
case was reported in the papers. A carrier was summoned for not having his name painted on his van as
the Act directed. By way of showing that he had not
offended, the carrier brought the board, when it was
seen that the name was painted in Old English. The
bench objected that the spirit of the Act had been
infringed, whereupon the carrier retorted that he had
seen a true copy of the Act, and had ordered his board
to be painted in the same lettering as that in which
the Act was written. He got off.

It may possibly be taken as a hint that the amateur
coachman was getting abroad at this time, as the 4th
section forbade the coachman, under a five-pound
penalty, to allow any one but himself to drive without
the consent of the passengers " within each coach "—
the outsides, who could see what was going on, were
apparently supposed to take care of themselves. Moreover, the coachman was not to quit the box without
reasonable occasion, or for a longer time than was
absolutely necessary. He was not to drive furiously,
nor was he by any negligence or misconduct to overturn the carriage, or in any manner endanger the
persons or property of the passengers. Then, section
5 provided that no guard should fire off the arms he
was intrusted with, either while the coach was going
on the road, or going through, or standing in, any
town, except it was for the defence of his coach. The
penalty for any causeless firing was twenty shillings—
just one-fifth, it will be observed, of the maximum
penalty imposed upon the coachman for letting somebody else drive, or for quitting his box without reasonable excuse.

This subsequent Act, like the first one, was in 1806
admitted to have failed to achieve its object; consequently a third was passed, and by it a concession was
made to coach proprietors by allowing twelve people to
be carried in summer and ten in winter; but this Act
was again repealed by another passed in 1811, which
contained, *inter alia*, a provision that no driver or proprietor might permit any luggage to be carried on the
roof of a coach, or any person to ride as an outside
passenger, if the top of the coach should be more than
8 feet 9 inches from the ground, or the bearing of
which on the ground should be less than 4 feet 6 inches
from the centre of the off wheel to the centre of the
near wheel. The penalty for infraction was five pounds ;

and it is curious to note that the top of a modern coach
is barely 6 feet 11 inches from the ground; so what a
vehicle, the top of which was 8 feet 9 inches from the
ground, must have looked like one can only guess at.

The modern coachman, too, may smile on reading
the 5th section, which deals with the object of lowering
the height of stage coaches, so that more luggage might
be carried. It says that it should be lawful to carry
luggage and parcels on the roof of any coach to a
greater height than two feet, so long as the top of the
burden was not at a greater height from the ground
than 10 feet 9 inches; and then by a further Act—2nd
and 3rd William IV., cap. 120—passed in 1832, ten
outside passengers were allowed as the maximum for a
four-horse coach. Other provisions were also made ap-
plicable to pair-horse coaches, and to vehicles licensed
to carry more than four inside, while the top of the
luggage carried on the roof was not to be more than
8 feet 9 inches from the ground. There were, in addition, other provisions. More than the proper number
of persons could not be carried inside a coach—a regula-
tion made in the interest of the comfort of the passengers; but a child under seven counted as half a passenger, and might be carried with the others. These
and other Acts of Parliament dealt with licences, duties,
and various matters, with which it is unnecessary to
trouble the reader. This last mentioned Act gave the
whole penalty to the Crown; but it left power to the
Court to give a common informer what portion of the
penalty it thought fit.

CHAPTER IV.

THE BRIGHTON ROAD IN THE LAST CENTURY.

ONE may very fairly say of stage-coaching, on the
Brighton as well as on other roads, what Eutropius
said of Rome—that it originated in a very small way;
but when it arrived at its highest state, there was
nothing bigger in the whole world. Our easy-going
forefathers, some of them, at least, were thankful for
small mercies. Had the worthy Chamberlayne, for
instance, lived in later years, how he would have
enjoyed himself in the era of fast coaches, and what
spirited descriptions he would have written of the
Devonport Mail, the Manchester Telegraph, the Brighton
Age, Magnet, and others! He must have possessed a
real love for coaching, for he saw much to admire in it
as long ago as 1649, when he published "The Present
State of Great Britain." "Besides the excellent arrangement of conveying men and letters on horseback," he wrote, "there is of late such an admirable
commodiousness, for both men and women to travel
from London to the principal towns in the country,
that the like hath not been known in the world; and
that is by stage-coaches, wherein (not whereon) any one
may be transported to any place sheltered from foul
weather and foul ways, free from endangering of one's
health and one's body by hard jogging or over-violent
motion; and this not only at a low price (about a
shilling for every five miles), but with such velocity
and speed in one hour as that the post in some foreign

countries cannot make in one day." Happy indeed
was the man who regarded four miles an hour in the
light of an express.

Thirteen years after Chamberlayne wrote his panegyric
on stage-coaching, that is to say, in 1662, it is said that
there were but half-a-dozen stage-coaches in England,[1]
and this number was six too many in the opinion of a
certain Mr. Cressett. This pessimist, who lived in the
Charterhouse, wrote a tract in which he pointed out
the injury coaches would cause to society at large. By
this rapid mode of travelling—in 1640 it generally took
three days to get from London to Dover—gentlemen
would come to London upon the slightest pretext—to
get their hair cut, for example—which, but for these
abominable coaches, they would not do "but upon
urgent necessity." Nor did the impending evil end
here, for their wives would come too ; and when a man
and his wife found themselves in London, they would
"get fine clothes, go to plays and treats, and by these
means get such a habit of idleness and love for
pleasure that they are uneasy ever after." Poor Mr.
Cressett ! he must have been a direct ancestor of
Mr. Wightman, who, just before the commencement
of the London and Brighton Railway, wrote a book
and proved, entirely to his own satisfaction, that no
train could ever travel faster than at half the speed
of the fast coaches !

Brighton's earliest visitors must have ridden on
horseback ; travelled in their own carriages ; have been
content to travel by the primitive stage-waggon ; or
be drawn by oxen.

Chamberlayne's passage in praise of stage-coaching

[1] This oft-made statement would appear to be rather erroneous,
unless the argument be that there were no more than six vehicles
whose build and construction could be called coaches.

was so highly approved of by a later writer, a Mr. De
Laune, who in 1681 put forth "The Present State of
London," that the latter annexed Chamberlayne's paragraphs in their entirety.   De Laune, however, is useful
for our purpose, inasmuch as he gives a list of coaches
and stage-waggons running out of London.   Nearly at
the head of the list I find that Thomas Blewman, a
carrier, came from Bredhempstone to the Queen's
Head in Southwark on Wednesday, and went out
on Thursday, "Shoreham same day."   It must be
admitted that "Bredhempstone" cannot be said to do
more than bear some resemblance to Brighthelmstone;
but I feel pretty sure that the two places are identical.
In the first place, De Laune spells very many of his
places in a manner peculiar to himself; secondly,
"Shoreham same day" would almost lead one to suppose that the Bredhempstone van ran on to Shoreham;
and thirdly, because in the list we read what were the
means of communication with Croydon, Clapham, East
Grinstead, Horsham, Petworth, Reigate, and Wad-
hurst, all of them places on, or bordering on, the road
to Brighton.

The next earliest reference to public conveyances
between London and Brighton that I can find is
contained in an old work called "New Remarks on
London," compiled by the Company of Parish Clerks,
and issued in 1732.   From that ancient publication
I gather that a coach left the Talbot, Southwark, for
Brighthelmstone on Thursdays, and that a van departed
from the Talbot and George inns on Tuesdays.   Both
these conveyances must have travelled *via* Lewes,
inasmuch as the same conveyances left the Borough
for that place on the same days on which they were
announced to start for Brighthelmstone.   Possibly
this coach and van took three days to compass the
distance.

The "Traveller's Pocket Companion," published in
London in 1741, purports to give a list of all stage-
coaches and carriers from London, and includes a
waggon to Brighthelmstone from the George, Southwark, on Thursdays, no mention being made of the coach
which seems to have been run when the Company of
Parish Clerks compiled their "Remarks," nine years
earlier. Nor do we find any record of a coach in an
old broad-sheet to which no date is attached, but to
which the British Museum authorities assign the date
1750. This print professes to give all the coaches;
but Brighton is served by a waggon only. Lewes was
slightly better catered for, as there was a coach thither
from the Talbot on Tuesdays and Saturdays; but this
may have run on to Brighton. There was a waggon,
too, on Thursdays. The waggon from the George
may probably have been the "Flying Machine," which
in 1745 was advertised to leave the Old Ship, Brighton,
at 5.30 A.M. in summer, and was due in London on
the same evening. There is a convenient margin left
here; and the proprietor, whoever he was, declined
to bind himself to reach his destination at any particular hour. Still, all things considered, it was no
doubt something of a feat to do the journey in one
day, even though the pace did not exceed four miles
an hour. Another writer tells us that these machines
were fashioned something like the Brighton bathing-
machines. No one was carried on the roof; but
subsequently there was added a big basket contrivance, called a "conveniency," behind, for the
accommodation of half-price passengers: this "convenience," or something like it, was, we are led to
suppose, the invention of one Bonner, a Dutchman,
who was Queen Elizabeth's coachman; but it does
not appear to have come into general use till about
1767; about twenty years later it was also called the

C

"Back Gammon," and was in a larger form added to coaches as a receptacle for outside passengers, in order to avoid the spirit of Mr. Gammon's amended Act, which limited to three, four, or five, the number of passengers carried outside.

It is just possible that the conveyances to Brighthelmstone mentioned by the Company of Parish Clerks and the "Traveller's Pocket Companion" belonged to James Batchelor of Lewes, who, through the medium of the *Sussex Advertiser*, in the course of a newspaper controversy with a rival, informed all whom it might concern, "that our family first set up the stage-coach from London to Lewes, and have continued it from father to son, and other branches of the same race, and that even before the turnpikes on the Lewes road were erected they drove their stage in the summer season in one day, and have continued to do ever since, and now in the winter season twice in the week."

I am, however, rather letting the coach press upon the horses, and must go back a few years to show how Brighthelmstone was served by conveyances. In Mr. Bishop's interesting book, "Brighton in the Olden Time," all these early advertisements are set out at length; but, as they deal rather with carrying than coaching, except here and there in a very primitive form, it has not been thought worth while to reproduce them *in extenso*, though I may here acknowledge my indebtedness to Mr. Bishop's book, as from 1756 to 1770 I have availed myself of his labours as a means of lightening my own.

It seems, then, that about 1746 Thomas Smith, an old Lewes carrier, died, and his widow announced by advertisement that she still carried on the weekly stage between London and Lewes, and I presume that there was an extension to Brighton. At any rate, in

the *Sussex Weekly Advertiser* of the 12th May 1756
there is this advertisement :—

NOTICE IS HEREBY GIVEN, that the LEWES ONE DAY STAGE
COACH or CHAISE sets out from the Talbot Inn, in the Borough,
on Saturday next, the 19th instant.

When likewise the Brighthelmstone Stage begins.

Performed (*if God permit*) by

JAMES BATCHELOR.

Although, as already mentioned, this Mr. Batchelor
notified that for a long period his family had driven
their stage to London in one day, we find him in
May 1757 advertising his "two days' stage-coach," and
he apparently had the road to himself for another five
years, when competition, which subsequently became
so keen on the Brighton road, set in, Messrs. J. Tubb
and S. Brawne having made up their minds to start
the Lewes and Brighthelmstone new flying-machine
(*viâ* Uckfield). This "machine" is described as being
both light and commodious, and hung on steel springs.
It carried four passengers inside, and left the Golden
Cross, Charing Cross, at 6 A.M. on Mondays, Wednesdays, and Fridays for the White Hart at Lewes, and
the Castle, Brighthelmstone. On the alternate days the
machine returned to London. The fare was thirteen
shillings to Lewes, and sixteen shillings to Brighthelmstone. Each passenger was entitled to take 14 lbs.
of luggage free; but all in excess of this weight was
charged for at the rate of a penny a pound for the
entire journey. Children "in lap" and outside passengers—the latter no doubt travelled in the basket
"conveniency" behind—paid half price.

At this time we learn that the "machines" were
not unlike the Brighthelmstone bathing-machines;
the coachman drove four horses in hand, and his

extra leaders were ridden by a lad ; but Batchelor, in response to the opposition of Tubb and Brawne, lost no time in starting "a new large flying chariot with a box and four horses, *viâ* Chailey, to carry two passengers only, except three should desire to go together;" and he reduced his fares. Then the rival proprietors rushed into print, and a series of blasts and counterblasts were published, which, though by no means unamusing reading, do not throw much light on coaching.

However, Tubb and Batchelor carried on their opposition vehicles till 1760, when Batchelor's death left the upstart Tubb master of the situation. His first step was to take into partnership a Mr. Davis, and these two proprietors seem to have carried on business in a state of brotherly love for a long time. Seven years later, that is to say, in 1767, the partners put on a double conveyance, a "Fly," leaving London and Brighton every day, the route being through Uckfield and Lewes.

In 1770, whatever the cream of the Brighton road may have been, it was apparently skimmed by Tubb and Davis, who had a "machine" and a waggon at work ; but in 1777 they had to encounter the opposition of Lashmar and Company ; and one firm or the other appears to have been most energetic, as in a London Directory for 1777–78 I find that a diligence ran daily between Brighthelmstone and the Bull and Gate, Holborn, leaving either end at six o'clock in the morning, and carrying passengers for fifteen shillings a head. Then, according to the same publication, a coach ran to Brighthelmstone from the Golden Cross, Charing Cross, at five o'clock on the mornings of Monday, Tuesday, Wednesday, Thursday, and Saturday during the summer, and at six on Tuesdays only in the winter. The proprietor of this conveyance charged but fourteen shillings for the journey. Another diligence ran daily from the Swan with Two Necks, Doctor's Commons, starting at four in the morning, and carrying three passengers at threepence a mile each. A couple of carriers, who left the Borough once a week at three and four respectively in the morning, appear to make up the list of Brighton's conveyances.

In the year 1780, Tubb and Davis's machine set out from the New Ship, Brighthelmstone, on Mondays, Wednesdays, and Fridays, returning on Tuesdays, Thursdays, and Saturdays from the Spread Eagle, Gracechurch Street. This coach passed through Steyning; the fare from London to that place was eleven shillings, and to Brighthelmstone fourteen shillings.

The same firm had also another coach which set out at five o'clock on Monday, Wednesday, and Friday mornings from the Golden Cross, Charing Cross, and took passengers to the Star at Lewes for twelve shillings each, and to the Castle at Brighton for fourteen shillings.

We now, for the first time, hear of Cuckfield on the route from Brighton to London ; and a quaint place it used to be, the White Hart having a sort of outdoor tap, at which subsequently coachmen waiting for up or down coaches, and as many of the villagers who were not better employed, used to congregate.

The Brighthelmstone and Cuckfield machine, then, started from the Swan with Two Necks, Lad Lane, London, at five in the morning on Mondays, Wednesdays, and Fridays, and returned from the Castle at Brighthelmstone on the other three days. The fare to Cuckfield was ten shillings and sixpence, and to Brighton fourteen shillings. A diligence, too, set out from the New Ship, Brighton, on Mondays, Wednesdays, and Fridays at six in the morning, and arrived at the Swan with Two Necks, Lad Lane, at about three in the

afternoon. It returned on the other three days, and
would thus appear to have been a two-end coach, as
no doubt the machine and the diligence were in one
and the same interest, judging from the hour of starting
and the destination.

During the summer of 1784, Tubb and Davis found
the increase in the traffic sufficient to warrant them in
putting on a second light post-coach; while in 1787,
three light post-coaches, two heavy coaches, three
machines, and three waggons ran on the London and
Brighton road.

The year 1789 appears to have been ushered in by
bad weather, as on New Year's day a high wind caused
the snow to drift to a depth of several feet in many
places, though not in such a manner as to interfere
with the main road, " as appears by the regular arrival
of our mails and stage-coaches—the mails at this time
were, on the Brighton roads, carried by boys on horseback—which have not yet been materially retarded."
A week later, the stage-coachmen working in and out
of Brighton declared that they had never been out in
weather like that which prevailed on Thursday the
8th January (1789). It was the keenest day they ever
remembered; it was only with the greatest difficulty
that the horses were induced to face the blizzard, and
the snow had drifted to such a height that the roads
were in some places impassable, while the London
coach, after leaving Lewes, had sometimes to " break
the road " and go over the fields !

Up to the time of which we write no mention can be
found of amateur coachmen on the road, possibly because
there was little or nothing to make stage-coach driving
the pleasure it subsequently became. The coach-boxes
had no springs under them until, at a later date, Mr.
John Warde, the father of fox-hunting, suggested the improvement, which was opposed by many of the coach

proprietors, upon the ground that if their coachmen were made too comfortable they would go to sleep.   Nevertheless four-in-hand driving must have been indulged in to a greater or lesser extent, because, in the *Sussex Advertiser* for 23rd February, 1789, it is recorded that " a singular wager is now depending between a driving baronet and a certain gentleman on the wrong side of sixty, with little conspicuity but what arises from the lower scenes of gallantry.   The former in his phaeton, and with six white coursers, is to trot thirty miles over the grounds at Newmarket before a snail, *now in training* by the latter, should have crawled from one end to the other of a stone three yards square, and covered with powdered sugar.   Great bets are depending, and the trial will come off next spring."   Whether the driving baronet paid forfeit, or whether the snail failed to survive the exigencies of training, does not appear ; but no record of the match having taken place can be found, though, if it had come off, it would have been a thousand to one on the horses.

During the summer of 1790, Messrs. William Henwood and James Scott ran, between London and Brighton, a new and elegant post-coach, carrying four inside and three out.   The route was through Cuckfield and Reigate ; the coach left the White Horse Inn, Brighton, at eight o'clock in the morning, and reached the Blossoms Hotel, Lawrence Lane, Cheapside, in nine hours ; the inside passengers paid eighteen shillings, and the outsides half that amount.

Meantime Davis & Co., as the firm was now styled, were not by any means idle.   They ran a " machine," which appears to have been a two-end coach, daily, between London and Brighton by way of Lewes ; the Castle and the Old Ship inns were the houses of start and call at Brighton, and the down-coach started from the Golden Cross, Charing Cross.   Both coaches left at six in the morning, and finished the journey at "about five" in the afternoon.

For those who liked quicker travelling, a "light" post-coach left the same places as the above, and at the same times, but finished the journey at three o'clock instead of "about" five. The "Ryegate and Cuck-field" coach ran as before, except that the up-journey was performed on Mondays, Wednesdays, and Fridays. The coach was nine hours on the road.

A new proprietary is now met with in Ibberson and Co., whose light post-coach ran from the George and Blue Boar, Holborn, at half-past five on Tuesday, Thursday, and Saturday *via* Lewes, arriving at the White Horse Inn, East Street, Brighton, at three o'clock. The up-journey was made on the other days; but it took less time by half-an-hour, as the coach started at six and arrived in town at three. The same firm also ran a "machine from the same places on alternate days with the post-coach," and this machine arrived at either end before five in the evening. When entering and leaving London, Ibberson's coaches called at the Swan, Charing Cross.

Wessen's coach ran from the "Spread Eagle, Grace-church Street, London," at six on the morning of Tuesdays, Thursdays, and Saturdays, travelling by Hors-ham and Shoreham, and reached the Gun Inn (now Harrison's Hotel) on the Cliff, at Brighton, about four in the afternoon. The coach returned on the other days. There was also a light coach from the Gun Inn at half-past six every Tuesday, Thursday, and Saturday, to the White Bear, Piccadilly, whither it arrived at three in the afternoon.

During the winter season the arrangements were sufficiently liberal; a machine ran to the Golden Cross, Charing Cross, on Mondays, Wednesdays, and Fridays; a post-coach (through Chailey) on Tuesdays and Satur-

days, and a daily post-coach from the Castle and New
Ship, Brighton, to the Golden Cross, Charing Cross,
viâ Cuckfield.

If, however, Chamberlayne and De Laune had nothing
but praise for the new mode of travel, there was at least
one individual who was by no means smitten with the
coaches of 1790 which carried six "insides." He had
learned the discomforts of these vehicles by bitter
experience, and to the *Public Advertiser* for Tuesday,
the 28th September, 1790, he forwarded the following
lines, headed :—

THE COMFORTS OF A STAGE-COACH.

A country friend to visit, I, a cit,
Bespeak my passage in a God-permit.
Th' impatient coachman warns us to prepare,
And, long ere sunrise, mounts his daily care.—
Scarcely awake, in dreaming mood I rise,
Enter the coach, and ope my wondering eyes
On two old females of the Falstaff size ;
No choice is left me, so, between the two,
On each side elbow'd, I am doom'd to stew.
A nurse, a child, a soldier swelled with pride,
And a fat landlord, fill the other side.
Day scarcely dawns, before the rugged road
From this to that side jolts the motley load,
One beldame coughs, the other scolds and stares,
The landlord snores, child pukes, and soldier swears.
Of God-permits, if these the comforts be,
My feet, thank Heaven, still can carry me.

With reference to the expression "God permit" in
the above lines, it is only necessary to state that the
old coaching advertisements invariably concluded with
the announcement that the journey would be "performed, if God permit,"[1] by So-and-so.

---

[1] Is it not Dean Ramsay who in one of his books quotes an
old advertisement to the effect, that the Glasgow boat would start
on Monday, God willing and weather permitting ; or on Tuesday,
whether or no ?

In the year 1791, Tubb & Davis no doubt kept on
their waggons and machines; but they at the same
time turned their attention to putting light and faster
coaches on the road.   At seven o'clock every morning
a coach left the Castle Inn, calling at the Old and New
Ship inns. and ran to London by way of Lewes and
Uckfield ; at eight o'clock a post-coach left the above-
named inns and reached town in eight hours; while at
nine o'clock another light Post-coach left the same
starting-places on Mondays, Wednesdays, and Fridays
for the Golden Cross, Charing Cross.

There was, however, opposition to be again encountered at the hands of Messrs. Henwood, Scott, & Holbrook, whose undertakings included the " original eight-
o'clock post-coach, *viâ* Cuckfield and Reigate, which, like
Tubb & Davis's vehicle, reached London in eight hours,
arriving at the Blossoms Inn, Cheapside, at four o'clock
in the afternoon.   Their other coach was a " new post-
coach with guard and lamps," which left at eight o'clock
at night ; carried four insides at twenty shillings a head,
and two outside at ten shillings each ; and arrived in
London at five o'clock in the morning, a branch coach
meeting her at the Elephant and Castle to take passengers to the West End.

The mail-coach system, as is well known, originated
with Mr. John Palmer, M.P. for Bath, and proprietor of
the Bath Theatre.   For some reason, best known to
the Post-Office officials of the time, Mr. Palmer's suggestions met with stern opposition ; but he at last
carried his point, and the first mail-coach ran between
London and Bristol on the 8th August 1784.   It has
frequently been said that there was no mail-coach on
the Brighton road till the year 1810 ; but this is a
mistake, as a mail-coach first ran between London
and Brighton on May-Day, 1791.   The coach which
was to make the first up-journey passed through

Lewes on Saturday the 31st April, *en route* for
Brighton, and, in the opinion of the Lewes critic, she
was elegantly finished, and presented a very showy
appearance, which, added to the expedition the mails
must observe on the road, might induce some people to
travel by them in the summer; but, during the winter,
the opinion was hazarded, it would be impossible that
they could be made to answer, unless the amount then
allowed to the contractors by the Post-Office were considerably augmented. There would appear to be some
doubt as to the hour at which the mail left Brighton.
According to the *Morning Chronicle* for the 29th April
1791, the hour was half-past eight; the *Sussex Advertiser* of the 9th May (the advertisement was surmounted by a woodcut of the royal arms) gave it as eight
o'clock; while a few days later the mail was announced
to leave Brighton at nine o'clock at night, Lewes at ten,
and to run to the Golden Cross. It would appear, too,
that Tubb & Davis horsed the mail out of Brighton,
as in the advertisement their other coaches are included.[1] Not quite all, either, as in another paragraph
it is announced that Messrs. Tubb, Davis, Shergold,
Tilt, Best, Hicks, & Co. had put on an elegant new
coach, to carry six people inside, at sixteen shillings
a head, to London. The Old Ship was the starting-
point, the hour of setting out was half-past seven in
the morning on Tuesdays, Thursdays, and Saturdays;
the route was through Cuckfield and Reigate, and, as
with Tubb & Davis's other coaches, the Golden Cross,
Charing Cross, was the London terminus.

On Tuesday, 12th July 1791, the royal mail was
requisitioned for the officers of the Guards, who had

---

[1] Were it not for this circumstance, I should have imagined that
the mail and Henwood's night-coach, " with guard and lamps," were
one and the same vehicle.

received instructions to join their respective regiments, " in case their assistance should be necessary at the Crown and Anchor on Thursday." This phrase occurs in both a London and a Sussex paper, and in neither is it stated in what place the Crown and Anchor was situate. The *Sussex Advertiser* continues, " And thus was their (the officers') pleasure interrupted to fight a phantom that vanished in smoke without fire." The *Morning Chronicle's* comment is, " How much it is to be lamented that the gentlemen were not ordered to take places for Birmingham," where some riots had just broken out. We are, therefore, left in ignorance why the Guardsmen were called away from Brighton ; it seems clear that they were not wanted, however, and they were, no doubt, back in Brighton without loss of time.

Owing to many causes, travelling by coach was not all beer and skittles in the last century ; but, at any rate, a limited number of persons had the opportunity of sitting outside in the fresh air when the weather was not too inclement. Coaches, however, toppled over with such unpleasant frequency that people grew alarmed, and the fault was laid to carrying people on the roof. There were not wanting suggestions how to overcome this liability to get wrong end upwards ; but the remedy would surely have been worse than the disease had coach proprietors fallen in with the ideas of a gentleman who wrote to the *Morning Chronicle*, of 10th October 1791, to urge the adoption of "an elegant long-bodied carriage, that conveniently contains four-and-twenty insides, which runs at a great rate with four horses. Why then the dangerous practice of carrying outsides ?" Fancy travellers from London to Brighton, a nine or ten hours' journey, in an elegant long-bodied carriage with twenty-three other "insides" !

Without, however, dealing with imaginary difficulties, stage-coach travellers of an early day were often confronted with some of a very real nature, and occasionally it took a court of law to settle the disputes. In the thirteenth volume of the *Annual Register* is an account of a case tried in the Common Pleas, wherein a passenger by the up P—— (probably Portsmouth) coach was the plaintiff, and the master of the coach defendant. It seems that the coachman pulled up for dinner at a "hedge ale-house," one of the coachman's favourite places. The passengers, however, declining to dine at such a place, walked on to another inn at Epsom, and sent word to the coachman where they were, bidding him at the same time to stop for them, as he would have to pass their inn when he resumed his journey. The coachman, however, drove straight through to London without stopping for his passengers, leaving them to return as best they might. The coach proprietor having refused to make any pecuniary recompense, a test action was brought, with the result that the passenger obtained £20 as damages, the others presumedly being requited on the same scale.

Drawbacks of various kinds would appear to have weighed upon the mind of a certain apparently philanthropic person, who may, for all one can tell, have been the owner of post-horses, and to have prompted him to insert, by way of advertisement, in the *Sussex Advertiser* and *Morning Chronicle* for the 3rd August 1791, a long document. It was headed "Travelling," and, as it sums up the situation very fairly, its opening sentences are given *verbatim* :—

"To those ladies and gentlemen who travel from London to Brighthelmstone, Dover, Deal, Ramsgate, Margate, and other places in the counties of Kent and Sussex.—The many gross impositions that are practised

upon strangers travelling in almost every country has
made it necessary to publish, for their benefit and
consideration, the different modes of conveyance from
London to Brighthelmstone, Dover, Margate, &c., and
the expenses of each.

" There are two modes of conveyance, either by
common stages or by a post-chaise. By the common
stage you are classed with company of every description,
and who may very frequently turn out very disagreeable.
You are also paid no attention to at the inns where
you stop, although you pay exorbitant for refreshment,
and are frequently insulted by the indecent behaviour
of the coachman ; and besides your fare, you have a
considerable sum to pay for luggage.

" On the contrary, if two or three persons choose to
travel together, they may, by travelling in a post-chaise,
not only avoid all these inconveniences in adopting the
first stile of travelling in the kingdom, but suit their
own convenience in point of time, and be at less expense, as the following statement will sufficiently prove,
besides meeting with the genteeler treatment at the inns
on the road :—

By post-chaise from London to Brighton, with three passengers and luggage, 54 miles from Westminster Bridge @ 1s. per mile	£2	14	0
Six turnpikes	0	3	0
Postboys, 5 stages	0	7	6
	£3	4	6
By the mail from London to Brighton, three passengers, and each 14 lbs. weight only of luggage	£3	0	0
Supposing each passenger to have only 50 lbs. weight of luggage more than the 14 lbs. allowed at 1d. per lb.—it is generally more	0	12	6
Coachman all the way at 2s. each	0	6	0
Guard ,, ,, 1s. each	0	3	0
	£4	1	6

"The balance in favour of travelling by post-chaise from London to Brighton is seventeen shillings."

Hitherto we have come across scarcely any instances of the Brighton coaches coming to any harm ; but on Saturday, the 13th August, 1791, one of them was overturned at Clapham Common on its way to London, owing to one of the front wheels coming off. Several passengers sustained somewhat severe injuries, and the coachman was so badly hurt as to be unable to drive into town. "The great attention shown to the distressed state of the passengers by the inhabitants of Clapham Common," says the Sussex paper, "reflects the highest credit on them." As, however, we get more news of coaching, we find that accidents were by no means rare ; and few of the old coaches ran for any length of time without coming to grief more or less often. It could not, however, have been pace which necessarily brought coaches to grief ; for the following description of a journey from Brighton to London about this time shows that it could not have been a very hurried affair. It is extracted from Mr. Shergold's "Recollections of Brighton in the Olden Time :"—

"There were three roads from Brighton to London. The first and chief passed through Cuckfield and Reigate. This was the Appian way for the high nobility of England. The other two were vulgar. The one passed through Lewes, the other through Horsham. The best method of conveyance on the Cuckfield road was by the pair-horse coaches. These started at eight o'clock in the morning, and, if nothing intervened, proceeded steadily and boldly as far as Preston, where they stopped at the public-house—it being a prescriptive right of all coachmen in those days never to

pass a public-house without calling. Coachmen were
also persons of much consideration, a great deal of the
business of the country being transacted by them.
After quitting Preston, the coach *snailed it on* to
Withdean and Patcham, stopping, of course, a little
time at each. The next stoppage was at the bottom of
Clayton Hill—the formidable Clayton Hill—where the
coachman descended from his box and civilly obliged
all passengers, outside and in, to walk up, on the plea
'that the roads were very heavy, it being absolutely
killing to his horses.' This walk to the top of Clayton
Hill took about half-an-hour, and was very fatiguing,
especially if a man had the gallantry to offer his arm to
a fat widow. From the top of Clayton Hill you had a
most delightful view. From Clayton Hill the coach
snailed it on towards Cuckfield, the coachman not
deeming it proper to ask the passengers to walk above
three or four times until he arrived at that little town.
At St. John's Common, on the hither side of Cuckfield,
was a neat little public-house where the coachman
usually took a snack, which consisted of a mouthful of
bread and cheese and five or six glasses of gin and
bitters, for that was the liqueur *par excellence* of
coachmen in that day. When the coach arrived at
Cuckfield, it was usual for some of the passengers to
say to one another, 'Well, as the coach will stop here
some time, we will walk on.' This walking on often
consisted of a hard tug, up hill and down, over five or
six miles of slimy, slippery road.

"Before the coach overtook the passengers who had
proposed to walk forward, they arrived at Hand Cross,
a complete rustic inn, of which the landlord bore the
impress of Sussex rusticity. With that kind and bene-
volent attention to the happiness and comfort of walking travellers which innkeepers by the roadside usually
possess, a number of stools and benches were always

placed in front of the inn to receive the wearied muscles of the promenaders.

" Bannister, the publican of Hand Cross, walked forth from his inn, carrying a gallon bottle of gin in one hand, and a small wicker basket of slices of ginger-bread in the other. 'You must be tired, gentlemen,' said he. 'Come! take a glass and a slice.' So we all partook of gin and ginger-bread; and I can safely aver that I never heard a gentleman's character disputed, or his reputation blackened, because he took a glass of gin and ate a slice of ginger-bread at the rustic hostelerie of Hand Cross.

" But the coach was soon seen tending towards Hand Cross, and the outside and inside passengers, leaping up, took each person his place, and off we went, at the quiet and everlasting pace of four miles and a half an hour! As we had a downhill passage from Hand Cross, and not above four or five public-houses to stop at, we soon arrived at Crawley, a miserable place, the sight of which always gave me the stomach-ache. At Crawley we delayed not more than was sufficient just to kick the dust from our feet, which Horace, or some other poet, mentions as a demonstration of contempt. We then bundled on to Reigate, and arrived at the King's Arms, the horses absolutely trotting up to the door as if they took a real pleasure in presenting their passengers in grand style. At the door of this com- fortable inn there was always standing (I mean in the days of coaching) a waiter, who, after handing out the passengers, informed them that dinner was ready, and would be on the table in five minutes. Every man felt hungry; for out of the thirty-two miles which lie be- tween Brighton and Reigate, they had walked twenty. When they entered the room where dinner was to be served, they found some other passengers, who had come by a downward coach, waiting to dine.

D

" Here, then, we were, about fifteen ladies and gentlemen of the coach-going community—and who were
not coach-goers in those simple and happy days?—
about to sit down to a plain dinner, with two bottles of
wine, at two o'clock in the day, at one of the best inns
of the sort in the kingdom. The waiters put everything expeditiously on the table, wine and all, and
said, very obligingly, ' Ladies and gentlemen, you have
just two minutes for dinner! The coachman is just
putting-to his horses, and he will be round at the
door immediately!'" [This almost occasioned a " scene ; "
but, the writer says, the coachman was appealed to,
" firstly, to the stomach, by a tumbler of sherry ; and
secondly, to his brains, by plain and solid argument,"
and "time was allowed."] "After dinner the coach
went on as fast as two horses could carry us. The
coachman, after we quitted Reigate, entered into an
able soliloquy, addressed to me, to prove that eating
dinner at two o'clock, and drinking heavy port wine,
was imprudent. I was sitting on the box, and perfectly
agreed with him. He did not say anything about
drinking sherry, so I did not allude to it ; but when he
told me that he was quite sure he should lose his place
through staying so long at Reigate, we on the outside
all gave him a shilling apiece ; so that, by delaying
ten minutes, he gained seven shillings and a tumbler
of sherry. The coachmen of those days were such
honest men—not at all cunning ! But those were the
days of the olden time, before the slippery railroads
came into fashion !

" When the coach arrived at Reigate Hill, the passengers, outside and inside, were requested to descend.[1]
This hill was the most formidable tug on the road.

---

[1] This sort of thing was in great contrast to the style of going
in later days, when some of the ground near Reigate was that over
which a little time could be, and was, made up.

The best and easiest way of arriving at the top of the
hill was to follow humbly the movements of the coach,
but some ladies and gentlemen ventured up a steep
path which led almost perpendicularly up the hill, and
joined the road by a transverse path. Here was the
trial of sound lungs and easy and comfortable lacing.
Ladies who looked more to dapper shapes than to easy
respiration were sure to be brought to a *non-plus* about
the middle of the path, and it was necessary sometimes
to despatch a deputation of the gentlemen, who were
walking near the coach, to aid in dragging the impeded
ladies up the path.   The fair passengers, however
squeamish, were obliged to submit to the pulling and
pushing movement, for there was only this method of
surmounting the difficulties, unless they preferred to
be rolled down the steep like a bundle of goods, and
thus rejoin their fellow-passengers below.   When we
arrived at the top of Reigate Hill, we—the travellers
of the ancient epoch—considered the journey to London
almost as completed ; for we were so accustomed to
slow travelling, that an hour in a coach was as patiently
borne as five minutes are now on the railroad.   At
' the Cock ' at Sutton we delayed a little half-hour, as
the French say, and then valiantly proceeded on to
the noted ' Elephant and Castle,' where we waited for
the completion of many businesses, such as change of
coach, if you were going into the City ; and other necessary duties.   The destination of the Brighton coaches
in those days was ' The Golden Cross,' Charing Cross
—a nasty inn, remarkable for filth and apparent misery,
whence it was usual to be conveyed to the place to
which you were going in one of those large, lumbering
hackney-coaches, with two jaded, broken-winded and
broken-kneed hacks, which were common in those
days, before the introduction of safety cabs and light
flys.   These vehicles were always damp and dreary, the

very epitomes of misery.   On arriving at the house you
were going to in London of some friends or relations,
the following conversation often occurred : ' Happy to
see you ; but what brings you so soon ?—didn't expect
you before nine, and it's now only seven.'   ' We have
been eleven hours on the road—is not that enough ? '
' Oh ! quite enough, but formerly the Brighton coaches
arrived at midnight.   Travelling improves every day.
I wonder what we shall arrive at next !   Only eleven
hours from Brighton to London !   Wonderful !   Almost
incredible ! ' "

In 1792, Tubb, Davis, & Co., and Henwood, Scott,
& Co. were the proprietors who ran coaches to London;
and, so far as I can make out, each firm ran one or
two during the winter, Tubb & Davis going the long
road by Lewes and Uckfield.   In the summer, however, both proprietors put forth their best energies :
opposition was keen, and directly one firm made an
alteration, its rival followed suit.   For example, in June
1792, Tubb & Davis started a Sunday-coach *via* Lewes
and Uckfield to the Golden Cross, Charing Cross,
whereupon an opposition concern was at once put on
the road by Henwood & Co. ; but, whereas Tubb &
Davis took off theirs towards the end of October, the
other ran up to December.

Independently of the Sunday-coaches, however, the
following appear to have run during the summer of
1792 between London and Brighton :—

TUBB, DAVIS, & CO.'S COACHES.

From the Castle Inn, and the Old and New Ship Inns.

A Coach *via* Lewes and Uckfield to the Golden Cross, Charing
Cross.

Post-Coaches at 7, 8, and 9 o'clock, *via* Cuckfield and Reigate, to
the Golden Cross, Charing Cross.

Post-Coaches *via* Lewes and Chailey, at 7, 8, and 9 o'clock, to Golden
Cross, Charing Cross.

HENWOOD, SCOTT, HOLBROOK, & CO.'S COACHES.

From the White Horse Inn, East Street.

Post-Coach *viâ* Cuckfield and Reigate, at 8 A.M., to Blossoms Inn, Lawrence Lane, Cheapside.

This coach appears to have been accelerated, as she now reached London at three instead of at four o'clock.

An Elegant and Light Post-Coach, carrying four inside and three out, at 9 o'clock, arriving at Hatchett's New White Horse Cellar at 5 P.M.

The Original Eight o'Clock Post-Coach, *viâ* Cuckfield and Reigate, to the Blossoms Inn, Cheapside.

Ibberson's & Wessen's coaches ran as before.

The above list, it will be seen, gives a total of a dozen coaches a day running between London and Brighton during the summer months. In the winter, the "Original Eight - o'Clock Post - Coach" ran but three times a week—up on Mondays, Wednesdays, and Fridays, and down on the alternate days.

At the time of which we are speaking the coaches seldom carried guards ; comparatively few passengers were carried on the post-coaches, which, like all other coaches, down to the very last, had to depend greatly for their receipts upon the carrying of parcels. These parcels were, in the early days, stowed away anywhere and anyhow ; they were tucked in just where room could be found for them ; and the only wonder is that robberies were not of more frequent occurrence, as it would seem possible to commit them with something like impunity, if, at least, we may judge from the papers of the date. In the *Sussex Advertiser* for the 6th February 1792, for instance, there is an account of how one Sarah Baxter booked herself as an outside passenger by one of the London coaches. In the course of the journey she thought that she would like to ride inside, and as there was no one else, on or in the coach, the coachman allowed her to change. In the

seclusion of the inside Sarah Baxter at once began to
examine the contents of some of the parcels ; and, while
manipulating one, she was seen by the coachman, and
in answer to him said that the package was her own—a
statement the truth of which was readily accepted ;
but farther along the road she slipped out. The coachman did not miss her till a short time after she left
the coach, and then, becoming suspicious, he went in
pursuit of his missing passenger, whom he caught, and
on her was found some property she had extracted
from a parcel. She was prosecuted, and duly imprisoned ; and possibly the coachman learned to be more
careful of his parcels in future.

On the 30th of October in this year (1792) there
occurred what has been known as the "Robbery of the
Brighton Mail," a heading suggestive of a well-mounted
highwayman stopping a mail-coach and four, and getting
away with his booty before the guard had time to discharge his blunderbuss. In reality, however, instead of
a dashing highwayman, we have a couple of very ordinary footpads, and in place of the mail-coach, guarded
and lighted, we have a lad twelve years old riding on
horseback from Horsham to Steyning and Brighton,
carrying the mail-bags.

A certain habitual criminal named Howell became
aware of the fact that a farmer who lived near Goldstone Bottom, not far out of Brighton, would be returning home on the aforesaid 30th October with a large sum
of money about him, and it occurred to Howell that,
with assistance, he might possess himself of the farmer's
money, so he induced a young man named Rooke to be
his accomplice. As good luck had it, the farmer was
persuaded to stay in Brighton for the night ; but while
Rooke and Howell were waiting in Goldstone Bottom,
the "Brighton Mail," in the person of the above-
mentioned small boy, came by. He had ridden for

some distance behind the Brighton coach, on which
the Steyning post-mistress was a passenger; and she,
for some reason or other, directed the boy to part company with the coach, and to take a short cut which
turned out to be down the very lane in which Rooke
and Howell were in waiting.

The chance was too good to be lost; so the boy
was stopped, and the bags taken from him; but the
whole of the plunder consisted of half-a-guinea in a
letter. The lad "conducted himself very properly,"
we are told. He made his way to the nearest farm-
house; the farmer, like a good fellow, sent to Brighton
to acquaint the post-master of the robbery, and that
functionary at once sounded the alarm, with the result
that a band of horsemen at once turned out to scour
the country. In the early morning two of the horsemen met a suspicious-looking person whom they at
once captured, and he, "after sinking to the ground
with fear," not only confessed to his share in the
robbery, but informed his captors where they would
find his accomplice. The boy's horse and the bags
were recovered, but not the contents of the latter.
This is one version of the capture of the thieves; but,
according to another, Rooke was caught through the
information given to the authorities by an old woman.

Rooke and Howell were tried at the Horsham Spring
Assizes in 1793; were found guilty, and sentenced to be
hanged near the spot at which the robbery took place.
They were taken in a post-chaise from Horsham, and
the sentence was duly carried out, the bodies being
afterwards hung on gibbets twenty-five feet high.
Howell, as already mentioned, was a hardened and
habitual criminal. During the interval which elapsed
between his capture and the carrying out of the sentence, he was proved to have been concerned in a
number of burglaries and other crimes. Howell was

forty years of age, while Rooke was but twenty-four;
though, young as he was, he had been several times "in
trouble." He lived at Old Shoreham with his mother,
a hard-working and respectable woman, and the only
pathetic part of the story is that when the flesh had
decayed from the bodies, Rooke's mother would go
to the gibbets night after night to collect the bones
which the wind scattered, and these she ultimately
buried in a chest in Shoreham churchyard.

The little post-boy was scarcely as lucky in his
adventure as another lad whose doings are related in
one of the old volumes of the *Sporting Magazine.*
He had been sent to market with a cow which he was
to sell for seven guineas; but he was lucky enough to
dispose of her for more than that sum, and, in his
inexperience, while having his dinner at an inn, was
unwise enough to boast of what he had done. A "road
inspector," as highwaymen sometimes called themselves, happening to be present, very naturally made
his arrangements accordingly, and before the boy had
gone very far he was requested to hand over his money;
but, instead of doing so, he scattered the guineas on the
ground. The highwayman hurriedly dismounted to
pick them up, and then the boy is said to have mounted
the highwayman's horse, and to have galloped off
home, where, on making up a profit and loss account,
it was found that though he had lost about eight
guineas of his father's money, he had become the
possessor of a horse worth about twenty guineas; while,
on further examination, sixteen guineas were found
sewn up in the saddle!

In the main, the coaching arrangements of 1792 were
repeated in 1793. Mr. John Baulcombe, maltster, of
the New Ship Inn, Brighton, advertised that he had
become a partner with Tubb & Davis, and the firm
put on a new post-coach, carrying eight passengers,

four inside and four out ; while Henwood, of the
White Horse Inn, North Street, after returning thanks
for the patronage extended to him, announced that the
coaches ran as usual from his house, and that firm now
appeared as Johnstone, Whichelo, Scott, & Henwood ;
but in subsequent advertisements the names appeared
in different order.

In 1794 there appeared for the first time an advertisement of a coach running to London through Ditchling
and Lindfield ; but as its anonymous proprietors stated
that it " continues running," it must have been on the
road during the previous year, and possibly longer than
that.   She started from the White Lion and Golden
Cross, Brighton, and ran to the George and Blue
Boar, Holborn, leaving Brighton at eight o'clock on
Mondays and Fridays, returning at seven o'clock in
the morning on Wednesdays and Saturdays ; though
when the summer set in, the coach ran thrice a week
each way.

Messrs. Law, Grenville, & Crosweller had for some time
run a service of waggons between London and Brighton,
and, in 1795, Crosweller, whose name subsequently became famous in the annals of stage-coaching as the proprietor of the " Blue" coaches and " Blue" office, as well
as a partner in many other concerns, flew at higher
game than a waggon, and joined Henwood & Scott,
Henwood's former partner soon after going out of the
business.   Henwood & Crosweller kept on the post-
coaches, which now left the White Horse Inn at
eight and nine o'clock in the morning, running to
Hatchett's New White Horse Cellar, and to the Cross
Keys, Wood Street, instead of to the Blossoms Inn, as
in previous years.   This firm also ran " the long coach
as usual ;" but whether this means that it ran by the
long road, or whether it was one of the long-bodied
vehicles, I am unable to say.   At any rate, it ran three

times a week, leaving Brighton at eight o'clock in the
morning.

Meantime Scott, having severed his connection with
Henwood, lost no time in becoming coach-master on
his own account, as in November 1795 (the dissolution
of partnership was announced in October) he thanked
the public for the support accorded to his coaches and
diligences, and announced that during the winter he
would run a light post-coach or diligence to the Blossoms Inn and the Old White Horse Cellar every morning at a quarter to eight o'clock, at the reduced fare
of half-a-guinea inside and six shillings out.

Tubb had apparently made his fortune, or amassed
a competence, for he announced that he had retired
from every kind of business ; but Davis & Boulton kept
on the coaches, which appear to have run as usual ; and
now for the first time we find mention of a " coach-
office," Davis & Boulton's coaches starting from the
establishment which they appear to have themselves
founded at the bottom of North Street.

During all this time the Sussex paper contained
lengthy weekly lists of fashionable arrivals ; but we
meet with no mention of any of these great people
travelling by coach ; in fact, whenever an accident, a
dispute, or some other cause leads to the mention of a
name, it is invariably that of a " respectable tradesman,"
or some one not known in the highest fashionable circles.
Travelling with post-horses either in one's own carriage or in a post-chaise was the " first stile," and
it was not till later that stage-coaching was regarded
as anything more than third-class travelling.   Post-
chaises in great numbers travelled along the London
and Brighton roads, and on the return journeys the
post-boys were in the habit of picking up people walking in their direction, and keeping the money given to
them by their informal fares.   The practice appears to

have attained to such large proportions that the Brighton
and Lewes post-masters clubbed together, and offered a
reward of half-a-guinea to any one who would inform
them of an instance of a post-boy picking up a return
fare. It afterwards became illegal for post-boys to take
up any one while on their way home ; but the above
form of " shouldering " must have been very common, as
the advertisement offering a reward for information appeared for more than a year. At the end of the Brighton
season there was a great exodus of all classes, and one
writer declared that the coaches " go up as full as a
vicar's belly, and return as empty as a curate's kitchen."

In 1796 Henwood, Crosweller, & Co. kept on the
coaches already mentioned, and early in June announced
their intention of putting on a night-coach to London
in July. Davis, Boulton, & Co. (who also kept to the
arrangements of the previous year) likewise determined
to start a night-coach ; but the two firms had the sense
not to run on the same night, so Henwood & Crosweller
started on a Monday, and Davis & Boulton on the Sunday.

A " diligence on a new construction," carrying three
inside and three out, was advertised in July (1796) to
run to London by way of Lewes and Uckfield three
days a week, leaving Brighton at half-past seven, to
reach the Blossoms Inn at seven ; and the coaching
news of the year is completed by the announcement
that Henwood, Crosweller, & Co. had taken in some
more partners. In the autumn the firm was Henwood, Crosweller, T. Pockney, R. Cuddington, and
J. Harding ; and they appear to have signalised the
inauguration of this large amalgamation by starting a
coach to match ; for, like some of the older vehicles,
it carried six passengers inside, though two only on
the roof. It left the White Horse and New Inns,
Brighton, and the New White Horse Cellar (Hatchett's)
at eight o'clock in the morning, calling at the Blos-

soms Inn *en route*, and travelling *viâ* Cuckfield and
Crawley. The fares by this coach were fifteen shillings inside and nine shillings outside; but scarcely
had New Year's Day 1797 passed before the firm were
compelled to give notice of an increase of fares, owing
to the imposition of extra duty on coaches. Insides
were now charged nineteen shillings; half-a-guinea
was demanded for " children in the lap; " outsides
were also charged half-a-guinea, and parcels twopence
each; but the last-named charge must, I presume, be
taken to mean twopence in addition to the tariff previously in force. These additions, however, the firm
with many names somewhat sanguinely hoped would
meet with the approbation of their patrons. It need
scarcely be said that the rival firm made a corresponding advance in their prices; and in the summer of
1797 Davis seems to have followed the retired Tubb
into private life, as the firm was now Boulton, Tilt,
Hicks, Baulcombe, & Co., the last-named being proprietor of the New Ship Inn. W. H. Henwood, jun.,
had succeeded his father at the New Inn, and William
Allen, who described himself as late butler to Lord
Torrington, and who subsequently blossomed into a coach
proprietor, had become landlord of the White Horse Inn
in 1798, and at that house coaches for London called at
eight, nine, and ten A.M. The coaches of Boulton & Co.
started from the General Coach Office at the bottom of
North Street; and those which ran *viâ* Cuckfield and
Reigate went to the Golden Cross, Old White Horse
Cellar, Gloucester Coffee-House, Piccadilly; and the
Swan with Two Necks. Post-coaches ran to London
by way of Lewes at 6.30 and 8.30, returning from London at seven and eight A.M. As already mentioned,
some of the coaches covered the distance between London and Brighton in eight hours, which, all things considered, was not bad work; and the coachmen of that

day, when the improvement in pace and organisation
was taking place, were fully justified in priding themselves on the superiority of their undertakings over
those of a past age. For example, in the twelfth volume
of the *Sporting Magazine* is this passage :—" Formerly it appears, from ancient records, that the Shrewsbury flying waggon came to London (if God permitted)
in twenty-one days, and the coach in nine. Now
(1798) the waggon comes in four days and a coach in
about twenty hours."   On the whole, therefore, the travellers of nearly a century ago may have congratulated
themselves that they were " born so late."

The usually comprehensive columns of the *Sussex
Advertiser* tell us little or nothing of the Brighton road
during the year 1799. Coach proprietors seem with one
accord to have abandoned advertising, while the pen
of the paragraphist was still.   Coaches started as usual
at eight and nine o'clock from the New Inn in North
Street, and that is one of the very few items of coaching
news given in connection with the main road.

Hay and corn had risen in price, and in consequence
Shelley & Son, and William Bradford (the latter ere
long turned " 'rioter," as a coach proprietor was termed,
as we shall see in the next chapter), together with
several other carriers, announced that they would be
obliged to charge an additional sixpence per cwt. for
the goods they carried after the 1st of January 1800 ;
while, on the other hand, the innkeepers on the road
advertised that, notwithstanding the high price of
forage, post-chaises could still be hired to Brighton *via*
Epsom, Dorking, Horsham, and Henfield at the old
price of a shilling a mile.

Mention has already been made of the establishment
of a coach-office, for, as business and traffic increased,
it was found that the limited space at the different
inns was insufficient ; and now Henwood, Crosweller,

Pockney, & Co. notified that, for the better accommodation of the public, and for the more expeditious
conduct of the coaching business, they had engaged
the New General Coach Office, 44 East Street, at the
corner of Steine Lane; and, as will be seen later on,
coach-offices grew and multiplied in and about Castle
Square. The history of stage-coaching between London and Brighton for the eighteenth century ends,
therefore, with the distinct advance of the establishment of public coach-offices.

On the whole, it must be admitted that, if stage-
coaching had not advanced with the proverbial leaps
and bounds, it had at any rate undergone considerable
improvement in the seventy years which had elapsed
since the two-day conveyance ran in 1731. At the
close of the last century there must have been about ten
or a dozen coaches running daily to and from London;
a mail-coach up and down had been on the road for
eight years; night-passenger coaches ran in the summer; and the fastest coaches were timed to run between
London and Brighton in eight hours, though, as a
matter of fact, it was rarely that a coach crossed the
Thames under nine hours. Still, roads were then a
long way from being at their best; heavy horses and
long stages were doubtless the rule; and the driving of
four horses could not have been the art it afterwards
became.

CHAPTER V.

FROM 1800 TO 1809.

THE nineteenth century appears to have opened
without bringing with it any startling change in
the coaching arrangements. One at least of Crosweller's coaches seems to have started half an hour
later than before; but, beyond that trifling deviation
from the programme of 1799, things appear to have
gone on as before. Then, as now, the average Briton
was evidently inclined to keep himself to himself while
on a journey, and from the *Sussex Advertiser* for the
3rd March 1800 I extract this paragraph:—" A few
days ago two persons, strangers to each other, took
their departure together in one of the public carriages.
After some time one of them said, ' Here is a fine
morning, sir.' The other remained silent. They rolled
on a mile or two, when the first spoke again, ' Well,
how do you do now, sir?' ' I am very well, thank
you, sir,' was the answer, but no more. Some time
afterwards the talkative gentleman accosted his silent
companion with, ' Well, my friend, and how are you
now?' ' I am as well,' was the reply, ' as when you
asked me before, and if I ail anything I will let you
know.'" Here is a story guaranteed to be at least
ninety-three years old, and it must have stood sponsor
to numberless others of later date; but it is scarcely
surprising that in olden days people should have been
chary of entering into conversation with strangers, for
then, even to a greater extent than at the present time,
one was liable to make undesirable acquaintances. "I

always feel very nervous in a coach," said a highly respectable female to a fatherly old gentleman, who was
the only other inside passenger, "on account of these
dreadful highwaymen. I have now with me a gold
watch I am taking as a present to my sister, and
the sum of twenty guineas, and I confess I scarcely
like to have so much about me." The gentleman very
politely replied, " Madam, you may rest assured that
no highwayman shall touch your property ; I never
travel without a brace of pistols," a speech which tended
to reassure his companion. Some distance farther
on the road the gentleman said, "I alight at the end
of this stage, and before I take my leave I must
trouble you for the gold watch and your twenty
guineas, and I warn you to say nothing of the matter
when the coach stops."

On looking through the old newspapers, one cannot
help being struck with the number of apologies which
are met with in the advertisement columns. Here, for
example, is one, headed " Caution to Stage-Coachmen,"
and the apology proceeds, " Whereas I, William Wager,
late driver of the Brighton and Lewes stage-coach from
the Golden Cross, London, did on Wednesday, the 7th
November, grossly, and without provocation, abuse and
otherwise ill-treat a gentleman on horseback opposite
Loughborough House, near Brixton Causeway, for which
offence he has justly commenced a prosecution against
me ; but in consequence of my (thus publicly) asking
pardon and acknowledging my offence, and out of com-
passion to my wife and family, the same gentleman has
humanely condescended to stop proceedings against me,
for which act of lenity I beg to return my thanks, and
publish this as a caution to all other coachmen not to
offend in like manner." Turnpike gate-keepers were
very prone to lose their tempers and become abusive,
but were generally brought to book when proceedings

WHITE HORSE CELLARS

were commenced against them, and an abject apology
in the Sussex paper was the inevitable sequel.

The extract given on a previous page graphically
described a journey from Brighton to London ; and in
Mr. Bishop's book appears an account of the down-
journey ; but if the opening sentence means that the
two pair-horse coaches were the only vehicles running
between London and Brighton, the writer is clearly
wrong. The Directory of Brighton for 1800 by Mr.
Edward Cobby—it is reprinted in Mr. Bishop's book—
shows that there were half a dozen coaches daily, and
one which ran but three days a week.

" In 1801 two *pair*-horse coaches ran between London
and Brighton on alternate days—one up, the other down
—and they were driven by Crosweller and Hine. The
progress of these coaches was an amusing one. The
one from London left the ' Blossoms' Inn, Lawrence
Lane, at seven A.M., the passengers breaking their fast
at the ' Cock,' at Sutton, at nine. The next stoppage
for the purpose of refreshment was at the ' Tangier '
(Banstead Downs), a rural little spot, famous for its
elderberry wine, which used to be brought from the
cottage ' roking hot,' and on a cold wintry morning
few refused to partake of it. George IV. invariably
stopped here, and took a glass from the hand of Miss
Jeal as he sat in his carriage. The important business
of luncheon took place at Reigate, where sufficient
time was allowed the passengers to view the Baron's
Cave.

" Handcross was the next resting-place, celebrated
for its 'neat' liquors, the landlord of the inn standing
bottle-in-hand at the door. (He and several other
Bonifaces, at Friar's Oak, &c., had the reputation of
being on pretty good terms with the smugglers who
at this period carried on their operations with such
audacity along the Sussex coast.)

E

" But the grand halt for dinner was made at Staplefield Common, celebrated for its famous black cherry-
trees, under the branches of which, when the fruit
was ripe, the coaches were allowed to draw up, and the
passengers to partake of their tempting produce. The
hostess of the hostelry here was famed for her rabbit-
puddings, which were always waiting the arrival of the
coach, and to which the travellers never failed to do
such ample justice, that ordinarily they found it quite
impossible to leave at the hour appointed ; so grogs,
pipes, and ale were ordered in, and, to use the language of the fraternity, ' not a wheel wagged ' for two
hours. The coach then went on to Clayton Hill, and
as the passengers had to walk up this ascent, a cup of
tea was sometimes found to be necessary at Patcham,
after which Brighton was safely reached at 7 P.M."

At the beginning of the year 1802 Boulton & Co.
and Crosweller, Pockney, Henwood, & Co. ran their
coaches as usual during the winter. The fare by the
post-coaches was a guinea inside, and eleven and sixpence outside ; while the Blue coaches (Crosweller's),
which started at eight o'clock in the morning from the
Blue Coach-Office, in East Street, charged the same
amount. The Blue coaches ran to the Blossoms Inn,
Lawrence Lane, Cheapside, and Hatchett's New White
Horse Cellar, returning at a quarter to eight every
morning. By the time May came round, the inside
fare by Crosweller's post-coach (Vallance & Co.,
brewers and coal merchants, of West Street, had now
joined the firm) was reduced to nineteen shillings, but
one could travel by the " accommodation " coach (six
inside) for fifteen shillings, or for half-a-guinea outside ; this vehicle left Brighton at nine in the morning. The rival firms were also busy, for Boulton & Co.
started their coaches at seven, eight, and nine in the
morning from the General Office, North Street, to the

Golden Cross, Charing Cross, the Old White Horse Cellar, and the Gloucester Coffee-House, Piccadilly, and the Swan with Two Necks, Lad Lane.

A fortnight later, however—that is to say, on the 24th May 1802—a fresh opposition sprang up in the shape of the "New Royal Union Four-Horse Coach Company," who gave notice that their commodious coaches would commence running between London and Brighton at eight o'clock every morning on Monday, the 31st of May.

Messrs. Crosweller, Henwood, Vallance, Pockney, & Co. had, however, a shot in their locker, and promptly advertised that a coach on a new construction, built on a safe, elegant, and commodious principle (it had need to be commodious, seeing that it carried six passengers inside), and drawn by four horses, would start from the Blue Office for the Blossoms Inn, and Hatchett's New White Horse Cellar, and would carry people for half-a-guinea inside and seven shillings out; while Boulton, Tilt, Hicks, Gourd, Baulcombe, & Co. likewise reduced their fares; like the proprietors of the Blue coaches, they ran post-coaches, and each firm again ran a night-coach thrice a week.

With three, or possibly four, rival establishments in full work, there were seven day-coaches to London, a night-coach, the mail, and Scott's diligence with its three passengers inside and one outside. It started from the White Lion, North Street, at half-past eight on Mondays, Wednesdays, and Fridays, and ran *viâ* Cuckfield and Crawley to the Belle Sauvage. There was, of course, bitter rivalry—in fact, from this time until the opening of the railway there was possibly more competition on this road than on any other in England. The newly-started company would appear to have obtained their share of public support, if at least we may credit their own statements, as in July

(1802) we find them begging "to return thanks for the very liberal support they have experienced," and they followed the time-honoured precedent in stating that they would always study to have "their coaches safe with good horses, and sober, careful coachmen." The company also took the opportunity of contradicting a statement made, to the effect that one of their coaches had been turned over a week previously, by which accident it was reported that a gentleman's leg had been broken. The company modestly pointed out that the mishap really befell one of the Blues (Crosweller's); and, as several mistakes had occurred through their friends booking at the wrong place, patrons were invited to note that they should betake themselves to the Royal New Coach-Office, the Catherine's Head, 47 East Street, Brighton.

This new body showed commendable enterprise, as they appear to have done a good stroke of business by running "an elegant" post-coach from Lewes to London *viâ* Brighton. This new venture made its first journey on Monday, the 22nd November 1802, starting from the Bear Hotel, Lewes; but unfortunately the advertisement does not give the hour of departure, though it does tell us that the coach reached London at half-past four in the afternoon, so that passengers could write letters in town in time to catch the evening down-mail. It left the Bull Inn, Holborn, every morning at seven; called at the Green Man and Still, Oxford Street; the old White Horse Cellar; the Mecklenburgh Coffee-House, Cockspur Street; and the Elephant and Castle, proceeding thence to the Royal Coach-Office, Brighton, and on to Lewes. The probability is that the coach started from Lewes at a somewhat uncomfortably early hour in the morning; so by way of tiding over the difficulty to some extent, the proprietors, with rare foresight, allowed the more sloth-

ful of their passengers to go overnight to Brighton,
where they were "accommodated with a good bed free
of expense," and could proceed comfortably to London
by one or other of the Company's morning-coaches.
The fare from Lewes to London through Brighton
was twelve shillings inside and eight shillings outside.

In different parts of the country both the mail-boys
and the mail-coaches had been stopped with too great
frequency ; so on the Brighton road an attempt appears
to have been made to remedy this state of things ; for
in the *Sussex Advertiser* for the 30th August, 1802, is a
paragraph stating that "any attempt on the mail passing between London and Brighton will now be extremely dangerous, as the persons travelling with them
are armed in a manner that enables them to bid
defiance to the attacks of all ordinary robbers, which
adds much to the safety of the conveyance, and does
great credit to Mr. Aust, one of the principal surveyors,
on whose suggestion, we understand, this mode of
defence was adopted. The post-boys have all lately
been presented with a uniform dress and helmet, similar to those worn by the artillery-drivers, which gives
them a very fierce and formidable appearance," though
it may be doubted whether on the cross-roads many
mails were saved by reason of a boy looking like a bad
imitation of an artillery-driver.

During the years 1803, 1804, and 1805, there is a
remarkable dearth of coaching news ; so we may presume that no very great change took place in the
previously existing arrangements. In 1804 the unex-
pired portion of the lease of the Bolt-in-Tun, the inn,
in Fleet Street, where at some of the coaches called
on their way to Brighton, was sold by Mr. Aldridge at
his repository ; and the alteration was made in the
road at the entrance to Brighton for the convenience of

the Prince of Wales, by whose order several houses in
the rear of Church Street were bought, in order that
they might be pulled down. A Mr. Howell, who combined the callings of builder and lodging-house-keeper
on a large scale, and who also had a wheel in one of
the London coaches, died, and so did Mr. Pockney, a
member of Crosweller's firm. In 1805 "New Telegraph and Post Coaches" ran to London every morning
at seven, eight, and nine o'clock, _viâ_ Cuckfield and
Reigate, to Cheapside, Charing Cross, and Holborn,
and there was still a night-coach at ten o'clock.

During the year 1807 there are comparatively few
coaching advertisements beyond those put forth by
Messrs. Boulton, Tilt, Gourd, Baulcombe, & Co. During
the summer of 1807 that enterprising firm ran "post
and accommodation coaches to London at seven, eight,
and nine o'clock in the morning, the route being
through Cuckfield and Reigate, and the destination
the Golden Cross Hotel, Charing Cross, and the Swan
with Two Necks, Lad Lane. They also ran, through
Lewes, a coach which left Brighton at half-past six
in the morning, and the night-coach left Brighton at
nine instead of at ten.

As the season progressed, Boulton & Co. determined
to take a new departure, and so they announced,
"Uncommonly quick travelling to London by coaches
from the Royal Clarence Coach-Office, Castle Square."
A coach left at eight in the morning, and ran to the
Golden Cross, Charing Cross; and the Spread Eagle,
Gracechurch Street. This coach went by way of the
Devil's Dyke and Henfield, described in the advertisement as being the most pleasant and cheerful route to
London—as it no doubt was—and the plan, we are
told, upon which this undertaking was conducted had
been frequently attempted, but never punctually acted
upon. Messrs. Boulton & Co., however, were confident

of succeeding where others had failed ; they had introduced sundry reforms, and had each year shown themselves ready to move with the times. With that confidence, therefore, which is the secret of success, they
guaranteed that these long-route coaches should "arrive
at the stones-end of London in eight hours ;" but
then came in a saving clause—the eight-hours bargain
would only hold good if there was "no general disposition of the passengers" to delay on the road. Hence
it would appear that the time-bill was really in the
hands of the public. If, however, the passengers did
not delay the coach, and if the coach did not reach
the "stones-end of London" at the specified time,
then Boulton & Co. engaged to return the fares—an
offer which, as we shall presently see, was made in
1816 by another firm anxious to secure patronage.

We occasionally read in the papers of people suing
railway companies for the expenses they have been
put to for horse-hire, or hotel-expenses, when they miss
trains, or when the connection between two lines fails,
and there were persons who did the same sort of thing
in the old coaching days. In the spring of 1808 some
very bad weather was experienced, and on one particular day all the London and Brighton coaches had
to return, consequently one of Mr. Pattenden's was not
in London to make the down-journey as far as Horsham
on its proper day. Two *gentlemen*—the *Brighton Herald*
is careful to italicise the word—appear to have booked
places ; and as no coach was forthcoming, they posted
down to Horsham at the cost of £3, 2s., and "insisted"
on Pattenden reimbursing them this sum, which he did,
coach proprietors of that time possibly finding it expedient, like insurance offices, to establish a reputation
for liberality rather than for stinginess ; but the demand seems to have been rather an unjust one.

The night-coaches to and from London were an-

nounced to start for the season in the middle of April
1808; and the other proprietors worked on the lines
of the previous year until Pattenden, whose office
was in St. James's Street, decided to try his luck with
a ten - o'clock coach, this being an hour later than
any morning - coach had started at before; he also
decided to run one at noon.   Crosweller at once
replied with a ten-o'clock coach from the Blue Office,
44 East Street.   Meantime, Pattenden ran a light
four-horse post-coach on Mondays, Wednesdays, and
Fridays at seven o'clock in the morning, by way of
the Devil's Dyke, Henfield, Horsham, and Dorking,
to the Angel Inn, St. Clement Danes, in the Strand,
the down - journey being undertaken on Tuesdays,
Thursdays, and Saturdays.

   The success of Pattenden's and Crosweller's ten-o'clock
coaches had the effect of calling forth further opposition; and, after the above-mentioned concerns had
been running about a month, Waldegrave & Co.
announced that on the 13th August 1808 they would
run an eleven - o'clock coach from the St. James's
Tavern to the Bull Inn, Bishopsgate, whence the down
coach would return at noon.   The proprietors stated
that they, being anxious to render their conveyances
the most complete on the road, "combining the
greatest convenience with the quickest despatch,"
would be happy to receive, from time to time, any
observation or information from passengers "tending
to promote such desirable objects."   Leaving Brighton
at eleven, it was proposed to reach Cuckfield about
one P.M., Crawley about a quarter - past two, Reigate
at about half - past three, and Croydon about five,
reaching London at about seven.   In those days the
Brighton horses commonly ran to Cuckfield, about
a fourteen-mile stage.   The fares by this coach were
twenty-three shillings inside and thirteen shillings

outside; while, following a not uncommon practice,
parties booking the whole of the coach had the privilege of starting at what hour they chose.

Mr. Shergold, whose name has figured in sundry
coach advertisements, was twice proprietor of the
Castle Hotel, Castle Square, which afterwards became
the coaching centre of Brighton, for in the Square,
and close to it, were all the coach booking-offices.
As we have already seen, the first regular coach-office
to be established away from an inn was the General
Office, North Street, founded by Boulton & Co. in
1795; but that firm seems subsequently to have
migrated to the Royal Clarence Office (afterwards
known as the Red Office), in Castle Square. Secondly
came the Blue Coach-Office at 44 East Street; it
stood nearly on the site of Messrs. Treacher's premises :
Pattenden's town office was in St. James's Street.
These are all that were open up to this date, but others
followed in due course, as will be seen farther on.
On Mr. Shergold's second tenancy, business increased
to such an extent that he took Messrs. Tilt and Best
into partnership, and the three carried on the house
till the year 1791,[1] when they gave up hotel-keeping,
and confined themselves to the coaching business,
with which they had been previously connected.
After the fashion of the firms of coach proprietors,
the *personnel* of the confederacy underwent several
changes; and in course of time, Messrs. Samuel
Shergold, John Hicks, Richard Wood (of Reigate),
and Mr. John Davis were gathered to their fathers,
the surviving partners paying to their respective
executors the value of their shares. In 1808 the
members of the firm were Stephen Gower one-sixth,
Thomas Tilt one-sixth, William Tylish (of Lewes),

---

[1] Brighton in the Olden Time, by J. G. Bishop.

one-sixth, George Boulton (of Lewes), one-sixth, and
half of one-sixth, and James Gregory half of one-
sixth.

In the *Brighton Herald* for the 19th November
1808. there appeared an advertisement announcing
that there was for sale, by private contract, the good-
will of one-twelfth part or share of the above coach
business, carried on for nearly fourteen years in North
Street; at the Swan with Two Necks, Lad Lane,
London; and the Golden Cross, Charing Cross, London. Included in the share to be sold was one-twelfth
part of all the horses, harness, straw, hay, corn, and
stage-coaches, and the beneficial leases of stables.
lands, and premises, both on the Cuckfield and Lewes
roads to London.

Some idea of the magnitude of such a comparatively
small coaching business may be gained from the statement in the advertisement that the returns of the business were more than £12,000 a year. From Christmas
1794 to Christmas 1808 it had paid more than £7, 10s.
per cent. upon the capital invested, besides buying up
the shares of the deceased partners.

Coaching intelligence for the year 1809 opens with
an announcement that the proprietors of the " Original " coaches had removed from their office at the corner
of North Street to Castle Square (the house near the
entrance to the Castle Inn) ; while, taking a jump to
London, we find that the Bolt-in-Tun, an old coaching
house in London, the lease of which has been mentioned above [1] as being for sale, passed from Mrs. Carter
to Mr. Croom, while at the same time the former also
gave up the Sussex Coffee-House in Fleet Street.

During the month of June 1809, Mr. Shee, a well-
known Brighton wine merchant, mysteriously lost, while

travelling by one of the night-coaches, a parcel containing £700 or £800 worth of bills and notes. The package was eventually found in the hollow of the road which led to the common sewer, in the Steyne, by an employé of Mr. Scrase, of Brighton, and this person kept the parcel for several days before notifying the owner that he had found it. The bills and notes were, when lost, sealed up in other packages; but, in the interval which elapsed before the safety of the parcel was made known, the finder had opened and examined everything, a circumstance which led Mr. Shee to limit the reward to five guineas, the amount advertised. Had the enclosures not been opened, he said that he should have considered the man would have had a still stronger claim on his liberality. Honesty, one sees, is the best policy, because, as a rule, it pays best. It would have done so in this case; but the examination of the parcels by Mr. Scrase's man was rather suggestive that had he found in the package coin, which could not have been traced, it would not have been restored.

So far as it is possible to ascertain from the newspapers, comparatively few accidents had hitherto overtaken the Brighton coaches; but what appears to have been quite a preventible one befell, in August, 1809, one of the coaches belonging to Messrs. Waldegrave & Co. She had arrived from London, carrying a good load, and the coachman had pulled up to set down Mr. Hoare, the banker, at his house in Pavilion Parade. In order to get into Church Street and the New Road, *en route* for North Street and St. James's Street, it became necessary to turn the coach, and this always delicate operation in a confined space seems to have been undertaken so hastily that the vehicle locked and turned over. One of the inside passengers, a lady, sustained a fracture of the collar-bone; and her companions were slightly injured; but an undertaker's man, who "had come down with the sable plume to attend the removal of the remains of Mr. Baillie, a merchant," had his thigh broken ; while one of Waldegrave's horse-keepers, who had just climbed on to the back-seat, fell under the coach, and was so dreadfully crushed that his life was in great danger. The coachman, who caused the accident, of course escaped unhurt, nor was the vehicle as much shattered as might have been expected. Pattenden, too, the proprietor and coach-man of one of the London coaches, met with an accident while on the up-journey. Pattenden was very much respected on the road, but this occurrence appears to have given rise to rumours not altogether of a compli-mentary kind ; whereupon one of his patrons sent to the papers the following outspoken letter, in which the incident is fully explained :—

"SIR,—I hope you will not deem me intrusive when I beg leave to offer a few observations respecting the late accident which happened to Mr. Pattenden, a pro-prietor of a Brighton coach, and the consequent effect of it in prejudicing the public against him. He was, when the accident happened, passing through Ewel (*sic*) at a very moderate speed ; and, as he was turning the corner by the church, one of the wheel-horses fell, on which Mr. Pattenden, with the intention of making him spring up again, applied the whip. This, however, failed in the effect of raising the wheel-horse, and unfortunately occasioned the two leaders, very spirited animals, to dart forward, drag the coach upon the fallen horse, and overturned it. The horse, which had but last summer cost Mr. Pattenden £35, was killed on the spot, and one of the passengers was slightly hurt ; Mr. Pattenden himself was violently precipi-tated from the box, and his head thereby was so much bruised that he was for some time in great danger, but from which situation he is now happily recovered. Can any blame here attach to the unfortunate proprietor? He was driving very moderately, and was quite sober, so that he cannot be accused either of rashness or inebriety. The place where the coach was overturned was a very wide and level piece of ground, which saves him from the blame of unskilfulness. Yet, notwithstanding the plainness of these facts, malicious reports have been circulated, which have so much prejudiced the public that Mr. Pattenden has, in consequence, lost a great deal of that custom upon which he depends for his own support, and that of his wife and family.

"If this misfortune were a single, or an unprecedented one, my surprise would cease; but when I see a liberal public prejudiced against a man whose misfortune was evidently the effect of chance, I cannot help concluding that some of those wretches who disgrace society by secretly injuring the fair fame of individuals—the vendors of private scandals—have been levelling their envenomed shafts against his character; and, like base assassins, stabbed his reputation in the dark. I will conclude, Mr. Editor, by observing, that I would as soon go myself, and recommend all my friends to go, by Mr. Pattenden's conveyance from Brighton to London as by any other, so much am I convinced of his skill, his care, and his attention.

"JUSTICE."

CHAPTER VI.

FROM 1810 TO 1814.

WITH the opening of the new year (1810) came
the happening of a curious accident at the Angel
Inn, St. Clement Danes, Strand. While some men
were putting a quantity of oats in the granary over
the stables, the floor gave way, and all the vast stock
of grain was precipitated into the stable, in which
stood four mail-coach horses. Three of them were
with difficulty rescued without their sustaining any
injury, but the fourth was completely smothered, and
was found to be dead by the time the oats were removed. The horsekeeper had only just left the stable,
and was in the act of locking the door on the outside
when the collapse occurred.

In Mr. Bishop's book I find it stated that in, or
about, 1809, a certain Mr. Bradford, known as "Miller"
Bradford, became associated with about a dozen others
in starting a two-end four-horse coach, the speed of
which "revolutionised the trade." Although a careful
search has been made through the files of all papers
extant at the date, I have been unable to find the
paragraph upon which the above statement is based;
but it is certainly the fact that, a year or two later,
Bradford started an office at 53 East Street, and had
a share in one or two coaches. Before this, however,
the firms of Crosweller & Boulton had done what they
could toward increasing the speed of coaches.

It has already been mentioned [1] that a mail-coach

---

[1] *Ante,* p. 42.

ran between London and Brighton so long ago as 1791,
leaving Brighton at half-past eight, and going *viâ*
Lewes to the Golden Cross, Charing Cross. How long
that mail ran I have been unable to discover; but
probably the prediction of the *Sussex Advertiser*, that
the speculation would not answer unless the subsidy
from the Post-Office were increased, was verified, for
we hear nothing of the old mail during recent years;
or it perhaps became amalgamated with the two night-
coaches run by Crosweller & Boulton. When, therefore, in the spring of 1810, it was announced that a
night-mail would be put upon the road, it was spoken
of as quite a new, and very convenient, institution.

The mail—I fancy it was a pair-horse concern—
made its first journey from either end on the evening
of Monday, the 21st May, 1810. It left Brighton at ten
o'clock at night, arriving in London at six in the morning, being thus eight hours on the road. The down-
mail left London (the Bull and Mouth) at a quarter
to eight, and reached the New Inn, North Street,
Brighton, at four in the morning, the route being
through Cuckfield, Crawley, Reigate, and the new cut
to Croydon. The Brightonians, seeing that their
town had materially increased year by year both in
size and population, rejoiced at the new arrangement,
and anticipated that great advantages would accrue to
the town and neighbourhood from the establishment of
the mails. They regarded with satisfaction the pro-
spect of an early delivery of letters, and a post open
till nearly ten at night, conveniences which the local
papers, in forgetfulness of the old mail, declared had
never been enjoyed before. Nor was it Brighton alone
that profited by the new arrangement. Reigate,
Cuckfield, and Crawley had up to this time been sub-
offices only; but, now that the mails ran through those
places, they were promoted to the dignity of general

offices, and shared with Brighton the advantages of a
late post and early delivery. In the advertisements relating to the mails, they are said to have been horsed,
in part, that is to say, by J. Willan, of the Bull and
Mouth, and Mr. Phillips of the New Inn, Brighton ;
but J. Willan was no connection of the Mr. J. J.
Willan who afterwards became a famous amateur on the
Brighton road. Willan of the Bull and Mouth was, I
fancy, a man who began life in a small way, and made
a good start afterwards by selling a perfect hack to the
Prince of Wales ; subsequently he horsed some of the
coaches, and gradually acquired a large business.

Prior to the establishment of the new mails, letters
were not delivered till between eight and nine in the
morning ; but now, notwithstanding the fact that all
Brighton was talking about the new departure, there
was at least one simple soul to whom early deliveries
and late posts appeared to be matters of no consequence. This East Street tradesman had done very
well under the old order of things, and bothered not
his head about new-fangled arrangements. He was,
however, the recipient of a letter after the mail had
been running but a day or two ; and, on the postman
knocking at his door a couple of hours earlier than
usual, he jumped from his bed, put his night-capped
head out of the window, and, according to the *Brighton
Herald* for the 26th May, 1810 (the mails only started
on the 21st), threatened to beat the disturber of his
rest *into a post* if he were not off ! The departure
of the mails from the General Post-Office was always
one of the sights of London. The mail-coaches were
drawn up outside, and as their respective bags were
made up, were summoned by the name of the place
they ran to—Oxford, Birmingham, Brighton, and so on.

Just as the mail was about to leave the New Inn,
Brighton, on the night of Tuesday, the 6th November

"A LONG LINE AWAITING THE POST OFFICE."

(1810), a soldier who had omitted the preliminary of paying his fare was discovered inside. " No pretences are permitted to cause a delay in the journey," said the mail notice ; so the stowaway was hauled out of the coach there and then. In explanation, he stated that he belonged to the German Legion ; had served in Spain and Portugal ; was for nine months a prisoner under the French ; and that, having made his escape, he was brought by an English transport to Portsmouth, whence he had that day walked to Brighton, a distance of about fifty miles. Lord C. Somerset, who then commanded the district, very kindly gave the destitute man money, lodgings, and food, the soldier announcing his intention of joining his regiment next day at Bexhill. It was discovered, however, that he had made off in the opposite direction—towards Portsmouth—so he was promptly pursued, and on the men approaching him he cut his throat ; but as the wound was not a severe one, he was brought back to Brighton, where subsequent investigation showed that, besides being a deserter, he had stolen several valuable articles. " Indiscriminate charity " was evidently as risky a thing then as it now is.

The cold weather, which came in with the year 1811, was so far productive of inconvenience to the London coaches that it froze the water at the mouth of the " Grand Arch " of the conduit which carried the water to the sea, and this being choked, the water overflowed the junction of the Preston and Lewes roads for nearly a quarter of a mile, thereby forcing the coaches to take a circuitous route to their respective destinations.

Though the professional side of stage-coaching had made great strides since the beginning of the century, we find no mention of amateurs, or rather, to use " Nimrod's " phrase, of " gentlemen coachmen," who in subsequent years added such great lustre to the Brighton

F

road. By 1811, however, amateur talent had begun
to take its place on the coach-box, for a contributor
to the *Brighton Herald* for the 2nd February of that
year wrote: "The education of our youth of fashion
is improving daily; several of them now drive stage-
coaches to town, and open the door of the carriage
for passengers, while the coachman remains on the
box. They receive the money also for the fare, and
many of them farm the perquisites of the coachmen
on the road, and generally pocket something by the
bargain. These young gentlemen will in time make
excellent hackney-coachmen."

Up to this period, however, there could have been but
little inducement for any one to take to coaching as a
pleasurable amusement. Long stages were the rule;
the horses could not have been first-rate, nor were the
roads; while there must have been at this time many
coaches the driving-boxes of which were not on
springs. This humane invention is generally credited
to Mr. John Warde, of Squerries, in Kent, the "father
of fox-hunting," and who was himself an enthusiastic
coachman of the then old school. He was accustomed
to drive, in addition to his own team, the old heavy
Gloucester coach, and must have endured much discomfort in consequence of the absence of springs
under the driving-box. Mr. Warde is reported to
have often suggested to coach proprietors the expedi-
ency of putting the driving-box on springs; but he
invariably received the same answer, "The beggars
will always be asleep." At last, however, his suggestion was adopted, but in what year the improvement
took place I am unable to ascertain. It may, however,
be noted that the members of the Benson Driving
Club, founded in 1807, and of the Four Horse Club,
established in the following year, did not drive what
we should call drags or coaches, but a kind of landau.

In his interesting book, "The History of Coaches,"
Mr. G. A. Thrupp writes : " The driving-box of the post-
coaches was placed high above the horses on a narrow
boot, something like what is called a Salisbury boot ;
this was placed upon the beds or timbers of the carriage,
with a tolerably comfortable seat for two persons upon
it ; but the jolting and shaking over rough bits in the
road must have been very trying.   In the Hall of the
Coachmakers' Company in Noble Street, Cheapside, is
a picture of Hyde Park Corner in 1796, painted by
Dagaty, in which is an old stage-coach : the hinder
part has a boot and guard's seat attached to the body,
as in modern stage-coaches ; but the box is detached
from the body, and on the beds, as described above."
Rowlandson has given us a drawing of a stage-coach
built on the above-mentioned lines, and Mr. Thrupp
has engraved it in his book.   The box-seat looks anything but a comfortable perch, and its rail is about
two feet below the roof of the coach ;[1] there are no
front seats, nor are there any back seats ; but suspended
over the hind-axle, which is some distance behind the
back of the body, is a large basket, of a shape resem-
bling a Ralli car, in which the outside passengers were
carried.   So long as these primitive arrangements prevailed, no wonder that amateur talent kept clear of the
stage-coach.

And now to go on with the Brighton road.   The
Herald for the 8th June 1811 tells us that "twenty-
eight coaches at present pass daily between Brighton
and London, conveying between fifty and sixty thousand persons in five months.   Thirty-five years ago
only one went daily to town, and that went by the
circuitous route of Lewes.   During the last twenty

---

[1] For notice on the height of coaches, see *ante*, in chapter on
Legislation, pp. 28 and 29.

years Brighton has quadrupled its population." This estimate of the coaches was under the mark, there being really thirty-four, including three-days-a-week coaches, on the road, as will be seen from the following lists :—

From the Blue Office, 44 East Street, Brighton :

CROSWELLER, CUDDINGTON, ALLAN, VALLANCE, & Co., Proprietors.

Coaches at 8, 10, and 12 o'clock, for Hatchett's White Horse Cellar (not Cellars), the Blossoms Inn, Lawrence Lane, Cheapside, and the George and Blue Boar, Holborn.

At half-past nine every night, a Four-Horse Coach, guarded and lighted, calling at the George Inn, Borough, and the Hope, Charing Cross.

From the Spread Eagle, East Street.

A Four-Horse Accommodation Coach, to carry four inside, at half-past nine, to the Bull Inn, Bishopsgate Street.

This coach was put on by a new proprietor, named Mackerell, who had formerly been booking-clerk to Marsh & Co., who had an office at the Bull, Bishopsgate, London. Mackerell bought Waldegrave's coach, and set up for himself; but, as will presently appear, the two became involved in a newspaper war. Shortly afterwards Mackerell started an eleven-o'clock coach to London, and opened a Brighton office of his own at 134 North Street, which he called the "only general office for four-horse coaches," whence also started the Royal Brighton and Telegraph coaches to the White Horse, Fetter Lane, and Bull Inn, Bishopsgate. These coaches he stated to be on an improved principle, and were particularly constructed for safety. Fares, twenty-three shillings inside, and fourteen out.

From the General (Red) Coach-Office, 10 Castle Square.

A Post-Coach every morning at eight, by way of Cuckfield, Crawley, Reigate, and Croydon to the Golden Cross, Charing Cross, Swan with Two Necks, Lad Lane, and the Spread Eagle, Gracechurch Street.

A new and elegant Post-Coach (four inside) at eleven on Mondays, Wednesdays, and Fridays, to the same inns, and taking eight hours for the journey.

A Post-Coach daily at ten o'clock in the morning to the Swan with Two Necks and Spread Eagle, Gracechurch Street.

A Post-Coach on Sundays, Tuesdays, and Thursdays, at 11 A.M., for the Golden Cross, Charing Cross.

A new and expeditious Post-Coach at ten o'clock every night during the season to the Golden Cross, Charing Cross.

A new Telegraph Coach through Lewes, Uckfield, Maresfield, East Grinstead, and Croydon, every morning at six, to the Golden Cross and Spread Eagle, arriving at half-past three, being nine hours and a half on the road. These coaches were run by Boulton, Barry, Gourd, Tilt, & Co., who were responsible for the statement that the coaches were new and easy, and travelled post.

From the old coach-office, North Street, William Pattenden ran a four-horse coach daily at eight o'clock along the new road so as to avoid the hills. The route lay through Henfield, Horsham, Dorking, Boxhill, Epsom, Ewell, Morden, Merton, Tooting, and Clapham, and the coach went to the White Lion, Talbot Court, Gracechurch Street, and the Angel, St. Clement Danes, Strand, calling at the Bolt-in-Tun, Fleet Street, and the Catherine Wheel in the Borough.

In addition to the above, Samuel Waldegrave ran a couple of coaches between London and Brighton, but though they are said to run to the Bull Inn, Bishopsgate Street, the Brighton starting-point is not mentioned.

It was said just now that Mackerell and Waldegrave engaged in a newspaper warfare, the beginning of which was when, in the paper of the 31st August 1811, Mackerell advertised that "the New Twopenny book-keeping office, adjoining the Old Bull Inn Gateway, Bishopsgate Street, has no connection whatever with his concern at Marsh & Son's Original and General Coach and Waggon Office, Bull Inn Yard, Bishopsgate

Street." Mackerell then circulated a handbill headed "Caution," in which he stated that he had bought Waldegrave's business; and that Waldegrave was dishonourably booking for other coaches to injure him (Mackerell), who had paid a great sum for the said business and coaches. To this Waldegrave replied that Mackerell's representation was false; for Mackerell had not only broken his agreement, but he had also omitted to pay a great part of the purchase-money, while he had also set up an opposition coach in another concern, and spread reports injurious to Waldegrave's good name. This brought Mackerell into print again to inform "his numerous friends that the statement given by S. Waldegrave, so far as it relates to the alleged breach of agreement on the part of Mackerell, is utterly destitute of truth;" and so the quarrel continued for a long time.

Meanwhile the lease of the New Inn in North Street was sold by auction for the small premium of £20, the rent of the house being 600 guineas a year; and a Mr. James Rickards became the new tenant of the White Horse, Fetter Lane.

Except that the royal mail, the contractors for which were J. Cross, of London, and Tilt, Barry, & Gourd, of Brighton, was removed from Bradford's office, 53 East Street, to the Original (Red) Coach-Office, 10 Castle Square, and that a new coach, named the Princess Charlotte, was started by Noble, Roberts, & Co., coaching would not appear to have undergone any very great change in the year 1812. Noble, Roberts, & Co. was probably Mackerell's firm, as in the previous year (1811) Mackerell & Roberts ran to London, and the Princess Charlotte, which left Brighton at half-past nine, called at Mackerell's old place, Marsh's office in Bishopsgate, as well as the White Horse, Fetter Lane, and the Belle Sauvage.

One of the coaching businesses seems to have been given up, or perhaps it was only one of the confederacies formed for the season, as on the 4th of November 1812, Mr. Aldridge sold at his repository "about forty horses, of different colours, all remarkably fast: also four coaches: these are part of a general stock;" and a month later the "residue of a joint-stock," consisting of fifty horses, mostly young and in high condition, were disposed of at the same mart.

When we come to read the accounts of the coach robberies of old, and see in how remarkable a manner the operations of thieves were facilitated, one cannot help wondering how it was that coaches were not despoiled much oftener. In February 1812, Brighton was all excitement on the fact being made known that a parcel containing notes to the value of between £3000 and £4000 had been abstracted from one of the Blue coaches. It appears that Messrs. Brown, Hall, Lashmar, & West, proprietors of the Union Bank at Brighton, had been in the habit of hiring— plenty of people, no doubt, were aware of the custom— of Crosweller & Co. a box beneath the seat of one of their London coaches, in order to allow of a small box containing cash, &c., being transmitted to their agents in London *with a greater degree of security!* Each box had two keys, for the convenience of the parties at either end. On the aforesaid 5th of February 1812, the notes—they having been cashed at the bank of Messrs. Weston & Co. in the Borough—were placed in the box for transmission to Brighton. In due course the Blue coach reached the Blue Office, Brighton, where Mr. Peacock, one of the Union Bank clerks, was, as usual, in waiting to receive the contents of the box under the seat. Provided with his key, he proceeded to unlock the box, when he made the discovery that it had been broken open and the contents taken. As there was no

guard, one is scarcely surprised to read that "the coachman was immediately applied to;" but he, poor man,
could, of course, do no more than tell the history of his
journey, and this is the substance of his simple narrative. The six inside places were booked at the London office, as the presence of a stranger would have
been fatal to the proposed operations. Two only of
the six passengers turned up when the coach started,
a gentleman and lady, "dressed in the first style of
fashion, and who seemed to be man and wife." Two
more of the six were picked up soon afterwards, and
then, in the cosy privacy of the capacious inside, the party
proceeded to anticipate the operations of Mr. Peacock,
of the Union Bank, Brighton. On the coach reaching
Sutton, about eleven miles from London, the lady was
suddenly taken ill, and was obliged to alight, she and
her husband being left at the inn. Finding that room
had unexpectedly been made inside, a foreign gentleman,
who had been riding outside, exchanged his seat for an
inside one, when he, of course, became the companion
of the two men who had been picked up on the road.
On the coach arriving at Reigate, the two men left,
while the horses were being changed, to inquire, as
they said, after a friend. They returned before the
coach started, and told the coachman that as the friend
they expected to find at Brighton had returned to London, it was useless for them to proceed farther, so they
paid their fares and took their leave. No sort of sus-
picion attached to the passenger who shifted from the
out to the inside, as he was a well-known resident
of Brighton; it was, therefore, as clear as the proverbial mud, that the robbery was committed by the four
insides between London and Sutton.

It is scarcely credible that business people should
have sent large sums of money up and down in this
casual way; they were as heedless of consequences as

those ladies who, in spite of the constant committal of
jewel robberies, persist in casually leaving thousands of
pounds' worth of trinkets on their dressing-table when
they go down to dinner. After the steed was stolen,
however, the proprietors of the Union Bank carefully
shut the stable door, and then for many months spent
large sums of money in advertising their loss, giving
the numbers of all the notes, and offering a reward of
£300. Some time after the robbery a few of the stolen
notes were found in circulation, but the reward was
never claimed.

The postmasters on the London and Brighton road
were, like those on other routes, in connection with
certain hotels to which their horses went; and from
them, if the passengers had no objection, the next
horses were taken, one of the advantages of this arrangement being that each postmaster got a chance of
business, and knew that his horses would be properly
looked after in his friend's yard ; but the proprietors of
rival houses were accustomed to bribe the postboys to
change at their establishments instead of at those to
which they were bidden to drive by the occupants of
the chaise or carriage. This state of things having
come to the ears of the postmasters on the road, several
of them combined, and advertised in the August papers
(1812) that, as investigation had proved the existence
of a complete system of bribing postboys, they had resolved to at once discharge any boy who induced a fare
to go to any other inn than that to which he was
ordered.

At the same time an old turnpike gate grievance
once more cropped up. Writing to the *Brighton
Herald* of the 25th July 1812, a correspondent signing
himself "Viator" complained that at one gate on the
London road appeared this notice : "Take a ticket
here to clear to Brighton." The artful keeper of the

'pike, however, managed to keep one of the gates shut,
and by turning the board managed to present its blank
side to the view of travellers proceeding in the direction of Brighton ; consequently they omitted to take a
ticket, unless they were up to the trick, and had to
pay again. " Whose business is it," asked Viator, " to
see to these things ? "

This letter called forth one from Sir R. Phillips,
who, writing as " Publicola," gave his experience of the
Shoreham Bridge Gate. The man there gave no
tickets ; he put up no name, as he should have done ;
and, when asked, he declined to give his name ; from
which it would seem that the authorities who farmed
out the tolls cared very little what went on so long as
they got their money.

Brighton at this time was not without its humours.
Four gentlemen, said to be officers, passed along the
front in a chaise drawn by " four spanking ponies."
Two of them sat inside the chaise, the other two acting
as postillions ; an outrider preceded the turn-out, and
a party of friends rode on horseback in the rear of the
conveyance, to the amusement of the people about.
" On the same day," we learn, " the Countess of
P—— partook of the healthful exercise of riding in
a donkey-cart, attended by one of her livery servants
mounted on an asinine charger, which, in a manner
peculiar to those frisky animals, threw his rider in
North Street with all the neatness imaginable, to the
infinite *delight* of the spectators ; " possibly the reporter
meant amusement.

There was yet another free show for the Brighton
lounger. A chaise drawn by six horses, all of which
were profusely decorated with favours and coloured
ribands, was seen to be travelling at a quick pace
through Brighton's principal street. There were naturally many inquiries as to whom the vehicle contained.

and it subsequently transpired that one of the post-
boys in the employ of Crosweller & Blaber had that
day been married at Worthing, and was bringing home
his bride in " bang-up stile," as he phrased it.

In 1812 the only London coach running through
Horsham was that run by William Pattenden from the
General (Red) Office, 10 Castle Square; but in 1813
we find a coach called the Duke of Norfolk running
the same route from the same office; but its destinations were the Angel, St. Clement Danes, Strand, the
Belle Sauvage, and the Spread Eagle; while the proprietors were John Eames, William Horne, & Co.;
but whether this was a new coach, or only a continuation of Pattenden's, I am unable to say. From the
advertisements, however, one gleans that one could
travel expeditiously to London—that is to say, in eight
hours—from the same Red Office by the old original
coach, which carried four or six passengers inside, and
travelled *via* Cuckfield, Crawley, and Reigate to the
Golden Cross, Charing Cross, Holborn, and the City.
John Cross and Co. were said to be the proprietors;
but the coach was advertised as being conducted by
Charles and George Newman. In August (1813), however, for some unexplained reason, the Red coaches
were removed, temporarily only, it would appear, from
the Red Office to the New Inn (now the Clarence),
North Street.

Meantime there was the usual amount of activity
at the Blue Office, whence Crosweller, Cuddington,
Pockney, & Co. ran three London coaches a day, at
eight and ten o'clock, and at ten at night, all three
apparently travelling by the Cuckfield and Reigate
route. In the summer, however (1813), Boulton,
Horne, & Co. started a couple of new coaches from
the Red Office. They were named respectively the
Defiance and the Prince Regent; both left at nine

o'clock, and both ran to the Ship, Charing Cross; the
White Bear, Piccadilly; the White Horse, Fetter Lane;
and the Bull Inn, Bishopsgate. The routes, unfortunately, are not mentioned; but the two coaches no doubt
travelled by different roads. By the Defiance the fares
were fifteen shillings inside and ten shillings out, and
by the Prince Regent "cheap and expeditious travelling" was exemplified by the charge being brought
down to twelve shillings inside and eight shillings outside; but according to an advertisement in the following November, the Prince Regent's fares appear to have
been fifteen shillings inside and eleven shillings out.

Private carriages were not exempt from the misfortunes which occasionally overtook the stage-coaches,
as in July 1813 Lord C. Somerset and his family
nearly came to grief while his private travelling carriage, drawn by four horses, was descending Pyecombe
Hill. The leaders' reins broke, and away went the
horses down the decline. A butcher driving a cart,
in which was a fat calf, failed to get out of the way
in time, and into the cart the carriage crashed; the
pole went through the tail-board and ran into the
calf, of course turning the cart over, while Lord
C. Somerset's horses joined in the general confusion
on the ground. When all had been righted, it was
found that the leaders of the coach were not materially
injured, nor were the butcher and his horse; the calf,
however, was killed. It was only a few weeks after
this mishap that Mackerell's coach had a very narrow
escape in Church Street. By the time it reached
Brighton from London, in October, darkness had set
in. The road opposite the old barracks had been
undergoing some repairs, and a big hole was very
carelessly left unguarded. Into this excavation the
leaders fell, and it says something for the skill of the
coachman that he was able to prevent the wheelers

going into it too. He managed to stop them, however, and the coach was not overturned, but the leaders were much cut and injured. It was by accidents like these that the profits of those who horsed the coaches were so often reduced or turned into a loss; for it depended upon the luck a man had with his stock whether the amount he drew every month paid him or not.

The coaches depended for their success as much upon parcels as passengers, if not more, and in very early times the coachman was often asked to undertake the duties of postman. To put a stop to this once common state of things, which interfered with the revenue receipts, the Act 42 Geo. III. c. 81 was passed; it provided that all letters must be sent through the Post-Office, and not by ordinary public conveyances. A certain mercantile house in the City, however, appeared to think that a printed circular letter did not come within the provisions of the statute, so they sent it by coach, with the result that the Postmaster-General proceeded against them, and recovered penalties to the amount of £75.

To turn to another matter, in 1814 the Thames was frozen over, and the severity of the weather was greatly felt by the coachmen on the different roads, while travelling was of course much impeded by the snow. One of Brighton's visitors, a Mr. Whitbread, amused himself by sleighing, and was one day, while driving a little way out of the town, considerably surprised to find his horse suddenly stopped by a countryman, who hoped the gentleman was not hurt. Mr. Whitbread was naturally at a loss to account for the man's evident interest concerning his welfare; but it turned out that his would-be rescuer had never before seen a sleigh, and was under the impression that the horse had bolted; that the wheels of the carriage had become detached;

and that Mr. Whitbread was in imminent danger of being turned over.

So far as the coaching arrangements of the year are concerned, there ran from the Red Office, 10 Castle Square, Newman's Prince Regent (*viâ* Cuckfield and Reigate) at nine in the morning; the Princess Charlotte at ten, put on by Whitchurch, Thorpe, & Co.; the Duke of Norfolk, run by Barrett & Burgess, leaving Brighton at nine, and travelling by way of Horsham and Dorking; Painter & Simcock's coach ran through Lewes and Uckfield; and a night-coach started at ten P.M.   A new and fast coach called the Eclipse, doing the journey in six hours, was started—seven coaches in all running from the Red Office.   The Eclipse, by the way, was put on the road to run opposition to a coach called the Hero, owned by Whitchurch & Co., of 135 North Street, this being the very first coach to make the journey to London and back in the day.

The Blue coaches appear to have run as usual; while the Dart, taking a leaf out of the Eclipse's book, left 18 Castle Square, Brighton, at six in the morning, and returned from the White Bear, Piccadilly, at three in the afternoon; while the Times left 9 and 15 Castle Square at one, reaching the Four Swans at eight, and leaving the latter place at one daily.

Although it has nothing to do with the Brighton road, it may be of interest to some to learn that, according to a notice in the *Brighton Herald* for the 21st May 1814, in the year in which a stage-coach first ran to town and back in a day, early green peas were being sold at four guineas a pint in Covent Garden Market.

At this time the Emperor Alexander, during his visit to England, made a tour in Sussex, and, under the heading " Imperial Condescension," the above-mentioned journal narrates how, while driving on a Sunday in the neighbourhood of Hellingley, His Majesty was much struck with an old house described as the residence of Mr. R., a wealthy yeoman. The party stopped, and were shown over the premises by Mr. and Mrs. R., after which the Emperor "condescended" to express his surprise at finding "so many of the elegancies of life in the house of a farmer!" Later in the day another stoppage was made for refreshment near Battle, and the presence of His Majesty having somehow or other become known inside the church, the congregation forthwith rushed out to see the Imperial visitor, the service thus rudely interrupted being suspended while those who had, but a few moments before, been devout worshippers satisfied their curiosity.

CHAPTER VII.

THE table given below affords all the information that
can be gleaned in connection with the starting and
arrival of the several coaches. It is compiled from
Cary's "New Itinerary," which was published for the
benefit of travellers to, rather than from, Brighton;
consequently the hours of return are not in all cases
given. The Brighton and Sussex papers, on the other
hand, generally give the times at which the coaches
left Brighton, leaving out in many cases the times
of the departure from London, while both Cary and
the Sussex papers omit many of the names of the
coaches. Further uncertainty is caused by the fact
that, at both ends, the coaches called at several offices
and inns; it has not, therefore, been possible to fill
in the blanks in every instance. It may also be pointed
out that the table does not profess to show how
many coaches ran between London and Brighton.
As I stated just now, all of them called at more
than one place, and it has been found impossible
to identify each coach; but the number running each
way was about eighteen. The following (pp. 98, 99),
however, is a table showing the coach accommodation
in 1815.

In the county of Sussex the price of oats has seldom
or never been high, but Bradford, the coach proprietor,
looked further afield for some of his supplies, as he
bought two hundred quarters of French oats of the

primest quality at eighteen shillings a quarter, a price at which, at that date (1815), running a coach could profitably be carried on. At the present time (1893) the contract price for foraging horses varies between sixteen and twenty shillings.

In one or two other places I have ventured to make mention of the driving of the ancients. Judging from an account in the papers for the 2nd September 1815, the coachman of the Comet appears to have been guilty of an amount of carelessness which would have done discredit to the youngest and least experienced amateur of to-day. The coach had completed its journey from London, and had set down the greater number of its passengers at Whitchurch's Office, 18 Castle Square, and, on leaving there, was about to proceed to some other places. The coachman, however, in turning, came round so abruptly that he got the coach on the lock, and she capsized. The coachman was very much hurt, and so were a gentleman who was riding outside, and a lady who was an inside passenger; but the hardest luck of all was that which overtook Mr. Walker. He had gone to the office to meet a friend bound for the Old Ship, and had climbed on the coach as she moved away from the office in Castle Square. Scarcely was he seated than the accident happened, and he had his leg broken, but subsequently returned thanks in the columns of the *Gazette* for kind inquiries, and stated that he was getting better.

A rather good story is told in the *Brighton Gazette* for the 2nd September 1815, in connection with that really remarkable man John Gully. While travelling from London to Brighton, he stopped for refreshment at Reigate, and soon after he had begun his meal a heavily laden coach drew up at the inn—most probably the White Hart, the terminus of the present Magnet. " Well, gentlemen," quoth the waiter, " you are just

G

1815.

Depart from	Coach.	Hour.	Route.	Place of Arrival.	Hours on Road.	Return to London.
Angel Inn, Strand. Belle Sauvage.	A coach.	8.45 a.m.	Ryegate, Cuckfield.	...	...	...
" "	„	8.0 a.m.	„	...	...	...
" "	The Hero.	2.30 p.m., 6.30 on Sundays.	„	{ Whitchurch's Office.	7 hours.	6.30 a.m.
Blossoms Inn, Laurence Lane, Cheapside.	A post-coach.	8.0 a.m.	Lewes.	...	...	...
„ „	Night-coach.	8.30 p.m.	...	Blue Office.	8 hours.	10.0 p.m.
„	Blue coach.	9.0 a.m.	{ Clapham, Sutton, Ryegate, Crawley, Cuckfield.	Blue Office.	7 hours.	10.0 a.m.
„	True Blue.	11.0 a.m.	{ Croydon, Ryegate, Crawley, Hickstead.	...	6 hours.	11.0 a.m.
„	„	1.0 p.m.	...	...	6 hours.	1.0 p.m.
Bolt-in-Tun.	A coach.	6.0 a.m.	{ Dorking, Horsham, Steyning.	Pattenden's.	4.30 p.m.	7.0 a.m.
Bull, Bishopsgate.	Dart.	2.30 p.m.	{ Croydon, Ryegate, Cuckfield.	Union Office.	6 hours.	7.0 a.m.
Bull, Holborn. Four Swans, Bishopsgate.	A coach.	8.0 a.m.	Sutton, Ryegate.	Old Ship.	8¼ hours.	9.0 a.m.
„	„	7.0 a.m.	...	...	7 hours.	9.0 a.m.
„	„	9.0 a.m.	...	...	7 hours.	11.0 a.m.
		11.0 a.m.	...	...	...	3.0 p.m.
George and Blue Bear.	Post-coach.	7.0 a.m.	{ Streatham, Ryegate, Crawley, Hickstead.	...	...	9.0 a.m.

From	Coach	Departure	Route	Office	Duration	Arrival
Golden Cross, Charing Cross.	Prince Regent.	8.0 a.m.	Croydon, Crawley, Cuckfield.	Red Office, 10 Castle Square.	8 hours.	9.0 a.m.
"	Eclipse.	3.0 p.m.	...	"	6 hours.	6.0 a.m. (6 hours).
"	Regency.	8.30 a.m.	Croydon, Ryegate, Cuckfield.	...	7½ hours.	9.0 a.m.
"	Defiance.	...	...	Red Office.	...	1.0 p.m.
Spread Eagle, Gracechurch Street.	Comet.	10.0 a.m.	Ryegate, Crawley, Hickstead.	14 Castle Square.	7 hours.	10.0 a.m.
"	Dart.	3.0 p.m.	"	14 Castle Square.	6 hours.	7.0 a.m.
Waldegrave's New Hotel and Bull Inn, Bishopsgate.	A coach.	7.0 a.m.	", Brixton, Croydon, Ryegate, Crawley, Cuckfield.	Blue Office.	...	...
"	True Blue.	11.0 a.m.	", Croydon, Godstone, E. Grinstead, Uckfield, Lewes.	...	...	...
"	"	7.0 a.m.	Croydon, Ryegate, Cuckfield.	Red Office, 10 Castle Square.	...	...
White Horse, Fetter Lane.	Accommodation coach.	9.15 a.m.	Dorking, Leatherhead, Horsham.	Union Office.	...	9.0 a.m.
"	Princess Charlotte.	10.0 a.m.	Croydon, Ryegate, Cuckfield.	135 North Street.	8 hours.	1.0 p.m. (7 hours).
White Bear, Piccadilly.	Times.	2.0 p.m.	"	...	6¾ hours.	1.0 p.m. (7 hours).
"	Duke of Norfolk.	8.45 a.m.	Horsham, Henfield.	...	8¼ hours.	9.0 a.m. (9 hours).

The hours of the arrival and departure as given in the body of the book are taken from advertisements in the papers. The above Table is copied from Cary. This will explain whatever discrepancies may be noticed.

in time to see John Gully set to with the Chicken."
"The Chicken," it is hardly necessary to explain, was
that chivalrous prize-fighter Henry Pearce, known in
the ring as the "Game Chicken," the man who rescued
Gully from the Fleet Prison, and who eventually lost
his life in rescuing some women from a burning building. Well, the coach-passengers crowded into the
hotel, and some of the more bold peeped into the room
in which Gully was, and there, sure enough, he was
setting to with the Chicken—but it was a roast chicken.
In the event of there being any truth in this story, it is
but an illustration of how the names of well-known
pugilists were held in remembrance ; for the last battle
between Gully and the "Game Chicken" took place
just ten years previously, that is to say, on the 8th of
October 1805. At the time of the above story Gully
was landlord of the Plough Tavern, Carey Street, Lin-
coln's Inn Fields, whither he retired about 1809, after
his two fights with Gregson.

There is no reason to believe that the Brighton
mail-coach had ceased to run at this time ; but, in the
autumn of 1815, the Post-Office were anxious to find
some one to contract for carrying the mails between
London, Brighton, and other places in Sussex in "light
carts," and at a rate of seven miles an hour, stoppages
included.

In 1816 Hine[1] & Co. put on the road a new light
coach to carry four inside passengers ; for the old six
insides were now going out of favour. This new concern left 52 East Street, the corner of Steyne Lane,
at half-past nine in the morning, returning from the

---

[1] Hine senior and Crosweller drove the two "Blue" pair-horse
coaches which ran at the beginning of the century, and Hine was
a very popular and skilful coachman. It was said that he must have
driven 100,000 persons into Brighton without having had an accident. Amongst his more famous passengers were Mathews, who so

Bell, Holborn, at half-past eight in the evening, thus adding to the number of the coaches which made the double journey to London and back in a day. At this time, too, a decision was given whereby the stage-coaches were relieved of a kind of injustice under which they had for some time laboured. The turnpike people had long argued that if a coach returned with a different team to that with which it had previously passed through a gate, it was liable to pay toll a second time, and this view of the case had been upheld in more than one court of law. At last, however, some coach proprietors combined, and took a test case to the Court of King's Bench, where a victory was gained by the coach proprietors, the decision causing an annual saving of many hundreds of pounds a year to the coachmasters.

From a very early period of its history, the Brighton road had been the scene of a variety of matches against time. Horses had been ridden and driven along it for wagers of a greater or lesser amount, just as in recent years people have attempted, on a coach, in sulkies, in the saddle, and on cycles, to lower records. In the summer of 1816 a Captain Brodie drove a tandem from the Marsh Gate, Lambeth, to the King's Arms, George Street, Brighton, in four hours and fifty minutes; and a day or two later, Captain Wombwell, of the First Life Guards, backed himself for a wager of 500 guineas to drive a like team over the same distance, but in less time, without changing horses. Starting from the Marsh Gate at four in the morning, the gallant Captain reached Brighton at a quarter to nine, thus beating

severely caricatured the dress of the amateur coachmen of the day in " Hit or Miss ;" Munden, Emery, and Russell, as well as Bannister, Quick, Mr. Thornton, the Rev. Rowland Hill, Sir M. Tierney, and Mr. G. Faithful. Hine had only just given up driving the Bellerophon, started in 1811, and named after Captain Maitland's ship.

Captain Brodie's time by five minutes, and winning his
bet. One of the earliest matches between London and
Brighton was brought about by a bet made by a Sussex
parson with an officer of a cavalry regiment, the former
undertaking to ride his own horse between the two
places in a shorter time than would be occupied by his
gallant opponent in posting down, and the parson won
by a few minutes. The Prince of Wales, too, drove
that very senseless team a "random," *i.e.* three horses
one in front of another, from London to Brighton
in four hours and a half; while in later times a trotting
match, to which Mr. C. Webling, now (1893) proprietor
of the Excelsior Tunbridge Wells coach, and Mr. H.
L. Beckett, the well-known amateur coachman, were
the parties, took place. The late James Selby's drive
against time [1] is of course well remembered. Accounts
of different kinds of matches are to be found in such
numbers in the pages of the newspapers, that it has
not been deemed worth while to extract them.

In connection with stage-coaching, as in other matters, history repeats itself. Those who travel by the
modern coaches are familiar with the boys who turn
wheels, and who, by an exhibition of youthful pedes-
trianism, try to extract coppers from the passengers.
These little urchins, however, had their prototypes
upwards of seventy years ago, for "a great many indi-
gent parents," we are told, were in the habit of sending
out their children to places at which the stage-coaches
were in the habit of stopping, to beg money from the
passengers. At Hickstead, on the new road between
Pyecombe and Staplefield Common, nine or ten juve-

---

[1] On the 13th July 1888, Selby drove the "Old Times" coach
from Hatchett's, in Piccadilly, to the Old Ship, at Brighton, and
back, in seven hours and fifty minutes. The time from London to
Brighton was three hours and fifty-six minutes, and that from
Brighton three hours and fifty-four minutes.

nile mendicants between four and six years of age would be found waiting for coaches.

I must not, however, forget to mention that the feature of the stage-coaching of 1816 was the starting of a new fast coach by a confederacy called by the *Annual Register* [1] " some Jews." It was put on the road in the spring, and was timed to do the journey between London and Brighton, fifty-three miles, in six hours, with a pledge that, if the coach did not accomplish the journey in that time, the proprietors would carry the passengers gratis ; to accomplish this, the horses were kept upon a gallop all the way ; and, " notwithstanding the great risk," the coach was always filled with passengers. On one of the journeys the coachman broke three whips, and in one week fifteen horses died. The coach, however, was never once capsized, and no material accident happened, except overturning a fish-cart near Kennington Common, whereby the driver was injured, but not seriously. This coach ran for about three months, and excited attention and curiosity all along the road. A crowd used to collect at the Elephant and Castle to see it start and come in, and it always kept its time within a few minutes. Its pace, however, in populous places like Newington, caused information to be laid against it under the Act of Parliament for regulating stage-coaches, and this being followed up, speed was reduced, and the coach was afterwards about three-quarters of an hour longer on the road.

What reasons, beyond bad management and bad coachmanship, can be assigned for this alarming sacrifice of horseflesh and whips, not to mention collisions with fish-carts and authorities, I am at a loss to understand. Unless the time-bills of the other coaches

---

[1] Vol. lviii. p. 161.

are untrustworthy, several of them—the Dart and the
True Blue, for instance—did the journey comfortably
in six hours : so the gentlemen who were at the head
of this ill-fated undertaking were cutting no record.
The present Comet runs between London and Brighton
in six hours, and her stoppages are long in comparison
with those made on the six-hour coaches seventy-five
years ago. *They* went right through, and are said to
have allowed no more time at the end of each stage
than was necessary to put to the fresh horses. Mr.
Freeman, however, gives his passengers a full half-hour
for luncheon at Horley, thus reducing the time on the
road to five hours and a half. I have never timed the
stoppages on the road ; but if we allow three minutes
at Streatham, four at Purley, four at Merstham, four at
Hand Cross, and six at Albourne, we have twenty-one
minutes for changes, or fifty-one minutes out of the six
hours for stoppages, consequently but five hours and
nine minutes remain in which to travel the fifty-three
miles and a half which intervene between the Hotel
Victoria and the Old Ship. During this time scarcely
a horse is out of a trot from start to finish, and
perhaps a leader will not be touched all the way.
The roads are, of course, better than they used to be ;
but how about the three whips broken in the course of
a single journey ? The whip was an instrument upon
which it was claimed for the old performers that they
could play in a manner far beyond the dream of the
present race of coachmen ; yet the artist in charge of
this Hebrew coach seems to have made a terrible mess
of hitting his horses.

Racing has claimed a good many victims in one way
and another, and one is somewhat surprised to find
that, in the autumn of 1816, so experienced a coachman as Snow was a party to this dangerous sort of
thing. One Saturday night the Phœnix and Snow's

Dart, both heavily loaded, were sailing along at a great
pace between Patcham and Brighton, the Phœnix leading, when Snow foolishly tried to overtake it.   As
it was in the evening in October, the light was bad, a
circumstance which no doubt had something to do
with what followed. Snow failing to clear the Phœnix,
ran into her, and overturned her, the Dart losing her
dickey-seat in the scrimmage.   The crash was heard
a long way off, and the shrieking was described as
being very terrible.   Mr. Taylor, of the Golden Cross,
had his thigh broken ; some of the other passengers
sustained fractures ; and nearly all were more or less
damaged. Snow, through whose fault the accident
occurred, was much hurt, and there was some talk of
prosecuting him ; but whether the threat was carried
into effect, I cannot find out.

Several fresh arrangements are met with in connection
with the year 1817.   As soon as the summer coaches
were running in their full strength, the Golden Cross
Inn, Brighton, became the starting-point of coaches
which left for London at six, nine, ten, and three
o'clock. G. Barratt & Co. had the night-coach, which
left 10 Castle Square at ten at night; while from the
Blue Office ran the accommodation coach at nine and
the True Blue at two, the public being informed that
the object of the latter coach was to keep its time, and
not to indulge in the folly of racing other coaches,
which exposed the passengers to the most serious accidents. At eleven o'clock a light post-coach set out *via*
Pyecombe, Crawley, and Reigate, and it was claimed
for this vehicle that it had the merit of travelling
like a post-chaise. This coach carried four passengers
inside and four out, and, like several other vehicles of
small capacity, could be hired for the exclusive use
of private parties, who could then start at their own
hour. The Irresistible, a new light post-coach, run

by a Mr. Rugeroh,[1] was removed from the Union Coach-
Office, in Castle Square, to Whitchurch's Office, 135
North Street, and ran as in the previous year up one
day and down the next, the Boar and Castle, Oxford
Street, and the Gloucester Coffee-House, Piccadilly,
being the houses of call in London. The following
table (pp. 108, 109), to which the remarks already made
in connection with that of 1815 apply, shows most of
the places in London at which it was possible for a
passenger to book for Brighton.

The mail-coach system, as inaugurated by Mr. Palmer
of Bath,[2] appears to have commended itself to our
French neighbours, as, in the year 1817, the French
Government asked some of the London coachbuilders
whether they would contract to build for France 900
mail-coaches at the price of £150 each ; but I cannot
discover whether the offer was declined or accepted.

In another place I have ventured to make some
remarks about coachmen and their performances ; but
in connection with a couple of paragraphs I find in
the papers of this date (1817), it will for the present
suffice to say that we have as yet found very little
information, in praise or otherwise, of coachmen. They
have hitherto no individuality ; we are told the names
of very few, and these we chiefly get through the
medium of police-court proceedings. I have, however, come across two paragraphs which are not quite
complimentary to the artists of 1817. The first is
from the *Sussex Gazette*, in which journal a correspondent, after complaining of the extent to which
people suffered by the cupidity and negligence of stage-
coachmen, suggested that while the proprietors should
still be liable to pay damages, the coachmen should

---

[1] Mr. Rugeroh died in 1846 at the age of eighty, while his wife
died so long ago as 1787.   [2] See *post*, p. 110.

be imprisoned if it should be found that the accident,
in respect of which damages were claimed, was brought
about by overloading; and that accidents were sometimes due to this cause we may readily understand
on reading in the *Brighton Herald* that a "respectable
correspondent" had begged the editor of that paper to
give a gentle hint to coachmen respecting the quantity
of luggage which was piled up (often to the height of
four feet) on the tops of their coaches. The building up
of these luggage stacks, it was suggested, was not only
illegal, but rendered the coaches so loaded liable to be
turned over by the slightest accident. This warning,
however, would appear to have fallen on deaf ears, as
a few months later the *Herald* told its readers that on
one of the stage-coaches there was more than four feet
of luggage, while on the summit of all that reclined
a passenger, who must have looked like one of the
figures on the top of a wedding-cake.

The theft of the Union Bank notes, not to mention
other coach robberies which were taking place almost
daily in different parts of England, does not appear to
have induced coach and waggon proprietors to adopt any
means for effectually guarding the property committed
to their care. A deal box, containing jewellery to the
value of £150, was abstracted from Knowles's van
while the horses were being baited at Merstham; and
shortly afterwards a trunk containing a good deal of
valuable property was taken from one of the Blue
coaches soon after she had left the Elephant and Castle.
In this case the thieves proved to be two outside passengers, who, together with their plunder, were soon missed.
After a pursuit of two miles, and a stout resistance, however, the men were captured and committed for trial,
Crosweller, one of the proprietors of the Blue coaches,
being bound over to prosecute at the Surrey assizes.

So far as I am able to gather, a new coach—the

1817.

Depart from	Coach.	Hour.	Route.	Arrive at	Time on Road.	Return to London.
Angel Inn, Strand.	A coach.	9.45 a.m.	Ryegate, Cuckfield.	...	...	...
Bell and Crown, Holborn.	,,	9.30 a.m.	...	...	6½ hours.	...
Belle Sauvage, Ludgate Hill.	,,	8.0 a.m.	...	...	...	...
Blossoms Inn.	Night-coach.	8.30 p.m.	...	135 North Street.	...	11 a.m.
Boar and Castle.	Irresistible.	12.30 p.m.	...	Blue Office and White Horse.	...	10.0 a.m.
Blossoms Inn.	Coach.	9.0 a.m.	Clapham, Sutton, Ryegate, Crawley, Cuckfield	...	7 hours.	...
,,	True Blue.	9.0 a.m.	Croydon, Ryegate, Crawley, Hickstead.	...	...	...
,,	Blue coach,	1.0 p.m.	,,	...	6 hours.	...
Bolt-in-Tun.	A coach.	9.0 a.m.	,, Horsham, Steyning.	Pattenden's Office.	8½ hours.	7.0 a.m. (10 hours).
Bull Inn, Bishopsgate.	Royal Clarence.	8.30 a.m.	Dorking, Horsham, Henfield, Shoreham.	...	...	...
Bull, Holborn.	A coach.	8.0 a.m.	Sutton, Ryegate, Cuckfield.	Old Ship.	8¼ hours.	9.0 a.m. (9 hours).
Bull, Leadenhall Street.	Dart.	3.0 p.m.	...	...	...	...
,, ,,	Umpire.	7.0 a.m.	Ryegate, Crawley, Hickstead.	...	6 hours.	...
Cross Keys, Wood Street.	A coach.	9.0 a.m.	...	...	...	...
,, ,,	Princess Charlotte.	2.0 p.m.	...	...	...	...
Four Swans, Bishopsgate.		9.30 a.m.	Croydon, Ryegate, Hickstead.	2 Castle Square.	7 hours.	9.30 a.m.

George and Blue Boar.	Post-coach.	7.0 a.m.	Mersham, Ryegate, Crawley, Cuckfield.	Blue Office.	...	...
"	"	8.0 a.m.	...	"	...	...
Golden Cross, Charing Cross.	Original Red coach.	9.0 a.m.	Ryegate, Crawley, Cuckfield.	The Castle.	8 hours.	9.0 a.m.
"	Eclipse.	10.0 a.m.	...	"	7 hours.	{ 6.0 a.m. (6 hours).
Spread Eagle, Gracechurch Street.	Comet.	3.0 p.m.	Ryegate, Crawley, Hickstead.	New Inn.	7 hours.	{ 2.0 p.m. (6 hours).
"	Dart.	10.0 a.m.	Croydon, Sutton, Ryegate, Cuckfield.	"	6 hours.	...
Temple Coffee-House.	A coach.	1.45 p.m.	...	...	...	...
Waldegrave's New Hotel, and Bull, Bishopsgate.	"	8.0 a.m.	Croydon, Ryegate, Crawley, Cuckfield.	Waldegrave's Office.	...	...
"	"	8.30 a.m.	"	...	...	...
"	"	11.0 a.m.	Croydon, Godstone, E. Grinstead, Uckfield, Lewes.	...	...	...
"	"	7.0 a.m.	Dorking, Leatherhead, Horsham.	...	...	...
White Bear, Piccadilly.	Times.	9.30 a.m.	Croydon, Ryegate, Cuckfield.	9 Castle Square.	7 hours.	2.0 p.m.
"	"	2.0 p.m.	Horsham, Henfield.	...	8¼ hours.	9.0 a.m.
White " Horse, " Fetter Lane.	A coach. Princess Charlotte.	8.45 a.m.	Croydon, Ryegate, Crawley, Cuckfield.	Old Ship.	7¾ hours.	{ 1.0 p.m. (7 hours).
		9.15 a.m.				

New Times—was put on the road in 1818. She started
from the Union Office, 9 Castle Square, at six in the
morning, and ran to the Golden Cross, Charing Cross;
the Cross Keys, Cheapside; and the White Bear, Piccadilly, returning from the last-named place at half-
past six in the morning. Between the same points,
the Original Times, the Regent, the Royal Clarence,
and the coach through Lewes and Uckfield ran as
usual, Holmes, Horne, & Co. being the proprietors;
while the two night-coaches, from the Blue and Red
offices respectively, went on as before.

It is no longer ago than July of the present year
(1893) since some one advocated a horse-shoe which
had a hinge at the toe, so that it could be adapted, at a
pinch, to feet of various sizes.   There may or may not
be any merit in the idea, which, at any rate, was not a
new one, as I find that a precisely similar shoe was announced in the *Brighton Herald* of the 18th July 1818.

The year 1818 cannot be passed over without noticing
the death at Brighton, on the 16th or 17th August, of
Mr. John Palmer, whose introduction of the mail-coach
system was one of the most important events which
have been chronicled in connection with the history of
the road.   Before the introduction of mail-coaches the
mails were carried by post-boys on horseback, a system
introduced by. Mr. Allen.   Mr. Palmer was given to
state that the mails were almost invariably intrusted
to some idle boy without a character, and I have
given an instance of two of these boys being stopped;
but scarcely a week passed without the mail being
robbed in some part of England or another.   On the
ground of speed and safety, Mr. John Palmer proposed
to supplant these boys by mail-coaches, for he knew
that merchants and others were in the habit of intrusting valuable packages to the coachmen of stage-coaches
—a practice which led to the passing of the Act of

George III. already mentioned.[1] However, for some reason best known to themselves, the Post-Office authorities strenuously opposed Mr. Palmer's suggestions, which were not acted upon till 1784. When once mail-coaches were started, their advantage over the old system soon became apparent ; in later times the mails were the glory of the road, and Thomas De Quincey sang their praises as few men could sing them.

I know of no collection of pictures showing the change which gradually came over the stage-coach. Affairs like the old Bellerophon did not bear even a distant likeness to what we understand by a coach, while in the first quarter of the present century the changes were many. The year 1819 was, I am inclined to think, a somewhat remarkable one from a coachbuilder's point of view.

In March 1819, Robert Snow, Cooper, Boyce, and Chaplin advertised that they had bought the newly invented safety coach, carrying four insides only,[2] the first ever built. This new coach, which was called the Sovereign, left the Spread Eagle Office, 3 Castle Square, at three in the afternoon, and performed the journey to London in six hours. This new-fashioned affair made its first journey on Sunday, the 21st March 1819, when between two and three thousand people assembled to see it start. The *Herald*, in describing the coach, said, " The outside passengers are not placed on the roof of the body of the carriage, but have excellent accommo-

---

[1] *Ante*, p. 93.
[2] Some of the advertisements of a slightly earlier period than this speak of coaches carrying four insides " only." This does not mean that they carried no outside passengers, though in the time of the old machines such may have been the case, exclusive of those carried in the basket. The " four insides only " was intended as an intimation to the public that the vehicle was a light coach, in which the passengers would not be subject to the inconvenience and discomfort inseparable from the coaches which carried six people inside.

dation in a well-contrived compartment between that
and the box, beneath which there is a spacious lock-up
receptacle for the stowage of luggage."

Whether there was anything in the build of the new
coach, or whether there was not, it appears to have hit
the public fancy, if, at least, we may believe the local
papers of the date. "If," said the *Herald* for May
Day 1819, "the public continue to give the safe coach
the decided preference they now do, there can be no
doubt that coachmasters will very soon generally adopt
it as their present stock wears out. The luggage-box
can be made less or enlarged, according to the requirements of the road, so as to contain much more than
the present coaches in all their parts. The confidence
which manufacturers and dealers have of their valuable property being secured from wet and pilfering is
enough to secure for it the most decided preference,
independently of its personal safety; and it has a right
secured by Act of Parliament of carrying two more
passengers than coaches which carry luggage outside.

"The weight is so placed as to produce a saving to
the horses of 11 lbs. in every 25 lbs. in draught. The
base on which this coach stands is five inches broader
than others,[1] and the weight placed five feet lower, so
that, when the wheels on one side are thrown off, the
axle drags on the ground, and will allow the remaining
wheels to be lifted twelve inches or more before the
coach loses its balance. If a wheel had been thrown
off any other coach while going at the rate of nine
miles an hour with two outside passengers, it must have
gone over; but should it take place with the safe coach,
it will not incline on one side so as to make passengers
uncomfortable.

"It weighs only 1500¼ lbs., which is 400 lbs. lighter

---

[1] That is to say, this coach was five inches broader between the
wheels than others.

than the average of coaches built to carry luggage, and
800¾ lbs. less than some gentlemen's landaus. The
different coachmen who have driven it say that on level
ground it runs much lighter than others, and every
mechanic knows that small wheels have the advantage
at a hill; but it is difficult to compare it with other
coaches, as it is mostly laden twice as much as they
are; it always, however, performs its daily journey as
quickly as any of them. It has been reported that
coaches like this have been running in the North for
some time; but this is not the case; they are very dis-
similar in almost every particular, and all the luggage
is placed on the roof, having no luggage-box, only a
very small boot under the coachman."

In this notice it is not difficult to discern the hand
of an "inspired" writer.   It is a delightful little sentence that in which the contributor points out the
difficulty of comparing the safety concern with other
coaches, "as it is mostly laden twice as much as they
are." This is bold advertisement indeed. The most
curious thing about this coach—and it was five inches
wider than most coaches—was its lightness. It might
have been thought that the writer of the above had
cooked his figures; but they appear to be correct, for at
a later page mention is made of one of Ade's coaches
which weighed the same. Now 1500 lbs. is but six
pounds more than thirteen hundredweight and a half.
This safety coach was 400 lbs. lighter than an ordinary
coach, as the notice tells us, from which we are to
infer that the average vehicle, which carried such great
loads, weighed less than seventeen hundredweight.
Proverbially it is as well not to prophesy unless you
know; but it is certainly difficult, even in the face of
two express statements, to believe that any stage-coach
was ever built at about thirteen hundredweight and
a half, or that the old coaches, safety or otherwise,

H

scaled less than seventeen hundredweight. Our modern builders turn out coaches as light as is compatible with safety, but possibly not one weighs under eighteen or nineteen hundredweight; while the coach that "Mad Wyndham" used to drive between Norwich and Cromer weighed thirty hundredweight; and when I last saw her, she was running between Bude and Holsworthy.

The inexorable law of supply and demand applies to stage-coaching as well as to everything else, and as the public seemed to fancy safety coaches, these vehicles rapidly made their appearance; so, on the 26th of July 1819, "the Umpire, a light, elegant, patent stage-coach, for safety on a new principle," was put upon the road. She ran from 125 North Street to the Bull Hotel, Leadenhall Street, taking but six hours for the journey, and running up and down in a day; the Hero and Dart ran from the same office, and were owned by Whitchurch. I do not know whether the Coburg was a safety coach or not; but, at any rate, she turned over at Cuckfield on her way to London. Horses had been changed; the leaders started in "an unruly fashion," and brought the coach into collision with a waggon. Eleven passengers were on the roof, and all were more or less hurt, a Mr. Blake, a "well-known London gentleman, dying next day;" another passenger broke his arm, and five had to remain at Cuckfield, where the King's Head was, not for the first time, turned into a hospital, as was so often the case when coaches upset. However, the inside passengers, on this occasion three in number, were unhurt.

There was in the autumn of 1819 a further addition to the list of patents in connection with locomotion in the shape of a "Trivector," a curious machine, invented by "Mr. C. Birch of London." This was one of the first, but by no means the last, of the curious road carriages which successive inventors brought out, with the object of superseding horse-power. As we shall

presently see, Brighton was often taken by surprise
by the arrival of a steam-carriage ; but none of these
contrivances came to anything. The "Trivector,"
however, was not a steam-carriage ; it was impelled by
three men sitting on seats "formed out of the body,"
whatever that may mean, with their feet resting on the
bottom ; and with either hand each man worked a
lever, with an action which resembled that of rowing
a boat, and the machine's course was directed by the
foremost man, who steered with his feet. Here, at any
rate, we have the principle of the coxwainless four—
the idea that one man shall, in addition to contributing
his share of propelling power, do the steering, and so
obviate the necessity of a person whose weight must
be carried, but who contributes nothing to power or
speed. This conveyance, which was capacious enough
to carry luggage, weighed, with the men, seven hundredweight ; it left London at half-past five in the morning,
and reached Brighton at four in the afternoon ; but the
party stayed for four hours at Crawley, being by that
time of opinion perhaps, like the Irishman after his
experience of the sedan-chair with the bottom out,
that, were it not for the honour of the thing, they
might just as well have walked. On reaching Brighton,
the "Trivector" went round the Steyne—afterwards this
became quite the stereotyped journey for all newly
invented carriages—and then started for Lewes on its
way back to London. Some of the coachmasters reduced their stock of horses as the winter approached,
and with an announcement that a dozen horses from
the Alert coach, together with three goats and some
miscellaneous effects, would be sold, the coaching news
for the year 1819 comes to a close as far as the newspapers are concerned.

The following table shows, as far as ·I have been
able to ascertain, the coaches which ran between
London and Brighton during the year 1819 :—

1819.

Depart from	Coach	Hour.	Route.	Arrive at	Time on Road.	Leave for London.
Angel Inn, Strand. Bell and Crown, Holborn. }	Light post-coach. Irresistible. }	9.30 a.m. 10.0 a.m. (not Sunday).	Reigate, Cuckfield.	... 6 Castle Square.	{7 hours 20 minutes.	... 8.15 a.m. (7¾ hours). }
Old Bell, Holborn.	Albert.	8.30 a.m.	...	52 East Street.	...	9.0 a.m.
Belle Sauvage.	Post-coach.	8.0 a.m. (not Sunday).	Lewes.	...	...	...
Blossoms Inn, Laurence Lane, Cheapside. }	Night-coach. }	10.0 p.m.	Crawley, Reigate, Croydon. }	...	8 hours.	10.0 p.m.
,, ,,	Blue coach.	9.0 a.m.	Clapham, Sutton.	...	7 hours.	10.0 a.m.
,, ,,	True Blue.	9.0 a.m.	Croydon, Reigate, Crawley, Hickstead. }	...	6 hours.	11.0 a.m.
Bolt-in-Tun.	A coach. ,,	1.0 p.m. 9.0 a.m.	,, ,,	Blue Office.	6 hours. 7 hours.	1.0 p.m. 9.0 a.m.
Bull, Bishopsgate.	Royal Clarence. }	8.30 a.m. (not Sunday). }	Horsham, Henfield, Shoreham. }	...	...	9.0 a.m.
Bull, Holborn.	A coach.	8.0 a.m.	Sutton, Reigate, Cuckfield. }	Old Ship.	7½ hours.	9.30 a.m.
Bull, Leadenhall Street, and Old Black Boar, Piccadilly. }	Dart.	3.0 p.m. (not Sunday). }	...	...	...	6.0 a.m.
,, ,,	Umpire.	3.0 p.m.	Reigate, Crawley, Hickstead. }	125 North Street.	6 hours.	7.30 a.m.
,, ,,	Hero.	8.45 a.m. (not Sunday). }	...	...	7 hours.	11.0 a.m.
Cross Keys, Wood Street, Cheapside. }	Regent.	9.0 a.m.	...	...	7 hours.	10.0 a.m.
,, ,,	A coach.	2.0 p.m.	...	...	...	...
Four Swans, Bishopsgate.	,,	9.0 a.m.	...	...	...	...

„	„	2.0 p.m. (on Sundays 9 a.m. only.)	...	...	...	...
George and Blue Boar.	Post-coach.	8.0 a.m.	Ryegate, Crawley, Cuckfield.	Blue Office.	...	...
„	Original Red coach.	9.0 a.m.	Croydon, Ryegate, Crawley, Hickstead.	Castle.	9 hours.	9.0 a.m. (8 hours).
Golden Cross, Charing Cross.	Original coach.	9.0 a.m.		„ „	7 hours.	6.0 a.m. (6 hours).
„	Eclipse.	2.0 p.m.		„	6 hours.	6.0 a.m.
Saracen's Head.	New Times.	6.45 a.m.		9 Castle Square.	6 hours.	...
	Telegraph (goes by New Road).	2.0 p.m.				
Shepherd's Original Office, 90 Bishopsgate Street Within.	A coach.	8.30 a.m.	Croydon, Ryegate, Cuckfield.			
„	„	9.0 a.m.	Croydon, Godstone, E. Grinstead, Lewes.			
„	A light coach.	9.30 a.m.				
„	„ „	12.0 a.m.				
„	„ „	2.30 p.m.				
Ship, Charing Cross.	A coach.	9.0 a.m.		10 Castle Square.		
„	„	11.0 a.m.				
„	„	1.45 p.m.				10.0 p.m.
Spread Eagle, Gracechurch Street.	Sovereign (Royal patent safe coach).	8.0 a.m.	Ryegate, Crawley, Hickstead. (Not on Sunday).	3 Castle Square.	6 hours.	3.0 p.m.
„	Dart.	8.0 a.m.	„ „			
„	„	2.45 p.m.	„ „			
„	Connet.	9.45 a.m.			7½ hours.	10.0 a.m. (7 hours).
White Bear, Piccadilly.	Times.	1.30 p.m.	Croydon, Ryegate, Hickstead.		6½ hours.	2.0 p.m. (7 hours).
„	Royal Clarence.	8.45 a.m.	Horsham, Henfield.	Red Office.	8¼ hours.	9.0 a.m. (8 hours).
White Horse, Fetter Lane.	Princess Charlotte.	9.30 a.m.	Croydon, Ryegate, Crawley, Cuckfield.	Old Ship.	7½ hours.	1.0 p.m. (7 hours).

CHAPTER VIII.

FROM 1820 TO 1824.

QUITE early in the year 1820, a Mr. William Milton, a clergyman of Heckford, in Hertfordshire, wrote to the *Brighton Herald* in praise of a patent coach of his own designing. Theory, he asserted, had led him to construct first a caravan, and secondly a stage-coach, in each of which the sum of the diameter of the wheels was twenty-four feet. Without any pecuniary gain to himself, said Mr. Milton, his invention had been tested over fifteen hundred miles of road; and, in the opinion of several very competent coachmen, these high wheels were calculated to effect a saving of one horse in every four, five, or six, according to the roads and hills encountered. This statement, it was claimed, had been borne out by experiments conducted by Messrs. Brooks and Dougall, coachbuilders, of the City Road, Finsbury, on the plan adopted by Mr. Edgworth; and on that gentleman's calculation, Mr. Milton declared that his coach would carry nine or ten more people than the ordinary coaches, with no extra labour to the horses. It is unnecessary to do more than mention these inventions in connection with the Brighton road, the details of practical coachbuilding being altogether beyond the scope of this work; but for some years there was a great deal of discussion about safety-coaches and their build. A good deal of it is interesting enough; but, in spite of new inventions and arguments, the majority of the coachmasters kept to the usual style, which appear to have been known as that of the light post-coach.

The terms "Accommodation" and "Post" coaches

118

have several times been made use of in the foregoing pages ; and I may take this opportunity of stating that nowhere has it been possible to find a definition of either word. From what can be gleaned, however, and from the fact that the accommodation coaches seem to have been almost invariably a long time on the road, the chances are that the accommodation coach was the largest-sized vehicle used for the carrying of passengers, and in consequence of its great size and weight would necessarily have to travel somewhat slowly. With respect to the post-coaches, there is no hint that they had anything to do with the Post-Office, or the carrying of mails, so I think that the term post-coach simply meant a light coach, which in construction originally bore some resemblance to a post-chaise, and travelled at a quicker pace than the heavier and more capacious concern—it was, in fact, a sort of co-operative post-chaise. In after days the term appears to have been retained to signify a light and fast coach.

The first procession of the royal mails in honour of the King's birthday took place in the year 1791, and continued to be an annual function for about thirty-six years.[1] This procession is mentioned here for the sake of saying that, according to the *Brighton Herald* for the 29th April 1820, Mr. Waterhouse, one of the mail contractors, was offered 800 guineas for the two teams of greys which drew the Bristol and Holyhead mails. It has always been said that the London teams

[1] In 1892 the stage-coaches running in and out of London paraded for the first time on the Horse Guards Parade in St. James's Park. The affair was so far successful that the intention was to make it an annual function. Accordingly, in the spring of 1893, arrangements were made for holding a gathering early in May, but owing to some misunderstanding negotiations fell through ; but subsequently the coaches met on the Horse Guards Parade, on Thursday, the 8th of June, after each of the Driving Clubs had met twice.

of some of the mails were exceedingly good; but it
may be doubted whether Mr. Waterhouse or any one
else ever put hundred-guinea horses into coaches
seventy years ago. It is as likely as not that these
greys did not belong to Mr. Waterhouse at all, or, if
they did, that they were not the regular mail-coach
horses. I have somewhere read that it was customary
for people who had fine horses to ask permission of the
contractors for the coachmen to be allowed to drive
them in the procession from St. James's Palace to the
General Post-Office. Then the fancy teams would be
changed for the regular horses, and the mails would
start on their respective journeys.

The following is an account of the procession of
mails given in the *Brighton Gazette* for the 26th April
1821 : "The general postmen appeared in new uniforms. Eighteen[1] new mail-coaches and ornaments
were launched from Mr. Vidler's manufactory in Mil-
bank Row, in a most complete and elegant style, drawn
by the finest sets of horses possible to be procured ;
amongst the best and most admired were the greys in
the Dover, the chestnuts in the Portsmouth, the bays
in the Norwich by Newmarket, and the greys in the
Leominster and Worcester. The coachmen and guards
had all new uniforms, with flowers in their bosoms, as
did also the extra guards, and the three-penny post-
boys. They all assembled at the manufactory to form
the procession. The boys' hats were decorated with
blue, orange, and purple ribbons. The mail-coach
contractors were also entertained with a handsome cold
collation, and a profusion of wines, &c.

"Then the King's health was drunk on the grass-plot
at the back of the house. The procession proceeded
about five o'clock to Charing Cross, Pall Mall, St.

---

[1] The number was sixteen in 1791.

James's Street, Arlington Street, Piccadilly, and returned through Piccadilly, down Regent Street, Waterloo
Place, halted opposite the King's Palace in Pall Mall
to make their dutiful obeisance, and then proceeded
through the Strand to the General Post-Office."

And now once more to the Brighton road. The
coach companies were, as we have already seen, constantly changing their *personnel*; and in the year 1820
we find that the Blue Office and the Blue coaches belonged to Crosweller, Rogers, Norris, Balchin, & Co.;
while Snow, Cooper, Boyce, & Chaplin owned the
coaches which ran from the Spread Eagle Office, 4
Castle Square, to the Spread Eagle, Gracechurch
Street; and Webb's Hotel, Piccadilly. These coaches
were the Dart safety coach, built on Wright & Powell's
system, and which left at six o'clock in the morning;
the Comet (in seven hours), at ten o'clock; and Wright
and Matthews's patent safety coach, the Sovereign aforesaid, at three o'clock.

Meanwhile Messrs. Whitchurch, Best, & Wilkins ran
a good service of coaches from their office (the Union),
135 North Street, Brighton, to the Bull Inn, Bishopsgate, and the office 222 Piccadilly. The list of Snow's
coaches just given is taken from the papers for 17th June
1820, Whitchurch's being advertised in the issues of
the 1st July in that year. At the head of Whitchurch's
stands the Defiance, which was timed to leave Brighton
at six o'clock, the same hour as Snow's Dart; but
Snow's Defiance did not leave until eleven. There can
scarcely be any mistake with advertisements, one would
think, as the respective firms must surely have known
the names of their own coaches; but save when the
Age confederacy split up, as we shall presently see, I
know of no time at which there were two coaches of
the same name undistinguished by some other word.
However, both these Defiances covered the journey in

six hours, and both left Brighton at the same hour; but the advertisements do not state that both ran to the same place in London. The original Dart left Whitchurch's office at eleven, and the Umpire at three in the afternoon, the hours of return from London being a quarter to eight, ten, and a quarter to three respectively. In putting forth the above advertisement, Whitchurch embraced the opportunity of reminding the public that he was the first person who "progressed," and ran to London in six hours, returning the same day,[1] and he was pleased to think that he had done so daily for six years without having had an accident; on the strength of which he further hoped that it would not be deemed presumptuous in him "claiming the privilege (if not a patent) of calling his a *safety* coach;" and this desirable safety was assured, as he explained, by having only experienced coachmen, steady horses, and allowing neither racing nor furious driving. One does not, of course, know all the secrets of the Whitchurch confederacy; but four years later the pioneer of fast coaching fell upon evil times, as in the *Brighton Herald* for the 3rd of January 1824 I find a paragraph headed "Distressing Case," and stating that "James Witchurch (*sic*), late coachmaster of Brighton, who started the first coach that ever performed the journey to and from Brighton in the day," had, by a series of unforeseen circumstances, been reduced to the greatest distress. Some of his old friends and patrons took the trouble to inquire into the case, and, having come to the conclusion that it was one which deserved "the commiseration and charitable aid of the public," invited contributions, which would be received by the Union Bank, and the money so subscribed would, it was announced, be applied by Mr. J. Mortlock. Whether this appeal was attended with success

[1] See *ante*, p. 94.

or not I cannot discover, nor have I been able to find
out what eventually became of Mr. Whitchurch.

The year 1821 was ushered in by another snowstorm, and on the 3rd of January so deep were the
drifts that neither the mail nor Crosweller's guarded
and lighted night-coach could get to London. The
mail, indeed, struggled on as far as Pyecombe, and
then had to return ; nor could she make a start till late
next day, while the early coaches on the following
day had to delay starting until intelligence reached
Brighton that the roads were fairly clear. Between
Crawley and Brighton some of the drifts were ten feet
deep, but the storm was so far partial that on the
London side of Crawley only little snow had fallen.

To say just another word or two about safety coaches.
It had been so conclusively proved that Matthews's
safety coach, run by Snow & Co., could not turn over,
that no one was surprised to hear that one of these
concerns had capsized, and it was immediately and
industriously reported that the mishap had befallen
Snow's coach ; but this turned out to be a mistake, as
it was Newman's patent safety which turned over near
Patcham, but luckily no one was hurt. In connection
with this accident, Mr. Genn, who seems to have owned
the coaches managed and driven by the Newmans, wrote
a letter to the *Brighton Gazette* of the 5th April 1821,
in which he explained that the accounts published
were not accurate, inasmuch as the coach did not
turn over ; the pole did not break ; nor was the coachman hurt as reported. Mr. Genn's version was that
while the coachman was turning round to address some
remarks to a passenger on one of the back-seats, the
horses started and "turned over a high bank." The
safety coach, however, true to its name, remained
right-end uppermost, and " reclined " against the bank.
The exertions of three male passengers were sufficient

124 BRIGHTON AND ITS COACHES

to right her, after which the coach proceeded on her
journey, and reached Brighton at the usual time. The
opportunity for putting in a good word for the safety
coaches was naturally too good to be lost, so he proceeded to point out that had this mishap overtaken
one of the old Telegraph coaches, the accident might
have been attended with more serious consequences,
though why one does not quite understand, because the
coach was prevented from turning over, not by virtue of
any contrivance about her, but because she "reclined"
against the bank and could go no farther. Mr. Genn,
like many another man, however, having been indebted
to the good offices of the bank, forthwith proceeded to
advertise his vehicles as being the only patent safety
coaches between London and Brighton; they were
the Royal Sussex, New Dart, and Royal George, which,
leaving Brighton at seven, twelve, and three o'clock
respectively, ran to town in six hours, from 3 Castle
Square; the Royal Oak, St. James's Street; and the
King's Head, West Street, to the Bull, Leadenhall Street;
the Ship, Charing Cross; and the Old Black Bear,
Piccadilly. These coaches ran by way of Crawley,
Sutton, Mitcham, and Clapham, the fares being one pound
inside and ten shillings outside. The coaches from
the Blue Office ran as usual, the firm now figuring as
Crosweller, Cripps, Wilkins, & Co.; while Snow & Co.
ran as before the Dart, Comet, and Sovereign through
Hickstead, Crawley, and Reigate; but, as the Comet
was not destined to run during the winter, sixteen of
the horses which had been working in her were sold
at the King and Queen Inn by Mr. Attree. During the
month of May in this year (1821) I find it stated that
some of the stage-coaches went from Brighton to London
in four hours and twenty minutes, which, as the *Gazette*
observed, was "running with a fury." The table on
pp. 126 and 127 summarises as far as possible the coaching arrangements for the year 1821.

William Hine, who had been for five-and-twenty years at least on the road, and therefore was one of the old school in 1822, then contented himself with running one coach only, the Alert; but the other affairs went on much as before. With the arrival of spring (1822), William Genn put on those of his coaches which had been in dock during the winter, and announced by advertisement that, in honour of the King's birthday, his entirely new patent safety coach, the Royal Sussex, would start on the 23rd of May, leaving 135 North Street at seven in the morning, and London (the Bull, Leadenhall Street) at two in the afternoon ; while the Royal George was put on the road a few days earlier, and the New Dart, which ran through the preceding winter, kept her place.

From the Red Coach Office, 10 Castle Square, went the two Times coaches at six o'clock and three o'clock ; while Matthews's patent, which appears to have been well thought of, was adopted for the Regent, which left Brighton at ten o'clock ; and these coaches, said Horne, Holmes, & Goodman, "are allowed to be far superior for safety, care, and convenience to any ;" but so also said William Genn and Bob Snow of theirs. Snow's coaches now consisted of the patent safety Dart, Comet, Sovereign, and Rocket. In the autumn (1822) the *Herald* reporter announced the breakdown of a London safety coach through the fracture of an axle ; but the occasion was one of triumph for the safety vehicle, as, though there were fourteen passengers in and upon her, she did not overturn. In that respect she was more fortunate than was the Brighton mail, which a day or two before Christmas 1822 capsized on the down-journey close to Peas Pottage Gate, about sixteen miles from Brighton. As will have been noticed, coaches had for some time been running at good speed, and this presupposes decent roads ; nevertheless this mail turned over through

1821.

Depart from	Coach.	Hour.	Route.	Arrive at	Time on Road.	Return to London.
Bell and Crown, Holborn.	Alert.	8.30 a.m.	...	...	7½ hours.	8.30 a.m.
"	,,	10.30 a.m.	...	...	7½ hours.	4.0 p.m.
Old Bell, Holborn.	,,	8.30 a.m.	...	52 East Street.	...	9.0 a.m.
"	Meteor (safety).	10.30 a.m. (not on Sunday).	...	...	...	...
Blossoms Inn.	Night-coach.	10.0 p.m.	Clapham, Sutton.	...	8 hours.	...
"	Blue coach.	9.0 a.m.	Croydon, Ryegate, Crawley, Hickstead.	...	7 hours.	10.0 a.m.
"	True Blue.	9.0 a.m.	,,	...	6 hours.	11.0 a.m.
"	Royal York.	1.0 p.m.	,,	...	6 hours.	1.0 p.m.
Boar and Castle, 6 Oxford Street.	True Blue.	8.30 a.m.	...	...	...	...
"	Royal Eagle.	12.30 p.m.	...	...	...	...
Bull Inn, Bishopsgate.	Royal Clarence.	8.30 a.m.	Horsham, Henfield, Shoreham.	...	...	...
Bull, Holborn.	A coach.	8.0 a.m.	Sutton, Ryegate, Cuckfield.	Old Ship.	7½ hours.	9.30 a.m.
Bull Inn, Leadenhall St., and Old Black Boar.	Royal George.	7.30 a.m.	...	...	...	...
"	Royal Sussex.	2.0 p.m.	...	...	6 hours.	...
,,	New Dart.	10.0 a.m.	...	...	...	...
Cross Keys, Wood Street.	Life Preserver.	8.45 a.m.	...	...	...	...
"	Royal Clarence.	8.30 a.m.	Horsham, Henfield.	...	...	...
"	Times.	2.0 p.m.	...	...	...	...
Flower Pot, Bishopsgate.	Regent.	7.0 a.m.	...	...	...	...
"	A coach.	8.0 a.m.	...	...	...	...
"	,,	8.45 a.m.	...	...	...	...
Four Swans.		9.0 a.m.	...	...	...	...

London starting point	Coach	Departure	Route	Destination office	Duration	Times
George and Blue Boar.	„	2.0 p.m. (on Sundays only, 9.0 a.m.)	...	...	...	...
„	Post-coach.	8.0 a.m.	Ryegate, Crawley, Cuckfield.	Blue Office.	...	...
Golden Cross, Charing Cross.	Original Red coach.	9.0 a.m.	Croydon, Ryegate, Crawley, Hickstead.	The Castle.	9 hours.	9 a.m. (8 hours). 6 a.m. (6 hours).
„	Eclipse.	9.0 a.m.	...	„	7 hours.	7 hours.
Shepherd's Office, 90 Bishopsgate Street Within.	A coach.	2.0 p.m.	Croydon, Ryegate, Cuckfield.	...	...	...
„	„	8.30 a.m.	Croydon, Goxstone, E. Grinstead, Lewes.	...	...	...
„	A light coach.	9.0 a.m.	...	...	...	...
„	„	9.30 a.m.	...	...	...	...
„	„	12.0 noon.	...	...	...	...
Ship, Charing Cross.	A coach.	2.30 p.m.	...	...	...	...
„	„	9.0 a.m.	...	...	...	...
„	„	11.0 a.m.	...	...	...	...
Spread Eagle, Gracechurch Street.	Sovereign.	1.45 p.m.	Ryegate, Crawley, Hickstead.	4 Castle Square.	6¼ hours.	3.0 p.m. (6 hours). 11.0 a.m.
„	Defiance.	6.45 a.m.	...	...	6 hours.	...
„	Dart.	...	Ryegate, Crawley, Hickstead.	...	6 hours.	...
Swan with Two Necks, Lad Lane.	Comet.	2.45 p.m.	...	...	7¼ hours.	10.0 a.m. (7 hours).
„	Royal Brunswick.	9.45 a.m.	...	135 North Street.	6½ hours.	8.0 a.m. (6 hours).
White Bear, Piccadilly.	Rocket (New Road).	2.30 p.m.	...	...	6 hours.	...
White Horse, Fetter Lane.	Princess Charlotte.	9.30 a.m.	Croydon, Ryegate, Crawley, Cuckfield.	Old Ship.	7½ hours.	1.0 p.m. (7 hours).

one of the off-side wheels getting into a rut *two feet deep*, which caused the axle to break. The box-seat passenger, a gentleman from Lewes, was badly hurt, as the off-wheel horse fell upon him. The account in the papers goes on to say that there were ten passengers on the mail, a number far in excess of that I thought the mails were allowed to carry. I always thought that prior to the year 1834 mail-coaches were restricted to three or four passengers, one on the box-seat, and two or three behind the coachman, none being allowed at the back anywhere near the guard.

These few particulars which are given are all that are to be found in the papers by advertisement and otherwise for the year 1822; yet, according to the *Brighton Herald* for the 28th of September, there were forty-two coaches running between London and Brighton —*i.e.* twenty-one each way.[1] A large number, therefore, were never advertised; and, as will be seen by the tables for the different years, it has been found impossible to supply the names of all the coaches, hence the frequent use of the phrase "a coach." Upon what principle the coachmasters proceeded in giving their advertisements to the papers I know not. In some years a considerable number of coaches are advertised, and many paragraphs of gossip are given; in other years one may search every number of a paper, and find scarcely anything in connection with the coaches. If one proprietor advertised, one or two more generally followed suit; but if no one took the lead, the proprietors kept their money in their pockets; and the year 1822 is a bad year for information. It is only through reading a report of the prosecution (instituted,

---

[1] There were altogether sixty-two coaches working in and out of Brighton at this time, including those going to places other than London.

of course, by a common informer) of a Mr. Dale, for carrying more than his proper number of passengers, that we know there was a coach proprietor of that name, as no advertisements from him appear in any of the papers. The facts of the information case were on all-fours with the hundreds of others heard all over the country, several of which are noticed in the following pages. The informer and his hirelings hung about the roads, and if they saw a coach carrying more people outside than the Act of Parliament allowed, they made a note of the fact, instituted proceedings, and took half the penalty in the event of a conviction. In this case the informer's witnesses deposed to seeing eleven passengers on the coach, none of them being under the age of seven, and so unable to count as half a passenger only. The defence was based upon a somewhat peculiar line of argument. It was contended that, as the coachman had accounted for no more than ten passengers in the waybill, and as he derived no pecuniary advantage from the extra passenger, he was not liable to the penalty imposed by the Act. The magistrates, however, had no difficulty in quickly disregarding that theory, and so they fined Mr. Dale £10.

Then, again, but for reading (17th May 1823) that John Lanton, part proprietor and driver, was examined on a charge of running over and killing two little girls at Newington Butts, we might have remained in ignorance of Price's coach, which ran from Brighton to Islington in six hours. The poor little children whose deaths formed the subject of the inquiry appear to have done what children of to-day are constantly doing—they jumped out from behind another vehicle at so short a distance from the horses, that, although Lanton pulled up at once, he was too late to save the children from injury ; and no blame whatever attached to him.

I

Neither William Genn nor Crosweller & Co. made any material change in their arrangements; but Mr. Edward Augur, of the George and Blue Boar, Oxford Street, acting in conjunction with one or two others, put on the New Comet coach, to run from 134 North Street to the George and Blue Boar; the Lamb Inn, Lamb's Conduit Street; and Price's Office, Islington. This new coach, leaving Brighton at ten o'clock, ran through Cuckfield, Worth, Balcombe, Horley, and Croydon. Bearing in mind the not unnatural desire of the public to travel in safety, Augur & Co. were not slow to point out that the construction of the New Comet rendered it infinitely superior to public carriages in general, because the luggage was carried beneath the passengers, "which materially assists in preserving its equilibrium, contrary to the usual and dangerous custom of loading it on the roof." At the end of his advertisement Mr. Augur gave a list of the coaches which left his London establishment, the George and Blue Boar, for different parts of England; and in the *Times* for the 13th August 1823, his neighbour, Mr. Sanderson, of the Boar and Castle, informed those whom it might concern that the best-regulated coaches on the Brighton road (in which he included the True Blue, Royal George, and the Royal York, all belonging to Crosweller and Co.) started from his house.

One of the new summer coaches for 1823 was the Tally-Ho! run by Gray, Nelson, & White from the Tally-Ho Coach-Office, at the Royal Exchange, corner of the New Road, at ten o'clock every morning, for the Bolt-in-Tun, and Sussex Hotel, Fleet Street; and the Black Bear, Piccadilly, returning at half-past nine every morning. The same firm also ran a coach to London at six o'clock every morning.

The booking-clerks at the different offices were naturally very useful servants of the public; and in at least

one instance the regular travellers by Genn's coaches
readily came to the rescue, as in the autumn of 1825
John Jones, bookkeeper at Genn's office, returned
thanks, "with feelings of the deepest gratitude, to the
Countess of Winterton and those ladies and gentlemen
who had so kindly assisted him in the hour of misfortune." With a straightforwardness which cannot too
highly be praised, John Jones gave out that the amount
of money subscribed was quite sufficient to cover his
loss ; and so he considered it his duty to decline any
further appeal to the charitable feeling of his patrons.

Half a century ago the Brighton season would appear to have extended well into the winter, as it does
now, as in January and February 1824 are advertisements announcing the then forthcoming sales of horses
which had come off the road at the end of the season.
At Dixon's, now Rymill's, Genn sold thirty horses which
had been running in the New Dart, and probably in
some of his other coaches ; while at Maitan's Repository, Golden Cross Mews, eight of the Tally-Ho's
horses were disposed of. The George and Blue Boar,
Holborn, was to let, and the description shows that an
extensive business must have been carried on there.
The coach-offices, the paper tells us, were fitted up in
a style equal to that of any merchant's office ; while
the proprietor's residence—men lived over their shops
in those days—was convenient for a small family. In
the yard was stabling for eighty horses, with granaries,
lofts, harness-rooms, &c. ; while the stock consisted of
300 horses and several coaches—for proprietors, not
confining themselves to one road, horsed a number of
coaches over a given distance of ground.

Some idea of the magnitude to which stage-coaching
had attained can be gathered from an article published
in the *Brighton Herald* for the 8th of January 1824.
According to the writer, a person had fifteen hundred

opportunities of leaving London every twenty-four
hours by stage-coaches, including the repeated trips
of the short coaches.   Rather over than under three
hundred coaches passed Hyde Park daily, about forty
of which were running between London and Brighton
(this was a little under the mark) ; eighty-four coaches,
of which number forty ran daily, plied between London
and Birmingham ; sixteen out of nineteen ministered
daily to the wants of Chester ; seventy coaches, thirty-
four of which were daily ones, ran to Manchester ;
Liverpool claimed sixty, all but four running daily ; a
dozen went to Preston ; eighteen to York ; a dozen to
Hull ; half that number to Newcastle ; thirteen went
to Glasgow ; and thrice that number to Edinburgh ;
while distant Inverness could do with three coaches.
There was at that time, the writer ventured to think,
the most perfect public arrangement as regards travelling ever carried out : it extended from Falmouth
throughout London to Thurso—in other words, a distance of 1082 miles.   On the occasion of the meeting
of Parliament shortly before the article, of which the
foregoing is the substance, was published in the *Herald*,
one posting house at Barnet had sent no fewer than
fifty-four pairs of post-horses to Westminster !

CHAPTER IX.

FROM 1825 TO 1829.

$\mathbf{F}$ROM the foregoing pages it will be seen that the uses of advertisement have in truth been very many, and with the opening of the year 1825 I find the Rev. T. Jessett, B.A., of the "Slinfold Parsonage Boarding-School, near Horsham," availing himself of the newspapers. Just before the conclusion of the Christmas holidays he informed parents, through the medium of the *Sussex Advertiser*, that the Comet, from London to Bognor and Littlehampton, the Independent, from Chichester to London, the Hero, from Oxford to Brighton, and the Sovereign, from Oxford to Brighton, passed through Slinfold daily. In those days taking a boy to school was somewhat of an undertaking, involving a good deal of time and money—Tom Brown's father took him no farther than the Peacock Inn, Islington, whence he made the journey to Rugby by himself. The Slinfold pedagogue did well, therefore, in informing the parents of his pupils, who might not have had a perfect acquaintance with the pages of Paterson and Cary, from what places there was direct coach accommodation to his house.

On the main road between London and Brighton a new opposition was started, and it is the second mention to be found of a "company," as distinct from the confederacy which commonly prevailed. It had been talked about for some little time, and the first step was taken on the 16th May 1825, on which

133

day the following advertisement appeared in the *Sussex Advertiser:*—

"WANTED immediately, for a Company now forming, upwards of 300 horses. Any person having horses from 15 to 16 hands, with good action, and suitable for post-coaches, and not exorbitant in price, may find a ready sale and prompt payment by applying at Dixon's Repository, Barbican, London."

On the 23rd of May there was another sign of the awakening of the coaching business in the appearance of another advertisement in the same journal, to the effect that a hundred and fifty horses were needed for the fast summer coaches then about to be put upon the road.

Meantime, on the 19th May 1825, there appeared in the *Brighton Gazette* the prospectus of "The General Stage-Coach Company;" and those who drew up the document could never have dreamed of the huge concern that was destined in later days to come into existence under the similar title of the "London General Omnibus Company."

By 1825 stage-coaching on the Brighton road, as on other roads, was about entering on its final stage—that is to say, driving had become a fine art; horses were good, the coach and its appointments perfect, pace was accelerated, and both coachmen and guards were superior to the men of ten or twenty years previously; yet, in the opinion of the promoters of the General Stage-Coach Company, something more remained to be done; and, as the prospectus sets out possible improvements, and gives a general view of coaching arrangements usual at that date, it may be worth while to reproduce it *in extenso :*—

"The necessity of better regulations for securing the comfort of passengers by stage-coaches has long been a matter of observation with all persons whose pleasure or occupation has compelled them to

THE TAP. PEAS-POTTAGE.

travel ; therefore the idea of removing those inconveniences arising
from impositions on the road is not by any means a new one, but
claims merely the originality of reducing into practice the suggestions which are common with every one, and which have so long
been urged in vain with the present coach proprietors. The inatten-
tion which is in all cases manifested towards any public or individual
complaint of neglect or abuse is so common, it can scarcely fail to
excite considerable surprise that men are so blind to their real
interest not to see that a perseverance in those illiberal measures
must sooner or later elicit that opposition to their progress which,
when once adopted, must either COMPEL them to act properly and
justly by the public, or to FORFEIT their claim to support. A well-
turned voluntary liberality would have availed them, when, on the
contrary, a compulsory one will not.

"These men have assumed a high tone because individual opposition is too weak to affect them ; and knowing that they are sure of
custom *when unopposed* induces them to indulge the elevated hope
of maintaining it; but public opinion is against them, however much
they may disregard it.

"The levies which coachmen and guards are allowed to make, with
the sanction of the coach proprietors, upon passengers, to supply
the inefficiency of their wages, and the monstrous charges of them,
even in short journeys, has become a tax of very considerable magnitude, and has long called for the interposition of some measures
which would put a stop to so great a grievance.

"The shameful imposition, also, at the road inns, where the
coaches stop for refreshments, is intolerable—the charge is usually
heavy—the fare bad—the attendance deficient—punctuality seldom
observed—and as to comfort, it has almost become proverbial ' that
a man must not expect comfort in travelling.' Yet he pays *more*
than sufficient to ensure it.

"These, and other equally crying evils, have induced the proprietors to establish a Public Company, to be called THE GENERAL
STAGE-COACH COMPANY, the objects of which will be to remove all
the disagreeable consequences arising from the present scandalous
system ; to pay the coachmen and guards full wages, and never
allow them, on any occasion, to receive money for civilities, which their
duty will command without—to continue the present rate of charges,
and NOT TO INCREASE THE FARE—whereby the money now spent upon
coachmen and guards will be saved to the passengers; to provide
suitable places for refreshments, and to fix a moderate charge,
including waiters, so that any person travelling by the COMPANY's
coaches may know to a fraction what money it will cost him to the
journey's end—to avoid delays on the road, by observing one regular
pace, equal to the present rate of travelling, and to prevent the

necessity of *galloping* when time is lost; from which latter circumstance much and serious danger is always to be apprehended.

"These are some of the advantages the public will derive from the establishment of this Company; and it must be manifest to every one that such a plan will unquestionably ENSURE that public SUPPORT and patronage necessary to the profit of the concern, leaving no doubt of the success which from such arrangements may be fairly and reasonably expected.

"The CAPITAL of the Company will be £500,000, in shares of £50 each, the deposit required on each share being £3.

"A COMMITTEE OF MANAGEMENT being already formed, no time will be lost in reducing this plan into practice; and as the Company must ensure quick return of capital, being entirely a ready-money concern, the accounts will be made up quarterly, at which time the dividends will be paid.

"It may be fairly expected, from the present influx of applications for shares, that the lists will be entirely filled, and the Company enabled to introduce coaches upon all the principal roads by the 1st of July.

"The Committee having received various suggestions from several highly respectable tradesmen, who are in the constant habit of receiving and forwarding packages and parcels by stage-coach conveyance, have taken into consideration the adoption of a plan which will operate as a powerful corrective to that liability of loss and delay that at present exists.

"The Company will also ensure the safe delivery of bankers' remittances at a less expensive rate than they now incur. In short, every facility will be given to the public and the trade that is within the pale of possibility.

"Applications for shares and other communications to be made, without delay, to Messrs. Dickins & Davidson, 30 Queen Street, Cheapside, Solicitors to the Company. Bankers :—Messrs. Frys & Chapman, Mildred's Court, Poultry, and Sir Walter Stirling, Stirling, & Hodson, Strand."

The coach-travelling public were no doubt a long-suffering race; and then, as now, folks hated the "fee system." The advantages offered by this new company, the promoters of which had probably felt the public pulse, must have been awaited with infinite interest: everything sounded so well—inclusive fares; careful coachmen, no loitering, no galloping; comfort and moderate charges at roadside inns; civility; and, above

all, no tips : surely the millennium was at hand. In
coaching, however, as in other matters, history repeats
itself; for in the *Newcastle Chronicle* for Saturday the
7th of January 1786, there appeared a prospectus of
the Newcastle Post-Coach, which took three days to
go between London and Newcastle. The following is
an extract from the document in question :—

> "The proprietors beg leave to acquaint the public that they have
> provided several superintendents, one of whom will constantly attend
> the coach in order to prevent the drivers from taking up inside or
> outside passengers on their own account" (this was technically termed
> shouldering), "stopping to drink, or otherwise loitering on the road.
> The coach arrives in London early in the afternoon of the third day
> from Newcastle ; and, as the proprietors allow very genteel salaries
> to their superintendents, they are neither to ask nor accept any
> gratuity from passengers."

So here was a set against the fee system forty years
anterior to the starting of the new General Stage-
Coach Company.

Considering how well the Brighton papers had been
supported by the already existing coach proprietors,
it was rather bold of them to back up the prospectus
of the new company with the paragraph—

> "Our readers will rejoice to find that the impositions to which
> travellers have so long been subject are likely to be put a stop to
> by the New Stage Company."

Competition, however, inures to the public advantage ; and so, in a short time, an older-established firm
were to the front with a displayed advertisement,
headed with the stock woodcut of a coach-and-four,
the horses going at full speed, and the coach laden
with passengers. It announced " very superior travelling to London in six hours from the Tally-Ho Coach
Office, 137 North Street." The Tally-Ho post-coach
started daily at six A.M., and the Eclipse at two P.M.,
the destinations in London being the New White

Horse Cellar and Gloucester Hotels, Piccadilly; the Angel Inn, Islington; and the Swan with Two Necks, Lad Lane. Waterhouse & Co. were the proprietors of these coaches.

The General Stage-Coach Company, having perfected their arrangements, despatched their first coach to London on the 26th August 1825, and on the 1st September there was a grand advertisement, surmounted by the now familiar woodcut of the coach-and-four.

No Fees to Coachmen and Guards.

GENERAL

STAGE-COACH COMPANY.

Brighton to London in Six Hours.

The Company's New Elegant Post-Coach, carrying four inside and ten out, leaves Mr. Wilkins's Booking Office,

No. 5 Castle Square, Brighton,

Every Morning at six o'clock precisely, Sundays excepted, to the *Axe Inn*, Aldermanbury, London.

FARES

Inside, £1, 1s.   Outside, 12s. 0d.

In case of incivility being experienced by the passengers travelling by the Company's coaches from servants of the Company, it is particularly requested that prompt notification will be given to the Secretary, as it is the anxious desire of the Company to render all the convenience to the public in their power; they will therefore feel obliged by any communication or suggestion which on any occasion may be considered deserving of report. One regular pace is observed, and no frivolous stoppages allowed on the road, whereby the Company's coaches are enabled to keep the present fast rate of travelling without the necessity of any galloping whatever.

By Order of the Board,

Clerke Burton, *Secretary.*

N.B.—Superior travelling by the Company's coaches to Bath and Bristol, through Reading, Marlborough, Calne, &c., in fourteen hours, every morning from the Axe Inn, Aldermanbury, at a quarter-past six o'clock, and the Old White Horse Cellar, Piccadilly, at seven o'clock precisely.

For some time there had appeared in the *Brighton Gazette* a series of papers headed "The Vampire," dealing with various social topics, and No. 11 in the issue of that journal for 1st December 1825 had stage-coaching for its subject. It may not be a composition of the highest class, but as an example of the "smart" writing of the period, and as giving some idea of the surroundings of coaching at that time, some of it may be worth transcribing, as, so far as I am aware, it has never been reproduced :—

"Few persons, I believe, pass through Castle Square at the time of the arrival of the Brighton coaches without stopping to give at least a transient glance at the various kinds of luggage, animate and inanimate, which these vehicles bring down from the metropolis.

"As for myself, I have so inveterate a curiosity to see what fresh inhabitants are coming to increase our population, that even on these cold afternoons I often take my station at the door of the Red Coach-Office, where I stand shivering for half an hour on the faith of a promise, renewed and broken every five minutes, that the stage will arrive in a moment.[1] All this time, the reader must know, I am speculating on the sentinels who pass to and fro upon the pavement opposite, and saying to myself, 'Thank God! I am not fool enough to be a soldier.'

"There, then, I stand, without any real necessity, amidst a group of habitual idlers" (of which "Vampire," from his own account, frequently made one), "loungers, shopmen, waiters, and pastry-cooks' boys, who jostle among the crowd, regardless of the burden on their heads. On one side of me is a party of frolicsome children awaiting the arrival of papa, and jumping about with cold and expectation. On the other stands a long unformed gawkey, half-footman, half-shopboy, with his mouth gaping as though he would swallow the parcel he is sent for. A low muttering kind of conversation is kept up around me among the various figures who are awaiting the arrival of their friends; and it is only now and then that a false alarm of 'Here it comes' directs our excited attention to some empty fly that rattles by us round the corner. Presently, however, the real, long-expected vehicle arrives, and its approach is greeted by a volley of nods and general discharge of smiles from my sur-

---

[1] If "Vampire's" statement is true, it would appear that strict punctuality was not observed, and that there was some ground for the assertion that coachmen loitered by the way.

rounding group, a salute which is returned from the top of the stage, whilst I, expecting no one, and caring for nobody, remain silent and unmoved amidst this universal rejoicing, like an old spiked cannon on a battery. As soon as the wheels have given their last turn and slide, the hubbub of voices begins, and the passengers, rejoiced at having arrived at their journey's end, descend from their travelling prison like the Grecian warriors from the wooden horse of Troy.

"The first person I observe is a smirking young man in a white greatcoat, with his neck enveloped in a gay worsted wrapper. He is evidently pleased with something that has occurred during the journey, and, as with a scornful anticipation" (disregard for, our friend probably meant) " of the steps intended for ten lively passengers, he flings himself out of the dickey to the great peril of the spectators' heads below. I perceive this show of alacrity is intended to fix himself in the good graces of a smart, painted, bold-looking, but pretty woman about thirty, who discovers her profession by her countenance and tight-fitting pelisse. Though not married, she runs no risk of leading apes in hell. As her beau assists her down the steps, I see she endures his attentions; but her eyes are still on the alert for any better game that may offer. I hear him roaring for a fly, and storming about her luggage, and see him fidgeting round her with all the awkward but conceited gallantry of a young fool who wishes to pass for an experienced man of the town.

" He in his vanity thinks her a conquest ; and she considers him a good take-in. She gets into a fly, and as she refuses his escort to her intended lodgings, gives him an inviting glance and a card through the window, whilst he remains looking as much like an ass as his conceit will suffer him. But I must not neglect the rest of the passengers. The next who gets down forms a pleasing contrast to the above. It is a modest-looking young female, with a little basket in one hand and a child in her arms, who, in spite of the cold, has eaten itself fast asleep, and is dozing away with the remains of a bun in its left hand. Two of the dickey passengers have got down on the opposite side and escaped my notice, but the sixth is slower in his motions; he is a huge, fat man, whose bulk, I can perceive, has completely protected those who sat on the same side with him from suffering by jolts. He rises with a loud grunt, gives himself a shake like a dog just out of the water, and proceeds cautiously to let his enormous body down the side of the coach, swaying about like a bale of merchandise dangling on a warehouse crane. Of the passengers who ride in front, I have only time to notice one, a young man in a splendid cloth roquelaure, with a cigar in his mouth, who, I conjecture from his look of importance, is

paying his first visit to Brighton. As soon as he touches the pavement, he throws his eyes round him with a wild look of surprise,
and seems perfectly astonished that nobody mistakes him for a
great man.

"The first who gets out from the inside is a consequential yet
good-humoured merchant, who is soon recognised as papa by the
giddy little urchins I mentioned, who literally pull him down the
steps; yet he stops when half way out, and turns to give a nod
to his travelling companions as he bids them good-day, and having
no luggage, is carried off in triumph by his children, who dance
down the street for pure joy. He is no sooner delivered from the
stage than a good-natured footman runs up with a warm cloak
to the coach-door, to welcome a substantial housekeeper who has
just come down, and who, half ashamed of her old acquaintance
in presence of the company inside, receives his hearty 'How d'ye
do, Mrs. Spicer,' with much dignity, and only replies by 'Oh! James,
my band-box is behind.'

" By this time the coachman is multiplying himself to answer all
the queries of his temporary family. With one eye on the waybill
and the other on the passengers, he turns about like a weathercock
in a variable wind, and seems to answer, 'Yes, ma'am,' and 'No,
sir,' at random, whilst his left hand is mechanically extended to
receive all donations, like a parish poor-box, or the prospectus of a
new institution.

"But now the noise begins to thicken whilst the passengers dis-
perse in as much confusion as the labourers of Babel. I can no longer
distinguish one thing from another, and, after jostling and hustling
with porters and portmanteaus, I leave the office, my ears ringing
with the sound of 'luggage,' 'square,' 'street,' 'hotel,' 'crescent,'
'porter,' 'No. 16,' 'wheelbarrow,' 'row of houses,' 'fly,' 'opposite
the Chain Pier,' 'shawl,' 'shoes,' 'pattens,' 'King's Head,' 'in my
bandbox.'"

Here, then, is a freely written, and possibly not too
coherent, account of the arrival at Brighton of a stage-
coach from London; an incident which perhaps did
not materially differ from the arrival of the " Husband's
boat " at Margate, or of one of the modern fast trains
from London to Brighton. At any rate, the pickpocket
of the period made the coach-office the scene of his
happy hunting-ground. One gentleman, we are told,
was robbed, on alighting from an afternoon coach, of six
five-pound-notes, a sovereign, and several bills of ex-

change for a large amount, while another passenger was robbed of cheques and notes of the value of about £300.

Before passing on to the year 1826, mention may again be made of the manner in which the common informer harassed the coachmen and coach proprietors of the time. In 1824, a man of the name of Johnson, an informer by profession, carried on war against the coaching fraternity under every discoverable head of the Acts of Parliament by which stage-coach travelling was governed.[1] Johnson had had in his service one Byers, who, leaving his former employer, appears to have himself become a master-informer, and in the month of August 1825 laid informations against several persons, including a Mr. Selby, owner of a coach, and the bearer of a name destined in later times to become famous on the Brighton road. The information charged Selby with having carried more passengers than were allowed by the Act.

It was doubtless a wise proceeding on the part of the Legislature to limit the number of persons to be carried on a coach. The proprietors had their living to make, and would naturally have carried as many passengers as they could crowd on and into their vehicles, with the result that the strength of axles, springs, and the stability generally of the coaches might have been overtaxed, and, when anything did break, a preventible accident of a more or less serious nature was the result. For example, the *Brighton Herald* for the 30th June 1810 relates how an accident overtook Waldegrave's accommodation coach while proceeding to London heavily loaded. "The hind-wheels," says the report, "were suddenly crushed by the load, and the coach overturned near Brixton Causeway." In this case the *deus ex machinâ* was a corn-waggon which chanced to

---

[1] Some of these are mentioned at pp. 24 to 29.

be passing at the time, and on to it were pitched the bulk
of the passengers. One gentleman, however, had his
thigh broken, and contusions were " evenly distributed."
Moreover, there was the question of cruelty to horses,
and Parliament would appear not to have been unmindful of this, inasmuch as fewer passengers were allowed on
a pair-horse coach than on one drawn by four horses.[1]

To return, however, to the case of " Byers v. Selby."
A witness for Byers, who appears to have combined the
calling of a journeyman informer with the keeping of
" a respectable shop at £40 a year near London," stated
that on the 28th July (1825) he saw a London stage-
coach drawn by two horses at Pyecombe, with eight
passengers on the outside. Selby's name was not painted
on the coach-door, and the coach was not one of those
exempted by Act of Parliament.

As is not unusual in the present day, an attempt was
made to drag in irrelevant evidence, which the magistrates, to their credit, at once refused to admit. The
coachman proposed to produce his waybill to show the
number of passengers booked, and therefore presumably
carried ; but the Byers party retorted that the waybill
would show only the number of passengers booked,
and not the actual number travelling, for the coachman
might have picked up one or more passengers on his
own account, without putting them in the waybill at
all ; and Byers also contended that the coachman was
an incompetent witness, on the further ground that, if
it should ultimately appear that he had taken more
passengers than he had accounted for to his master, he
was liable to be imprisoned for three months, and was
therefore an interested party in the case. The coachman's contention was that he had booked no more than
seven passengers and a boy under seven years of age,

See *ante*, p. 27.

who would not have counted as a full passenger; he
further averred that he carried no one who did not appear on the waybill, unless one of the informers jumped
up unknown to him. The Bench, however, came to
the conclusion that an attempt had been made on the
part of Selby to impose on them; they therefore re-
jected the evidence of the coachman, and convicted
Selby in the mitigated penalty of £5 and 16s. costs.

Having thus vanquished Selby, Byers betook himself to Bath, where, during the first fortnight of November (1825), he laid no fewer than thirty-four informations involving penalties, says the *Brighton Gazette*
for the 17th November 1825, amounting to nearly
£500 besides costs. This would mean penalties aver-
aging about £14 in each case!

Whether Byers, in seeking for more worlds to con-
quer, went to Bristol and thence to Oxford, or whether
there were in Bristol some who adopted the calling on
account of its returns, I know not; but a few months
later a couple of informers began business in Oxford,
and laid a number of informations against coach proprietors for carrying, during an election which had just
taken place, more than the legal number of passengers.
On the day appointed for the hearing of the case the
informers were not present in court; but their absence
was satisfactorily explained. On their way to the Hall
they had been interrupted by some patriotic coachmen,
who, roused to indignation at the number of informations laid against their employers, endeavoured to secure
the informers, and they, on realising the turn things
had taken, incontinently bolted. Thereupon ensued a
chase, and as the spirit of sport was ever strong in
Oxford, men, women, and children joined in the hunt;
and this mixed pack, in due time, ran down the informers. "They were then brushed down by a chimney-
sweep," says the report, "and afterwards well ducked

in the river." After this course of treatment, one is
not surprised to learn that "they started for Bristol,
and have not since been heard of." Possibly the Mr.
"Four-in-hand Fosbroke" of the period contributed his
share towards running down the informers.

Something will be said later on concerning the
profits and losses of coach-owning; but the penalties
which were continually being inflicted, as the result
of informations laid, must have made appreciable en-
croachments on the profits; and to the penalties must
be added the compensation paid to passengers. Only
a few months before the Oxford episode a servant-girl
brought an action against Sanderson & Co., proprietors of a Brighton coach, and was awarded £400
by a sympathetic jury as a solatium for a broken arm,
and other injuries, sustained by the overturning of the
coach. It is not for a moment suggested that the
compensation was excessive; the sum is merely mentioned by way of showing to what reductions the
profits of coach proprietors were liable.

So early as the year 1825, the idea had come over
the coaching world that it might, in the future, be
threatened with a serious opposition in the form of
railways; but a certain Mr. Wightman did his best to
allay these fears by publishing a pamphlet in which he
was bold enough to state that the velocity attained by
the locomotive could not exceed one half of that of the
best stage-coaches. "A complete illusion prevails,"
he wrote, "as to the possible speed of trains," and he
warned his readers that all money expended in railways would be thrown away. What would the worthy
Wightman have said to the "Flying Dutchman," the
"Zulu," and the "Flying Scotchman," not to mention
the unnamed express trains on the London and
Brighton and other lines?

It was in the year 1826 that the Cliff roadway between

K

East Street and the western extremity of the town was
first called King's Road.   On reference to Cary's " New
Itinerary," the coaches enumerated in the table on page
147 appear to have run between London and Brighton.

From this and former tables it is shown that several
of the coaches called at more than one office ; and there
were thirty-one opportunities of booking from London
to Brighton.   The number of coaches was eighteen;
there are seventeen names in the list; but there was
a Times both morning and afternoon.   The number
shows a falling off from previous years ; but the explanation probably is that the list is incomplete by
reason of its including but one summer coach in lieu
of the many which were put on the road during what
was then the season.   The most notable absentees,
however, are the coaches belonging to the General
Stage-Coach Company, of which mention has already
been made.   So far as I have been able to ascertain,
its first advertisement was its last; and we hear
nothing more about the company, which probably died
an easy death.

From Mr. Cary's list we miss the Monarch, which
may have been given up at the beginning of March
1826.   Thirty horses which had been working in that
coach were sold at Tattersall's, at an average price
of £37, 2s. 8d.   In these days of high-priced coach-
horses, it may not be uninteresting to note that a
brown gelding, which had been bought during the
previous summer for thirty-five guineas at Aldridge's,
now realised ninety-five guineas ; a piebald brought
seventy-six guineas, and a chestnut seventy guineas.
These, however, were the flowers of the flock ; there
must have been some very cheap ones amongst the
remainder.   Nor does the usually accurate Cary make
any mention of the Eclipse, which we hear about
in the summer in consequence of an accident which

1826.

Depart from	Coach.	Hour.	Route.	Place of Arrival.	Hours on Road.
Old Bell, Holborn.	Alert	8.0 a.m.	Sutton, Ryegate, Crawley.	...	7 hours.
„	Union.	10.30 a.m.	...	...	...
„	Times.	7.45 a.m.	...	...	...
„	„	1.45 p.m.	...	...	...
Blossoms Inn, Cheapside.	Royal Mail.	8.0 p.m.	Ryegate, Crawley, Cuckfield.	Blue Office.	8 hours.
„	Magnet.	9.30 a.m.	...	...	6 hours.
Boar and Castle, 6 Oxford Street.	Royal George.	10.30 a.m.	Croydon, Merstham, Balcombe, Cuckfield.	Blue Office.	...
„	True Blue.	8.30 a.m.	...	...	...
Bull, Holborn.	Alert.	8.0 a.m.	...	...	6 hours.
„	Times.	8.0 a.m.	...	...	7 hours.
Bull, Leadenhall Street.	Royal Sussex.	2.0 p.m.	Sutton, Ryegate, Crawley.	...	...
Bolt-in-Tun.	Dart.	2.45 p.m.	Croydon, Godstone, Lindfield, Ditchling.	...	6 hours.
„	Patriot.	9.30 a.m.	...	...	6 hours.
Cross Keys, Wood Street.	Regent.	9.45 a.m.	...	...	7 hours.
„	Times.	7.45 a.m.	...	...	6 hours.
„	„	1.45 p.m.	...	...	...
„	„	8.0 a.m.	...	...	...
George and Blue Boar.	Alert.	8.0 a.m.	...	...	7 hours.
„	Union.	10.0 a.m.	...	...	7 hours.
Gloucester Coffee-House, Piccadilly.	Summer coach.	...	Richmond, Kingston, Epsom, Leatherhead, Dorking on Tuesday, Thursday, and Saturday.	...	...
Golden Cross, Charing Cross.	Comet,	10.0 a.m.	Ryegate, Crawley, Cuckfield.	Castle-Sqre	6 hours.
„	Regent.	10.0 a.m.	...	...	...
„	Times.	8.0 a.m.	...	...	...
„	„	12 noon.	...	...	...
King's Arms, Snow Hill	Coronet.	1.45 p.m.	Ryegate, Crawley, Cuckfield.	...	...
Spread Eagle, Gracechurch Street.	Comet.	9.45 a.m.	...	...	6 hours.
„	Sovereign.	7.45 a.m.	...	...	6 hours.
Swan with Two Necks.	Dart.	2.45 p.m.	...	...	6 hours.
„	Post-coach.	9.30 a.m.	...	...	...
Wades, Camberwell.	Patriot.	9.30 a.m.	Croydon, Godstone, Lindfield, Ditchling.	...	7 hours.
White Horse, Fetter Lane.	Duke of York.	8.15 a.m.	...	...	7 hours.

overtook it. The coach had just arrived in Castle
Square from London; and at the end of a journey, the
late Mr. Birch Reynardson tells us, the coach-horses of
old were not likely to "move on," after having done
their ten miles an hour. The horses of the Eclipse,
however, seem to have been the exceptions which
proved the rule, as, in spite of the man at their heads,
they suddenly started off towards the Steine; and the
man having prevented them from turning the corner,
the leaders jumped the railing opposite the Club-House.
One of them fell, and the other further complicated
matters by turning back through the opening left for
foot-passengers. Luckily, however, the wheel-horses
were amenable to control, and, in spite of the presence
of a big heap of stones, the coach was not overturned.

In connection with accidents, W. Akehurst, saddler,
125 St. James's Street (till a few years ago, there was
a saddler of the same name on the King's Road at the
corner of Black Lion Street), notified that after a business experience of over twenty years, he offered his
newly invented bit to the public. "It united," said
the advertisement, "simplicity and power," and "with its
assistance the most timid rider may, in perfect security,
mount the hardest mouthed horse with the conviction
of being able at pleasure to stop it." On reading this,
one can only regret that, like the recipe for the trans-
parent amber varnish on the Cremonese violins, Mr.
Akehurst's valuable patent should have been suffered
to drop out of knowledge. There have, however,
been a good many patent bits since then, and still we
cannot always hold our horses. Mr. Akehurst further
informed his customers that his bit differed from all
others, inasmuch as it did not hurt the horse's mouth,
as all other patent bits did; and was consequently
recommended both for harness work, or as a bit for a
lady's horse, as not half the usual exertion was needed.

About this time we hear a good deal more about
safety coaches, an innovation which was later on not
a little condemned by some writers on coaching in the
Sporting Magazine. However, the *Leeds Intelligencer*
notified that a Leeds man had invented a "stage-
coach prop." In somewhat dubious phraseology it was
reported to be self-acting, and could be made to work
at the bidding of coachman or guard. The details are
not particularly clear, but it would seem as though
the invention consisted of an iron stay beneath the
coach, and when the vehicle leaned over, the prop
would come out, and force the coach back into her
proper position again; while, if a wheel came off, or
an axle broke, the prop was *expected* to keep the
concern right side up.

Taking a jump from North to South, we find the
Sussex press taking notice of an "improvement," rather
than an invention, which had been introduced on the
Brighton road. Than this particular "improvement,"
few are said to have excited more curiosity than the
new coach introduced by Messrs. Waterhouse & Co.
It was built on the lines of the German coaches, and
was the only one of the kind in use in England. "In
appearance it is heavy," said a critic, "but it runs very
light; and a peculiar advantage belonging to it is that
the outside passengers are, *by means of an awning,*
protected from the weather." Modern coachmen are
chaffed enough, goodness knows, by those stern critics,
the old school, about the absence of luggage from their
coaches, the patent brake, pulling up with two hands,
&c.; but they have so far kept the awning off the
coach-top. We can well believe the statement in the
Sussex papers that "among the modern improvements in travelling, few perhaps have excited more
curiosity" than this new concern of Messrs. Waterhouse & Co.

Mention has just been made of an accident which happened to the Eclipse coach through not having two men to mind the horses, and another coach nearly came to grief from the same cause. The coachman had driven in from London, and on getting down left the horses in charge of a boy. A butcher's cart, coming by in that happy-go-lucky style which is frequently characteristic of those affairs, frightened the horses, which started off at full gallop down North and East Streets. Luckily, however, the ends of the reins were flying loose, and an active pedestrian getting hold of them, he managed to bring the horses to a standstill. A little while before, the Magnet horses ran away— one porter only was left to look after the four horses —through some one cracking a whip close to them. Before they had gone very far, one of them fortunately fell, a circumstance which enabled the bystanders to secure the others. In this instance some ladies were in the coach, but, though frightened, they were not hurt. These mishaps, and many others which are not worth mentioning, occurred after the horses had done their stage into Brighton, by which time, one would think, they would not have been averse to standing still, especially as some of the coaches ran from Cuck- field to Brighton, fourteen miles, having changed horses at the King's Head.

Per contra, the mail very nearly came to grief soon after starting (April 1827). As she was leaving the town, the leaders got the better of the coachman, and, dashing out of the road, just as they reached the corner of Gloucester Place, ran against the wall with such violence as to knock down a few yards of it as well as the railing on the top. They do not, however, appear to have done themselves any very great injury, as the mail proceeded on her way to London without the light-hearted leaders being changed. Less fortunate,

KINGS HEAD CENTRE FOLD

however, than the Brighton mail was the Patriot,
which ran from the Bolt-in-Tun, Fleet Street, as on
reaching Patcham, on her way to Brighton, she collided
with a cart and capsized. One gentleman had his leg
broken ; but the other passengers got off with only
slight injuries. Shortly after this, the proprietor of the
Patriot adopted Cooke's "protection reins," an innovation which caused the coach to be watched with interest.

Although stage-coaching had now, as it had been
for some time past, worked so systematically, it was
deemed expedient every now and then to insert advertisements for the information of the travelling public.
Accordingly we find it announced that "light and fast
coaches, conducted upon the most improved system,
leave the Spread Eagle, Gracechurch Street ; and Spread
Eagle Office, Webb's Hotel, 220 Piccadilly, connected
with Snow & Co.'s Brighton Office, at seven and a
quarter to ten in the morning, and at a quarter before
three in the afternoon." The fares, too, as we shall see,
were constantly undergoing revision ; and in January
1827, the Comet safety coach, which ran from the
Spread Eagle, Gracechurch Street, to 18 Castle Square,
at the corner of the Steine, reduced its fares to 16s.
inside and 8s. out. By the modern Comet—that which
runs now—the inside passenger pays less than he who
goes outside. When the Comet and the Old Times
were both running to and from Brighton, the fare by the
former was 10s. and by the latter 15s. ; but from the
very beginning fares have varied : I think 25s. was the
most ever asked ; while in the heat of the opposition
5s. was often accepted, and sometimes passengers were
carried for nothing, to keep them off the other vehicles.

These advertisements were doubtless rendered necessary by the fact that, at any rate on the Brighton road,
the coaches occasionally changed their London starting-
places ; the booking-places changed hands, and were

put to other uses; while coaches were from time to time given up, and new ones were started.

For example, Messrs. Crosweller & Co., proprietors of the Blue coaches and Blue Coach-Office, begged to inform the public (September 1827) that a "safety and commodious post-coach, called the ' Rocket' "—a new addition to the list—would leave the Blue Office every day, except Sunday, for London, at one o'clock. The True Blue ran from the same place at nine o'clock; the Royal George (a safety coach) at eleven; and the Royal Mail at half-past ten at night. The latter, by the way, appears to have been accelerated, for whereas she was eight hours on the road when Cary compiled his list in 1826, she was now advertised to do the journey in six hours.

To most of the coach advertisements was appended a notice stating that the proprietor would not be answerable for any parcels or packages containing goods above the value of five pounds, unless entered as such, and paid for accordingly. In early times it was found expedient to make common carriers insurers of the goods intrusted to them: they were bound to deliver the goods safely and in as good condition as when they received them. But for this, losses would have been more frequent than they were, through carelessness on the part of the carrier, or collusion with thieves. But in course of time special contracts, which had the effect of limiting a carrier's liability, came into use, and in his book on "Bailments" Mr. Justice Story said, "The right of making such qualified acceptances by common carriers seems to have been asserted in early times." This license not unnaturally led to railway and other carriers unduly restricting their liability, and to remedy the hardships thus occasioned the Railway and Canal Traffic Act became law in 1854.

The limiting of their liability on the part of the coach proprietors was one of these qualified accept-

ances ; and even though they fixed their liability at five
pounds, unless the excess value were declared and in-
sured, proprietors must have paid a large sum by way
of compensation in the course of a year.   In November
1826 the London and Brighton mail was robbed of
several parcels which had very carelessly been placed
in the pockets inside the coach-door. There was no
inside passenger, but it subsequently transpired that a
fellow got in at the Hare and Hounds unknown to
the coachman, and got out some distance up the road
while the coach was bowling along at the rate of about
nine miles an hour. The coachman heard the door
shut, but saw no one.   About twelve months later the
Dart coach was robbed in the most barefaced manner
one November afternoon.   Two suspicious-looking
fellows were observed to be following the coach for
some distance in a dark-coloured chaise.   On reaching
some cross-roads the chaise turned off, and just afterwards, when the coach was a few miles from Reigate, the
property was missed from the hind-boot ; but how the
two suspicious-looking fellows could have abstracted
the parcels without being observed was probably as
great a mystery to the Dart people as it is to us who
read the account of the theft.

Reference was made just now to the starting of a
new coach, the Rocket ; but starting and stopping were
always going on in the coaching world, and by way
of compensation, one of the Brighton coaches, the
name of which is not stated, was given up, in consequence of the proprietor, Mr. Cooper, retiring from
the coach business.   Eighteen horses (from the number
we may gather that he, according to the usual custom,
horsed the coach for a portion of the distance only),
together with the harness, clothing, &c., were sold, in
October 1827, at Aldridge's, then in the hands of Mr.
Morris.

Coaching-houses, too, were often in the market.
An inn bearing the euphonious name of " The Leg of
Mutton and Cauliflower," at Ashstead, eighteen miles
from London, and on the turnpike road from Epsom to
Dorking, Horsham, Worthing, Bognor, Chichester, &c.,
did not long want a buyer, more particularly as some of
the coaches changed horses there, and there was a
flourishing posting business attached to the house.
The George Inn, at Henfield, too, had to be sold, owing
to the bankruptcy of Mr. Richard Pattenden, formerly
in the coach business at Brighton. This commercial
failure also necessitated the sale of a miscellaneous
collection of jobmaster's effects, including a hearse and
mourning-coach " with velvets," &c. The unfortunate
Pattenden also seems to have kept the New Inn,
Brighton, one of the earliest of the Brighton coaching
inns.[1]

Then some one who had too many irons in the fire
to attend to coaching, advertised " an excellent stage-
coach in good running order, for sale, *without reserve,
price forty guineas*," and the Old Red Coach-Office in
North Street was to be let.

In the summer of 1827 the ubiquitous and iniqui-
tous informer, Byers, once more visited Brighton. He
caused to be laid a whole batch of informations through
his journeyman, Aaron Rolland.

The first information was laid against William
Blunden, a van proprietor, for omitting to have painted
on his van the number of passengers he was authorised
to carry, as directed by 44 George III. c. 98, s. 3. The
full penalty for this heinous offence was £20, and it
would appear that for some time after the passing of
the Act the magistrates had no power to mitigate it;
but happily for Blunden's pocket, the disparity between

[1] See p. 59.

the crime and its punishment struck the Legislature, and shortly before Byers laid this information a statute was passed giving the magistrates power to mitigate the penalty to one-fourth, which they did in this case ; and as one half of the penalty went to the informer, Byers got fifty shillings and his costs.

Byers next had an unsuccessful shot against Mr. Crosweller, the coach proprietor, for driving against a gentleman on horseback. A third case against Mr. Osborne, for carrying more than his proper number of passengers on a pair-horse coach, resulted in a fine of £10 and costs ; but Byers was defeated by Mr. Snow, the coach proprietor, against whom he laid an information for carrying too many passengers. It turned out, however, that the coach was not carrying passengers for hire, but was on its way to a funeral.

During the hearing of one of the preceding cases, Sir David Scott, the chairman of the bench, told Byers that they had no particular leaning towards him, a sentiment in which a crowded court doubtless shared ; and on the 9th August the Brighton coaching fraternity must have experienced a feeling of intense delight on reading in their *Brighton Gazette* a paragraph taken from the *Hampshire Chronicle* to the effect that Byers had been labouring in his vocation *here*—no place named, but probably it was Southampton. On entering the office to proceed with some of his cases, he was arrested for debt by the sheriff's officer, and lodged in gaol, where, if the prayers of his victims could have availed aught, he would probably have remained till he died.

The arch-informer, however, contrived to get his liberty again, and made his appearance on his favourite hunting-ground, Brighton, in November 1827, where he lost no time in laying an information against Mr. Cripps, a stage-coach proprietor, for having on the rail of the Brighton coach a name which was not included in the license. This case possesses a certain amount of interest, because in it we hear for the first time of Mr. Henry Stevenson, destined in a short time to become famous as the proprietor of the Coronet and the Age. In fact, it was Mr. Stevenson's name which was on the coach, and not in the license ; but Mr. Stevenson was the coachman, and the proprietors, Messrs. Cripps & Wilkins, imagined that, by putting up the name of the "Cambridge graduate" as one of the proprietors, it would bring increased patronage. Whether this coach was the Coronet or not, I have been unable to find out. In the result, Mr. Cripps had to pay £5 and costs.

The truth of the saying that a converted poacher can, if he choose, be a good gamekeeper, was not inaptly illustrated by one of Byers's "journeymen" leaving his service and setting up on his own account as a coachman's "lawyer." He was naturally up to every wrinkle, and it must have been a proud moment for him when he defeated no less a person than Byers himself at one of the London police-offices.

In the papers of January 1828 we learn something of the fun of coach-travelling in winter. The new year was ushered in by heavy downfalls of rain ; and in the lower-lying districts the floods were productive of considerable inconvenience, as the coaches had to travel through water nearly the whole of the way from Brighton to Patcham : in some places the water was axle-deep. One of the coaches stuck fast in the water and soft soil, so extra horses had to be sent for. Then ensued a long pull, a strong pull, and a pull altogether ; but the net result was the breakage of the pole. After a while the waters subsided, and snow fell so heavily as seriously to interfere with the London and Brighton traffic ; but when the snow vanished, the roads

were so heavy that the coach-horses were very much
distressed. These were the good old days, which no
doubt possessed greater attractions for amateur coachmen than for the mere passenger.

Steam, which in a few years was to annihilate stage-
coaching, an industry which arrived at perfection in so
comparatively short a time, and fell away even more
rapidly, appears by this time (1828) to have offered a
little mild opposition to coaching. The following paragraph, which was no doubt funny to those conversant
with the facts of the case, appeared in the *Brighton
Gazette* for the 17th January 1828 :—

"The coachmasters are resolved not to be outdone by the steamers,
and a Brighton Company have started a new coach, that can do anything almost but hold a conversation with the passengers. A full
gallop down a hill is to be as safe as to walk up it. By the turn of
a screw all the horses can be put in *strait-waistcoats* in a moment;
the wheels take up a contrary revolution, and intersect the line of
progress."

On the other hand, there were rumours of the success
which had been attained by Burstall & Hill's steam-
carriage. The *London Weekly Review* gave currency
to the report that the patentees had made arrangements
for running one of these steam-carriages on the Brighton
road; but suggested that it might be better policy to run,
in the first instance, a steam-caravan for goods, by way
of experiment, to Brighton or Bath.

The west end of Brighton was beginning to grow
about this time, so by June 1828 some coaches were
arranged to run from London direct to that quarter of
the town; but the old places were still houses of call.
In addition to the mail, the True Blue, the Royal
George (*via* Balcombe), and Rocket, already noticed,
an elegant fast post-coach was put on to run between
the Blue Coach - Office, Brighton, and Sanderson's
Hotel, Oxford Street, and Hatchett's Hotel, Piccadilly,

leaving Brighton at six o'clock, and several other new coaches, the names of which are not given, were announced as having been put on the road; while a still further increase in the number was expected.

One of the new ventures—it ran for the first time on Sunday, 27th July 1828—was a night-coach to London, leaving the Red Coach-Office, 10 Castle Square (it had been moved from North Street), and the Spread Eagle Coach-Office, 18 Castle Square, at 10 p.m., for the Spread Eagle, Gracechurch Street, and some of the West End booking-offices, returning from town each night at ten o'clock. Seven hours was the time allowed on the journey, and Snow, Chaplin, Hume, & Goodman were the proprietors.

The *Morning Herald*, in one of its November issues —it copies, by the way, from the *Sporting Magazine*— says that during the summer and autumn of 1828 no fewer than forty-two coaches left Brighton daily for London, and as many down. This is evidently a mis-statement, as the number was twenty-one each way; and the newspaper goes on to state that of these sixteen run all the year round, and that calculation assumes that twenty-six extra coaches ran each way during the season months. The *Morning Herald* then proceeds to state that " to pay anything like their expenses up and down, each of them must earn £10 a day, which gives an amount of £100,000 per annum spent in coach travelling on that one road, the best and most profitable, perhaps, for its length in England."

It used to be said, in the olden days, that a coach could be run at a profit if she earned £5 per double mile per month. The distances between London and Brighton were measured from Westminster Bridge; so if we say fifty-three miles thence to Brighton, and allow two extra miles for reaching the different book-ing-offices, we have a total of fifty-five miles. The phase "double mile" meant a mile each side of the road, *i.e.*, up and down; or, in other words, a coach paid if she earned £5 per mile one way only, leaving the other journey to be paid for out of that sum. At this estimate each Brighton coach must have earned £275 per month; but "Viator Junior," the *Sporting Magazine* writer, puts down the expenses at £10 per day; and as they did things rather grandly on this road, his calculation was doubtless correct.

However, a ruinous opposition set in, and proprietors, in their thirst for patronage, would carry passengers almost at the latter's own figure. During the heat of the contest, the fares, with very few exceptions, were five shillings from Brighton to London, and seven shillings from London to Brighton, an index that even at that time, as is the case now, there was a greater demand for seats one way than the other, though it is not easy to understand why this should have been the case when there was no railway. Such, however, was the fact; and three sets of proprietors were losing respectively £50, £60, and £70 per week; while a few others galloped straight into the Bankruptcy Court. Then came an honourable truce, and the fares were raised to the level of twelve shillings outside and a guinea inside.

On reference to the *Sporting Magazine* for 1828, one is able to gather more of the gossip of the road than it is possible to collect from newspaper authority, so I make no apology for giving the pith of three papers contributed by "Viator Junior" to the above-named publication. This somewhat outspoken critic[1] ranked Goodman's Times and Regent as amongst the best-horsed coaches on the road; while Goodman himself, who drove one of the Times coaches, is not considered

---

[1] See, too, pages 161 and 170.

to be a very great artist; but Moseley, who drove the
midday Times, was thought well of. Gray, too, on the
Regent, satisfied "Viator Junior." It is, however,
for Robert Snow that the highest compliments are re-
served. He was spoken of as a brilliant coachman,
and with more knowledge of driving in his little finger
than his brother William had in his whole body.

George Sheward, it appears, was interested in both
the Magnet and the Age; and he was pretty sharply
called over the coals for letting one of his best coachmen, young Cook, slip away to the Regulator. We
have always been so accustomed to hear the Age spoken
of as the beau-ideal of a stage-coach, that it is at first
something of a shock to hear it spoken of as a "flash
concern," and Corinthian in its *tout ensemble.* Yet
when we recollect that the horses wore fanciful pad
cloths and elaborate silver-plated harness, and that a
servant played the part of guard, and handed round
sandwiches and sherry *gratis,* Viator's description may
well be true enough. As a light coachman, however,
Mr. Stevenson is admitted to be very good; "he beats
nineteen out of twenty of the regular working drags-
men into fits," was the verdict passed on him; yet
he could not at this time have been more than about
twenty-three years old. Charles Newman, who drove
Genn's coach, is damned with faint praise; but Bristow, Hind's partner, satisfied our critic, who was also
pleased to speak well of Crosweller's coaches.

There were a couple of pair-horse coaches on the
road at this time, the Hero and the Royal Exchange.
"I have never thought it worth while to inquire the
names of these pair-horse performers," wrote "Viator
Junior;" "but I believe that one Carter has something to do with the driving of the Hero." This is
quite correct; but "one Carter"—whose Christian
name, by the way, was Philip—drove two horses so well,

that Mr. Robert Nelson thought he might with practice drive four. Accordingly he put him under one of his best coachmen, and about six weeks later young Philip Carter was sent out of London with the Courier, a Yorkshire coach. Then he was changed on to the Stroudwater Mail, which he drove as far as Bensington, in Oxfordshire, and eventually Carter drove the Red Rover, between London and Brighton. This "one Carter" was none other than Philip or "Tim" Carter, who died in March of the present year (1893), at the ripe old age of eighty-eight; and if he was given to the idea that there were few, if any, coachmen as good as he was, he certainly had some ground for his opinion, for he was by common consent one of the best men that ever mounted a box. The late Mr. Samuel Sidney called him the "standing counsel" to the rising generation of coachmen.

To the above may be added a story told by "Viator Junior," who professed to have been present at the time. "As James Pickett was starting with his 'Union' (a safety coach) out of Holborn, up comes a fussy old citizen, puffing and blowing like a grampus. 'Pray, coachman, is this here the patriotic Life-Preserver Safety Coach?' 'Yes, sir,' says Pickett, not hearing above half of his passenger's question. 'Room behind, sir ; jump up, if you please ; very late this morning.' ' Why, where's the machinery?' said the old one. 'There, sir,' replied a passenger (a young Cantab, I suspect), pointing to a heavy trunk of mine that was swung underneath. 'In that box, sir, that's where the machinery works.' 'Ah!' quoth the old man, climbing up quite satisfied, 'wonderful inventions nowadays. We shall all get safe to Brighton, not having an accident by this coach.'" This makes a very good story, but it is suspiciously like one or two more told at an anterior date.

L

The accompanying table of the coaches running from Brighton is extracted from the *Sporting Magazine* for 1828 :—

Names.	Offices.	Hours.	Dragsmen.
Dart	18 Castle Square.	6.0 a.m.	Bob Snow, up and down.
Item	Blue Coach Office.	6.0 ,,	Mellish, ,,
New Times	Goodman's, Castle Sq.	7.0 ,,	Sam. Goodman, ,,
Royal Exchange	Beehive, Castle Square.	7.0 ,,	...
Royal Clarence	Goodman's, 52 East St.	9.0 ,,	The. Holmes and son.
Alert	,, ,,	9.0 ,,	Hine and Bristow.
Regulator.	Beehive, Castle Square.	9.30 ,,	Young Cook and Adams.
Comet	18 Castle Square.	10.0 ,,	Clary and Jordan.
Patriot	7 Castle Square.	10.0 ,,	Harding.
Magnet	5 Castle Square.	10.0 ,,	Womack and Young Callow.
Regent	Goodman's, Castle Sq.	10.0 ,,	Cray and Goodman's brother.
True Blue.	Blue Office.	10.0 ,,	Mellish and Scriven.
Union	52 and 53 East Street.	11.0 ,,	Pickett and Egerton.
Age .	5 Castle Square.	12 noon	Mr. Stevenson.
Coronet	Beehive, Castle Square.	12 ,,	Old Tommy and C. Newman.
New Dart	135 North Street and 18 Castle Square.	12 ,,	Geo. Deere and Ned Pattenden.
Royal George .	Blue Office.	12 ,,	Rugeroh and J. Newman.
Rocket	,,	2.0 p.m.	Houldsworth and young C. Newman.
Times	Goodman's Office.	3.0 ,,	Mosely and Ellis.
Sovereign	18 Castle Square.	3.0 ,,	Ned Russell, up and down; sometimes W. Snow.
Hero	Beehive, Castle Square.	3.0 ,,	...
Evening Star	18 Castle Square and Goodman's.	10.0 ,,	Penny and Rumble.
Royal Mail	Blue Office.	10.0 ,,	Farley and Allen.

N.B.—An extra coach, from 18 Castle Square, at 8 o'clock every Saturday morning, driven by William Snow.

The spirit of opposition, however, appears to have been strongly implanted in the nature of every one connected with the stage-coach business, as, in a milder form, the cutting-down tactics were again pursued in the summer of 1829, when the usual addition of summer coaches made their appearance at a time when business was at its height; but no new conveyance which made a name for itself appears to have been put on the road.

A great many of the coaches, contrary to the general
idea, had no guards; and there being no one to
look after things, robberies were necessarily frequent.
Reference has been made to one or two; but the
accounts for the close of the year 1829 include several
others. After one coach was well clear of Brighton,
two rough-looking fellows appear to have hung on
behind the vehicle; and, as an old lady sat on the back-
seat, she was immediately pitched upon as the victim
of a robbery. One of the hangers-on had provided
himself with a sharp instrument, says the account,
with which he cut into the old lady's pocket, and
allowed the knife to penetrate even a little beyond,
when the poor old lady, feeling herself wounded, is
reported to have shouted "thieves, murder," whereupon the two fellows dropped from the coach and ran
away. The coachman, however, with commendable
promptitude pulled up, handed the reins to his box-
seat passenger, and gave chase, eventually capturing
one of the thieves.

Another similar case was reported from London.
Two men, whom the passengers supposed to be porters,
hung on behind the coach; and when the Obelisk on
the Surrey side of the Thames was reached, a female
passenger discovered that her cloak had been cut
through, and her purse would have been taken had it
not been for the clasp becoming entangled in the cloth.

Here were two incidents which could never have
occurred had the coaches carried guards, and a no less
celebrated vehicle than the Comet came to grief not
long afterwards through the absence of that functionary.
On reaching Epsom, the coachman got down to take
in a passenger; and while he was on the ground the
horses turned round, backed the coach, and caused her
to turn over, a lady who was riding outside having
some of her ribs broken. Owing to the want of

proper assistance, an accident which might have been attended with very serious consequences happened to the Alert, which was driven by young Mr. Hine. The coachman had gone round to pick up passengers, and the leaders had not been put on, when Hine drove it round to Russell Square to take up a lady passenger, Mrs. Stewart; Hine then drove on to Belle Vue Mansion, in the King's Road, for some more passengers. As the coach porter required assistance in getting the luggage on the coach, Hine got down to help him. From some unexplained cause the horses tried to bolt. A passer-by seized one horse by the bridle, and the coachman hung on to the other; but, as a cart was driven by at a furious pace and close to the coach, Hine had to let go to avoid being run over. The horses then, turning short round, made straight for the cliff, dashed against the iron railing forming the protection, burst it through, and horses and coach toppled over. The pole broke while the coach was falling, and the vehicle turned right over. The horses alighted on their haunches, and, strange to say, were so little injured, that one of them, later in the day, ran the first stage out of Brighton in another coach. The coach itself was broken to pieces, poor Mrs. Stewart being picked up in an insensible condition; and seeing that the coach and horses fell a distance of twenty feet, the only wonder is that the unfortunate lady was not killed. She was removed to the Old Ship, and in a week or two had sufficiently improved to be able to leave Brighton; but she recovered the substantial sum of £400 from the coach proprietors.

Brighton, it would appear, was sufficiently well catered for as regards the style of its coaches. There were fast coaches and slow coaches, high coaches and low coaches, safety coaches and vehicles of the ordinary build; but some genius conceived the idea of adding still further

to the existing variety, by reviving the old suggestion
of an omnibus with a double body to carry twenty-four
inside and fourteen outside passengers, the strange
vehicle to be drawn by five, six, or seven horses, as
might be found requisite; while a large well below the
passengers was to contain the luggage.

By a curious process of arithmetic the twenty-four
inside fares at 15s. each were estimated to produce
£18, 14s., and fourteen outside fares at 8s. 6d. are
reckoned at £6, 9s. 6d.; but this intending speculator,
who must have carried more than his proper number,
assumed that his vehicle would be full on every journey.
Now a coach is one thing, an omnibus is another; and
the man who would ride fifty-four miles, or thereabouts,
in a full omnibus would be the man to do what any
living mortal dared.

The fast coaches of the time of which we have been
speaking answered to the quick passenger-trains of the
present day, and they went by both the near routes—
that is to say, by both Cuckfield and Albourne. Their
accommodation would not have sufficed to carry all the
heavy luggage of their passengers. This, as well as the
various articles of merchandise required for the use and
consumption of the inhabitants of Brighton, together
with some of the meat and farm and dairy produce
generally which was sent to the London markets, was
intrusted to the vans, which were practically carriers'
carts on a rather exalted scale. They were indeed
the successors of the old stage-waggons which ran to
Brighton and Lewes before coaches were put upon the
road; and, with few exceptions, these vans carried
both goods and passengers; while the van proprietors,
like the Pantechnicon people of modern times, advertised that they were ready to remove furniture and
goods to any part of England. If we may judge from
the woodcuts heading the advertisements in the papers

of the date, the horses running in the vans were of a much stouter build than those which worked in the coaches; but, as the van owners were common carriers (see *ante*, p. 152), they had to take every care of what was committed to them; and so they appear to have carried a guard, a functionary who, as we have seen, was not always found upon a coach.

In the early part of May 1826, a case was heard in the Court of King's Bench which seems to have established the right of carriers to escape liability to make good parcels of a value exceeding £5, unless the same was duly declared and paid for. A couple of boxes of silk, worth about £200, were sent to Bath. The value was, of course, known to the sender; and, in the report of the case, it is stated that he was aware of the general notice given by the carriers in connection with the £5 limit. The boxes were lost, and the sender sought to recover their value from the carrier, on the ground that no particular notice had been given to him by the carrier when the boxes were accepted for transit. "The jury," we are informed, "gave in a special verdict," though in what terms we are unfortunately not told, and the judge gave judgment for the carrier, "after citing several analogous cases."

As with the stage-coaches, so it was with the vans, opposition was rife, as we have seen it was in the days of James Batchelor (*ante*, p. 35). Towards the close of December 1827, an opposition van, called the Paul Pry, was started on the Portsmouth road, and being an opposition concern, it bore the legend "I hope I don't intrude." Apparently it did not, for in the February of the following year it was advertised for sale.

At this time, however, there was something in a name. Some of the van proprietors were apparently in the habit of charging fancy prices for carting goods

from the West End of London to the City, whence
most of the vans started for Brighton, and so the great
firm of Winch & Chaplin announced that they had
started a new Fly van, for luggage only, direct to the
Spread Eagle Office, Regent Circus, and Brown's
Gloucester Warehouse, Oxford Street, in addition to
their usual van to the City; and the new venture paid
well.

Chapter X.

READERS of Captain Haworth's " Road Scrapings "
will remember the account of " Old Lal," the leg-
less pauper, who, being of a sporting turn of mind, contrived to obtain for himself a sort of miniature " buck-
board." To this vehicle " Old Lal"—he was known
by no other name—was accustomed to harness four
foxhounds, and with this singular team, put together
with true coachmanlike skill, he would beat all the
fast coaches on the North road. The story, as told by
Captain Haworth, is a curious one; but in some
of its features it was reproduced on the Brighton
road.

At East Grinstead there lived one Dumsdale, a tailor
in a small way of business, whose son had been a
cripple from his childhood. As Dumsdale *père* could
afford a no more expensive equipage for his afflicted
son, he had built for him a light four-wheeled cart—
something after the fashion of " Old Lal's," possibly
—and this affair, drawn by a unicorn team of bull-
dogs, startled those who happened to be in the Strand
one morning at the beginning of February 1830. The
usual pace of this vehicle was said to be seven miles
an hour; but the team often went at the rate of ten
miles an hour. From East Grinstead to Brighton is
twenty-four miles, and, allowing for stoppages, the
bulldog team used to do this journey comfortably in
four hours; while very often it would beat the
Brighton coach that travelled by this road, just as

"Old Lal's" foxhounds would shoot by the North road coaches. At some of the gates the keepers would exact the toll; but young Dumsdale was generally permitted to travel toll-free.

At the end of the month of February 1830, the coaching world was shocked to hear of the death, at the age of twenty-six, of Mr. Henry Stevenson, proprietor of the famous Brighton Age. Mr. Stevenson had been at Eton and Cambridge; and, according to one account, he had got through most of his money before starting as a coachman. This, however, can scarcely be the true version; for, although nothing is impossible to the spendthrift, the proprietor of the Age must have run through his patrimony very quickly, inasmuch as he first of all started the Coronet in conjunction with a Mr. Crisp (possibly a misprint for Cripps), who was somewhat vaguely described as "of Piccadilly." It is said in Pierce Egan's "Book of Sports" that Mr. Stevenson's first coach was the Waterwitch; but I can find no confirmation of this, though, as will be seen presently (p. 179), a Waterwitch was started subsequently; but nothing is said in connection with that coach of Mr. Stevenson ever having had one of the same name.

The Age was put on the road regardless of expense. It was, I think, a blue coach, and the harness, unlike that of the ordinary coach-horse, was silver-plated instead of brass. Everything was turned out in the very best style. A private servant in livery, who may have officiated as guard, accompanied the coach; and on the road a silver sandwich-box was passed round to the passengers, and the sandwich could be washed down by a glass of very fine sherry.

When Mr. Stevenson first appeared in the capacity of coach proprietor and coachman, the professional element was strongly against him, partly, no doubt, on account of his youth, and partly, perhaps, because it was thought that, by reason of his connection, his coach would receive greater patronage; though the aforesaid "Viator Junior" says that the concern could barely have paid expenses for days together. He was, however, such a good fellow, and withal such an artist on the box, that the opposition to him did not last long, and he soon became one of the most popular men on the road.

The beginning of Mr. Stevenson's illness would seem to have been an accident; but eventually, if his biographers are to be believed, mortification in the foot, and brain fever, set in. He certainly appears to have been afflicted with the latter, as some time before his death it was found necessary for his attendants to use a certain amount of force to restrain him. When, towards the last, he seemed thoroughly exhausted, his watchers removed the bandages which bound him to his bed, and were somewhat horrified to find him raise himself, as nearly as his very feeble state would permit, to the attitude he assumed when on the box. Once up, and his nature seemed to revive. In imagination he again handled the reins. "Let them go, George; I have them," he exclaimed, as though addressing a favourite servant, who invariably stood at his leaders' heads, and then, overcome by the exertion, he sank again on to his pillow and passed away. There could be something affecting even in connection with stage-coaching; the ruling passion was certainly strong in death in Mr. Stevenson's case.

Only a month or two after Mr. Stevenson's death the passengers by the Age on Tuesday, the 11th July 1830, most probably regretted that the "Cambridge Graduate" was not at work, as, for the first time in the coach's history, she was turned over, the accident taking place at the bottom of Red Hill. The passen-

gers were shot into a field—nothing is said about the
" insides," if there were any—but neither they nor
the coach were materially injured. Modern coachmen
have occasionally experienced some difficulty in keeping their horses straight should there happen to be
some straw, blood, tan, or any other unusual thing on
the road ; and, in the case of the Brighton Age, some
furze was the cause of the mishap. The horses shied
at it, and landed the coach in the ditch ; while two
other Brighton coaches, which went the same road,
nearly came to grief at the same place from the same
cause. On the death of Mr. Stevenson, Mr. Thomas
Ward Capps appears to have found funds to keep the
Age going, but a dispute arose in connection with the
coach, as will be seen in a later chapter.

A little farther on we shall have occasion to notice
the writings of one who congratulated the public upon
the improvement which had unquestionably taken
place in the general conduct of stage-coachmen ; yet
the coachmen of this date (1830) occasionally kicked
over the traces, like their horses.

James Cross, for instance, who ranked amongst the
best of the Brighton coachmen, was summoned before
Mr. Minshull, at Bow Street, by Mr. Augustus Amiat,
for having used abusive language to him ; and the evidence given at the hearing of the summons shows us
some of the incidents of coach-travelling at this time.

Mr. Amiat, it appears, was waiting at the Ship,
Charing Cross, for some coach which would take him
to Croydon. Up drove Cross, who, in answer to the
question, " Any room for Croydon ? " promptly replied
that there was, and Mr. Amiat seated himself on the
coach, which in due course reached the Elephant and
Castle. At that point were several people wanting to
go to Brighton, so Cross asked his Croydon passenger to
get inside. Mr. Amiat, however, was one of those people

against whom an earlier writer had inveighed because
they preferred the outside to the inside of a coach;
but he at length agreed to get inside rather than deprive
Cross of a through fare.   Then Cross appeared at the
coach-window and begged Mr. Amiat to get out and
travel by a Croydon coach which had just come up.
The good-natured man, who, in the words of young
Cook, a notable Brighton coachman, had been " moved
about between Hell and Hackney," consented to shift
to the other vehicle, upon the understanding that Cross
would guarantee him an outside seat, which Cross,
anxious only to get rid of his short passenger, without caring a farthing whether there was room or not,
immediately undertook to do.

The Croydon coach being full, Mr. Amiat returned
to Cross's vehicle, and resumed his seat inside, when the
coach started with three insides; at Streatham they
picked up a fourth, and a fifth was pushed in soon
afterwards.   This last indignity seems to have upset
poor Mr. Amiat altogether, so when he alighted at
Croydon he asked Cross whether he was one of the
proprietors, and on receiving an answer in the affirma-
tive, told him that he would be summoned for carrying
more than his proper number of passengers; whereupon
the veneer of the swell dragsman dropped off, and in
true plebeian style he told his passenger that he should
"like to give him a d—d good hiding," adding, "It
is such fellows as you that, when you come down the
road, and can't find anything to steal, turn informers."
Opposition was, no doubt, very keen at this time, and
Cross urged, in explanation of what he admitted was
unjustifiable conduct, that he had lost two through
fares to Brighton; while, like people who have put
themselves in the wrong often do now, he tendered
the cheap restitution of an apology; and this not being
accepted, Mr. Cross had to pay the full penalty of forty

shillings and costs, the magistrate observing that he never felt less regret in imposing a punishment for an offence of this nature than he did on that occasion.

Coachmen of the time of which we are speaking are invariably represented as having been models of everything that is good; but not a few cases are on record which seem to suggest that, in many instances, theirs was a sort of cupboard love. To their box-seat passenger they were doubtless very civil and nice; but to those who did not happen to take an interest in horses or in the details of the coach, and who would tip but moderately or not at all, there is every reason to assume that many of them behaved as did Cross to Mr. Augustus Amiat.

In point of civility Theophilus Holmes, coachman of one of the London coaches, who entertained an angel unawares when he carried Mr. Robert Taylor, a Surrey magistrate, left something to be desired. Mr. Taylor drove to meet the coach, and found that there were on the box two persons, one of whom got down to enable Mr. Taylor to find room; but that gentleman declined to share with any fellow-passengers a seat intended for one only. Thereupon Holmes remarked that if Mr. Taylor did not choose to get on the box, he would go without him; but Mr. Taylor's answer was that if he did, he would take a post-chaise, follow the coach, and inform Mr. Goodman, one of the proprietors, of Holmes's conduct; to which threat Holmes replied that he did not care a d—n for Goodman or anybody else. In the end the magistrates called upon Holmes to pay the mitigated penalty of thirty shillings and costs. All these little matters tend rather seriously to discount the glowing terms in which coachmen were described; but in that calling, as in others, there were specimens good and bad. The famous Dick Vaughan, who drove the Cambridge Telegraph, was exceedingly civil when he liked ; but he had a rough side to his tongue, and it is said that, while talking to his box-seat passenger, he would break off to swear at somebody or something, stop in the middle of his oath to apologise, and then finish the oath. This rather reminds one of the Mother Superior of a French convent, who, when her mule provoked her to wrath, would utter one half of some naughty word, making the lay sister who sat by her side say the other half, by which expedient she hoped to escape the sin of swearing.

Meantime the dragsman's sworn enemy, Byers, was keeping his eye on all coachmen who ventured in the very least degree to infringe any law which governed stage-coaching, and one day in August 1830, he laid three informations against Francis Vickers for having carried more passengers than he was entitled to do. In one of the cases it was alleged that one of Byers's minions was in an upstairs room of a public-house, and could not see the coach for a sufficiently long time to swear to the number of passengers on the roof; but the hireling swore that he was standing on the pavement, that all the persons were seated, and he averred that he not only saw the coach passing him, but that he also "saw it out of sight." The informer, however, gained the day, and the unfortunate Vickers had to pay three penalties of £10 each in addition to costs.

Yet another stage-coachman found himself arraigned before the magistrates. This time it was Edward Bristow. He was part owner of the Alert, and drove one end, and was summoned for furious and improper driving, whereby a valuable horse belonging to Captain Fuller, R.N., was seriously injured. The horse, which was standing in front of Tupper's Library, was frightened by the horn blown by some one on the Alert, and turning round into the roadway, was struck by the step of the coach, whereby he was a good deal hurt; but

the Bench, considering that the affair was a pure accident, dismissed the complaint.

And now to the coaches. As there was an increased
demand for afternoon coaches to London, the Red
Rover was put on in August 1830, leaving Brighton
daily at four o'clock ; and, to meet the wishes of those
who liked fast travelling, it was decided to run another
which should accomplish the journey to London in
four hours and a half; while some bold spirits were
anxious to exceed even this pace, as the *Brighton
Gazette* for the 18th November announced that a wager
of £500 was pending that a certain coach, which was
not named, should run to London in three hours and
a half; but I cannot find that an attempt was ever
made to accomplish this feat.

Before this time (1830) the railway had been talked
about; in December the prospectus of the proposed
London and Brighton line was published in the papers ;
and the following extract may serve to show the extent
to which coach and waggon traffic—destined to be
completely run off the road in another twelve years—
was carried on between London and Brighton :—

> "It has been ascertained that more than 500 persons pass daily
> upon the average of the year from one town to the other. The present
> inside coach fares are 20s. to 24s., and the outside 10s. to 12s. ; and
> it is presumed that it would not be unreasonable to calculate upon
> 10s. per head; and taking this upon 400 only, it would produce a gross
> revenue of £73,000 per annum " (reckoning £200 per day for seven
> days in the week, the exact sum for fifty-two weeks would be £72,800).

Then, to the amount represented by passenger fares
must be added what was paid for parcels and excess
luggage, and the money expended on what would now
be called goods traffic, but which in those days went to
the vans ; so it will be seen that, when railways once
started, they immediately began with a twofold business.

By way of offering further facilities to the afternoon
traveller, it was announced that, during the summer of

1831 a coach would leave Brighton at five o'clock, and would arrive in London at about ten; but the local papers suggested that six would have been a more convenient hour, as it would have afforded intending passengers the very questionable advantage, as we should now consider it, of dining at five o'clock. Eventually, however, the new coach was timed to leave Brighton at 4.30; and it made its first journey on Monday, the 5th March 1831. It was run in opposition to the Red Rover, which, as mentioned above, started at four o'clock.

The Red Rover coach is so far of special interest to men of the present day in that its coachman was an artist who died no longer ago than the spring of the present year (1893). I refer to Philip, better known as "Tim" Carter, to whom reference has already been made.[1]

The Badminton Library gives currency to the oft-told story that when King William IV. opened Parliament in 1831, Tim Carter drove the Red Rover down to Brighton with the King's maiden speech in three hours thirty-five minutes; while other coachmen—that is to say, Charles Harbour and Israel Alexander—have been credited with having taken down another Royal Speech in three hours and forty minutes. According to the *Brighton Gazette* for the 23rd of June 1831, however, Tim Carter and the Red Rover left the Elephant and Castle at four o'clock on Tuesday the 19th June, and reached Brighton at twenty-one minutes past eight, being thus four hours and twenty-one minutes on the road. "This coach," said the journal in question, which would not be likely to understate the case, "brought the King's Speech."

While one section of the public were praising the rapid pace at which the fast coaches now travelled, another body apparently clamoured for something rather

---

[1] See *ante*, p. 161.

slower, and slightly more sure than the galloping concerns whose achievements, or accidents, as the case
might be, were recorded in print every now and then.
In coaching, as in other matters, there was a supply of
everything for which there was a demand, and, to suit
those who were of opinion that "it's the pace that kills"
—passengers as well as horses—a diligence was put on
to run to London, and omnibuses carried the timid to
Lewes. From Goodman's Office "a new coach on a
new principle" started for London, the new principle
being that the coach was "low, wide, and consequently
may be considered more than usually safe."

Another "safe" coach was the Royal Adelaide,
which covered the distance between London and
Brighton in six hours. In the words of the advertisement, "this coach claims the decided preference of
families and invalids, the proprietor having selected
steady horses that can trot the distance with ease,
without once breaking into a gallop, as well as steady
coachmen, thereby avoiding the danger incurred by
other coaches which profess to perform the journey
in less time ; and also from their engaging to set down,
and take up, passengers in any part of Brighton." No
doubt the "other coaches which professed" to go more
quickly were much obliged to "Robert Gray & Co.,"
the proprietors of the Royal Adelaide, for the character
given them ; but competition was keen, and in some
instances, despite the proverb, self-praise may have
been a recommendation. The Royal Adelaide started
from the Age Coach-Office, Castle Square, Brighton, at
ten o'clock, and ran to the Bolt-in-Tun, Fleet Street,
and the Lamb, Lamb's Conduit Street, branch coaches
conveying passengers to the West End of the town.
At eleven o'clock the coach left on the down journey.
A week after the above advertisement appeared, the
new undertaking was patted on the back by a local

M

journal : " A very neat and well-conducted coach, the
Royal Adelaide, has just been established between this
place and London, which rests its claim to public
patronage on a ground novel in the present day—the
steadiness with which it is driven, as opposed to the
rapidity that generally prevails."

A new coach called the Reform also made its appearance at this time, and presumably derived its name
from the fact that it carried passengers at reduced
fares.

On the subject of fast driving and coach accidents,
a contributor to the *New Sporting Magazine*, writing
under the signature of " Dashwood," made some very
sensible remarks, which, shortly summed up, mean that
he was quite on the side of Robert Gray & Co., of the
Royal Adelaide, in thinking that, for safety, one uniform pace should be kept up. During the wordy
warfare which for a short time raged between the Old
and New *Sporting Magazines*, " Dashwood " was very
rudely designated as " Donkey Dashwood." However, " Donkey " or not, here are some of his remarks
on pace and its effects, which are, I think, worth
reproducing :—

" One great mistake amongst people who do not see
much of the road is to imagine, when they hear of a
fast coach, that there must be galloping and racing.
These two sins, indefensible at all times, are never
committed on a well-regulated concern. It is by per-
severing from end to end at a regular steady pace,
losing no time at the changes, and making no stoppages
beyond what the business of the coach requires, that
the fast dragsman keeps his time to a minute, and
does justice to his stock. Look, for instance, at Robert
Nelson's *Brighton Rover*" (the Red Rover already mentioned in connection with Tim Carter), " time five hours,
distance fifty-four miles ; and, unless a springing them

up a shoot or two be called galloping, not a leader
is out of a trot from the river to the ocean. As to
racing, the etiquette of the road is now completely
against it; and, except in the provinces, where sometimes there is a little bad blood amongst the *pro-
periators*, as Ned Burford used to style them, we hardly
nowadays hear of such a thing. Whilst I am writing
this, however, a report has reached me that there is a
little taste of it just now going on on the Portsmouth
road, and if so, all I can say is, the sooner it is put
an end to the better, for no man, take even the best
and strongest coachman that ever sate on a box, is safe
with four horses let loose in a gallop."

There is a good deal of truth in this. It is all
right so long as the horses are galloping; the difficulty sometimes comes in when you want to stop;
and even in some of the modern coaches there are
occasionally seen teams that not many men would care
to gallop; with many a horse it is a case of *crescit
eundo*—the faster he goes the faster he wants to go.

In the *Brighton Gazette* for the 25th August, 1831,
appears the first mention I can find of the Waterwitch,
the coach which Mr. Stevenson is said to have owned
before he had the Age. This coach, which appears
to have been started only a few days before, is reported
to have travelled very rapidly, and to have found
general favour. In the issue for the 1st September it
is announced in grandiloquent terms. First comes
an illustrated heading with the name of Cooper, the
novelist.

THE WATER WITCH.

"Few novelists have excited more intense feeling or exhibited a
more perfect acquaintance with the taste of the day, or more completely arrested public attention and admiration in so short a time,
as the above author in his various works, more particularly with
the far-famed

WATER WITCH.

We know that Brighton is the residence of the Queen of Taste, that is, Fashion—that here her Court is held—that here she invariably appreciates, in the highest degree, each endeavour to please her votaries. This is evident in the astounding extent of admiration and patronage.

As though there were *witchery* in the name bestowed on the indefatigable and spirited proprietor of the

BRIGHTON WATER WITCH,

which here, and in the Metropolis, and on its intervening route, has excited a degree of extraordinary attention, which nothing but its unexampled adherence to taste and truth, the surprising and satisfactory concidence of its professions, and the regularity of its developments could have collected and commanded during so short a time. PUNCTUALLY at three o'clock every afternoon it leaves the

ROYAL BEDFORD HOTEL,

and following the "line of ocean track" to those of the

ALBION AND YORK,

It leaves precisely at half-past three the BULL AND MOUTH Office, 3 Castle Square, and passing through Hixtead, Crawley, Red Hill, and Croydon, endeavours to crown its various merits by most sedulously accommodating its patrons in their various destinations to

All parts of the CITY and WEST END.

GEORGE WAGNER ; EDWARD SHERMAN,
Proprietors.

This composition is, I venture to think, quite worthy of the pushing hairdresser whose advertisement is quoted in the first chapter; but the newspapers of this date gave the coach a free advertisement by remarking that the streets were rendered most melodious by the horns of the stage-coaches—it is to be hoped that they were tuned in one key—some of which were played extremely well. Among the best, it was pointed out, was that of the Waterwitch, "a new and well-conducted coach, which, as we last week mentioned, has just been started from this place to London."

Mr. Wilde, of the Clarence Hotel, had, for some undis-
covered reason, advertised in the *Brighton Guardian*
that the Red Rover coach was discontinued, a statement which drew forth a prompt contradiction from
Christopher Holmes, one of the proprietors, who explained that the office was removed to East Street,
where passengers and parcels could be booked as usual.
Just before this the Red Rover was very much in evidence through racing with the Waterwitch, a little
frolic which resulted in the Rover's coachman, Charles
Holmes, Christopher's son—Tim Carter was driving the
other end—having to answer an information laid by Mr.
Slight, Clerk to the Commissioners. Both coaches were
sailing along the New Road, and when near the theatre
the Red Rover passed the Waterwitch at a gallop.
Foot people fled in all directions, and Mr. Slight entertained serious apprehensions for their safety. The explanation was that there was a noise outside the theatre
which frightened the horses, and caused Holmes to
whip his horses to keep them on the proper side of the
road ; but as Holmes had previously pleaded guilty, the
Bench inflicted the full penalty of £5 and costs. One
of the local journals understood that the galloping was
due to a guinea bet having been made as to which coach
would arrive first, and asked the pertinent question
why an information was not also laid against the coachman of the Waterwitch.

At the beginning of January, 1832, Goodman put on
the " Four-o'clock Times " to London—it left at half-
past four—and, before it had been running very long, it
had a narrow escape from turning over, owing to the
pole breaking ; but, as this mishap occurred before the
horses had got into their stride—that is to say, by
Wright's Library in North Street—the coachman managed to pull up the horses and saved the capsize. The
Times was one of the fast coaches, and the irrepressible

Red Rover maintained its claim to be ranked in the same category by reaching London in four hours and ten minutes on Sunday, the 8th June 1832. As a refuge from all this expeditious travelling, the Earl Grey, another new coach, was started, to travel at a comparatively slow speed by way of Ditchling and Lindfield. Many times in these pages has it been stated that new coaches have been put on ; but the majority of them must have been merely butterfly concerns to meet the exigencies of the summer traffic.

"Dashwood," from whom I have quoted above, begins his article in the *Sporting Magazine* by congratulating the world at large on the few coach accidents which took place ; but, after a lengthened period of searching into coaching records, I fear that "Dashwood's" compliments were a little premature ; the wish was probably father to the thought. On every road in England mishaps, more or less serious, were chronicled with monotonous frequency. Many of them were doubtless accidents against which no human foresight could have guarded ; but racing, either against opposition vehicles or against time ; carelessness, insufficient examination of coaches, poor harness, and weak horses were, in their turn, productive of many accidents ; and they arose from all sorts of causes.

For example, Wilkins, the driver of the Coronet, got down at Horley to see to the harness of the leaders ; one of the wheel-horses took it into his head to misbehave, and startled the team, which overcame Wilkins, who was thrown to the ground, the wheels of the coach passing over his leg. By something little short of a miracle the bone was not broken, and the coachman was able to drive on. It would appear as though this were another case of no guard, otherwise he would have been directed to get down and make the necessary examination or alteration, while the coachman

remained on his box—a very much safer method of
proceeding. The sad death of a gentleman named
Schraeder, while travelling by the Comet, was entirely
due to his own act. The coach had reached Patcham
from Brighton, when the reins became "entangled;"
but whether one of the horses got its tail over a rein,
or in what manner the entanglement took place, is not
stated. Mr. Schraeder, who had the box-seat, appears
to have deemed the situation critical, as, in spite of
the remonstrance of the coachman, he attempted to get
down, before the coach had stopped, to adjust the reins.
In so doing he fell beneath the coach, and the wheels
passing over him, caused injuries which resulted in
death. Mr. Schraeder was on his way to Brighton to
join his family, who were living on the Marine Parade.
Next it was the turn of the Red Rover to be within an
ace of having a bad accident, as on turning the corner
at the end of Church Street the leaders came in contact
with a carriage. They then behaved as leaders often
do in such circumstances—they "began to plunge and
kick violently." The coachman, we are told, "losing
command of them, the consequences would probably
have been serious had not a person caught the leaders'
reins and succeeded in quieting them." The account
continues by informing readers that "the pole was
snapped asunder, and this was *happily* the only damage done." A new pole was provided, and the Red
Rover proceeded on her way after a twenty minutes'
delay.

The mails, we are informed, came to grief but rarely;
but, just as "Fortune knocks once at every man's door,"
so, apparently, does ill-luck. At any rate, it so happened to the Brighton mail, as on the 30th October
1832, while on her way from London to Brighton, she
was upset just as she entered Reigate while turning
a corner. The coachman, whose name is not given,

died on the spot, his skull being fractured against a
gate. Outside the coach were three passengers and the
guard, while there were also some inside passengers.
The latter escaped unhurt, but the former were all
more or less injured, one of them having three of
his ribs fractured. All the horses were thrown down,
and the harness was completely broken; but, Reigate
being a coaching centre, this portion of the damage
was repaired, and, after the dead coachman and the
injured passengers had been brought into the town,
a man was found to drive the mail—for the vehicle
itself was not much injured—on to Brighton. The
coachman unhappily left a wife and four children. Not
a very long time before this a somewhat singular incident occurred to the Brighton mail just as she was about
to start for London. "One of the hind horses," says
a local journal—so by the year 1831 the Brighton mail
had four horses instead of the two which had sufficed
in earlier years—got his leg entangled in the wheel
"in so singular a manner that it was nearly half an
hour before it could be extricated, the poor animal all
the time groaning most piteously." A year or two
before this, it was calculated that the mail-coaches
of England ran over twelve thousand miles—half the
circumference of the globe—in a single night. A local
journal remarked that a newspaper published in the
morning in London was read at a place a hundred
and twenty miles distant in the evening; and that a
traveller going at night from London, slept on the
second night four hundred miles off. As a tribute
to modern enterprise, however, I may mention that
I have bought the *Yorkshire Herald* for the day at
York Station at about half-past two in the morning.

If, however, the leaning of coaches, mail and otherwise, was towards fast travelling, the Government
of 1827 appear to have been content with a very

moderate rate of speed for their cross-country posts,
as we find the Post-Office authorities advertising for
tenders from those willing to convey the mails in light
carts between Brighton and Chichester, the pace to be
seven miles an hour, including stoppages. The contractor was to pay the Shoreham Bridge tolls and the
assessed taxes ; and it was pointed out that to convey
a passenger rendered the mailman liable to a month's
imprisonment.

In one of the April issues of the *Observer* for 1832, it
was stated that the Post-Office authorities had it in con-
templation to substitute light two-wheeled vehicles for
the mail-coaches. The improvement in road-making,
and the advance of stage-coaching in all its branches,
including the rate of speed, had tended to bring about
the result that the mails were no longer the fastest
coaches on the road. The contractors, therefore, both
complained and explained that the preference for mails
on the part of travellers, upon which they calculated,
no longer existed, and that they could not horse the
four-horse mails with any profit to themselves unless
the Post-Office were a little more liberal in their allow-
ance. In France the custom had for some time been
to convey the mails in light pair-horse vehicles ; and
it was reported that the English Government intended,
when the then existing contracts ran out, to try a fresh
experiment all the kingdom over, especially as they
were led to believe that the pace might be increased
by two miles per hour, while much expense might be
saved. Whether the Post-Office ever really contem-
plated the change or not, I cannot say ; but it is certain
that, on the main roads, no alteration was made in the
arrangements which then obtained, and the mails continued to be run on the lines which had made them
famous throughout the world.

I am sorry to say that more space will have to be

devoted to accidents presently, so, by way of relief, let me
turn for a moment from the tragic side of stage-coaching to the somewhat comic element of steam-carriages.

In the summer of 1831, Mr. Hancock proposed to
build a new and improved vehicle by subscription
of forty shares of £20 each; it was to ply between
London and Brighton. I can find nothing more of
importance in connection with this new invention till
November in the following year, when, as the steam-
carriage " The Infant," as it was called, was an accomplished fact, the presumption is that Mr. Hancock's
£20 shares were taken up. About the 1st of November
1832, it went from London to Brighton; but the fuel
ran short on the way, and a long time was consumed
in travelling " from the river to the ocean." At
Brighton, " The Infant " took in a supply of water, and
then steamed back to London at a pace which is said
to have been between six and eight miles an hour.

Our horses of to-day should be pretty well accustomed to steam, yet traction-engines are occasionally
as lions in our path, and one is not surprised to learn
that, in the course of its journey, Mr. Hancock's
steam-carriage was at least on one occasion a source
of terror to the Sussex horses. " The noise of the
engine," we learn, " so alarmed a gig-horse who met
this machine, that a gentleman driving him had much
difficulty in reaching an inn on the road." Had the
steam-carriage been *behind* this recalcitrant gig-horse,
the inn would probably have been reached in double
quick time. The house being gained, however, the driver
of the gig left his horse there, and posted to London,
from which we may infer that the gig-owner was not
much accustomed to horses. Some Brightonian, who
apparently took an interest in steam-carriages, wrote
a letter to the *Brighton Gazette* of which the following
is a copy :—

"Having received an intimation that Mr. Walter Hancock's steam-carriage, the ' Infant,' was on the way from London to this place on an experimental trip, I went to meet it eight miles on the road on Friday morning, and came with it from thence into Brighton. We travelled at the rate of between five and six miles per hour up the steep hill at Pyecombe, and descended at the rapid pace of full thirteen miles per hour, proceeding afterwards into the town steadily at about ten miles an hour. Mr. Hancock made a tour round the North Steine enclosure, up to the New Palace gates, and returned to the tank near the new church, where he waited a short time to take in coke and water, and proceeded immediately on his return towards London. This unexpected visit excited a lively interest on the road, and at the north end of the town it caused an instantaneous assemblage of the entire neighbourhood. I understand from some of the gentlemen who accompanied Mr. Hancock from London that the only inconvenience experienced on the road arose from the want of proper relay stations for coke or water, which would be readily obviated under an organised establishment. They travelled from nine to eleven miles per hour on the level parts of the road, from five to seven up the hills, and from twelve to fourteen going down. The coke for the first part of the journey was procured from London ; that for the latter part from Brighton. A fact worth noticing was elicited from this circumstance, namely, that it was much more difficult to keep up the fire with the Brighton coke ; and a much greater quantity of it was consumed than of the London coke in travelling equal distances,—a circumstance I have found, on inquiry, to be satisfactorily accounted for by the use of *clay* retorts at the Hove gasworks, which enable the directors to obtain 12,000 feet of gas from a chaldron

of coals, while the *iron* retorts used in London limit
the operation to 10,000. Thus the London coke is
obviously less exhausted of its carbon. This experiment may, I conceive, be considered as a decisive
proof of the practicability of travelling by steam on
common roads. Every one knows there are several long
and steep acclivities between London and Brighton, all
of which were gallantly ascended, and the roads were
generally wet and heavy.—C. A. BUSBY."

There is a P.S. to the effect that Mr. Hancock had
almost completed a steam-carriage which he expected
to run from London to Brighton in three hours and
a half.

In the summer of 1833 it was announced that several noblemen and gentlemen, members of Parliament,
were expected to arrive at the Marine Hotel on a
certain evening by the steam-carriage. This announcement was quite sufficient to bring together nearly as
many idlers as Brighton happened to contain. The
company, indeed, came—fourteen of them, including
Sir Charles Dance and Sir Henry Watson—but it was
on the time-honoured coach, and not in the new-fangled
steam conveyance. They started in the steam-carriage,
and travelled safely as far as Hand Cross, where, in
endeavouring to avoid one of the Brighton coaches
while descending a hill, one of the piston-rods snapped
and prevented farther progress. The party were forced
to complete their journey by coach. Amongst the
party were the stage-coach proprietors Messrs. Chaplin
and Sherman, who probably watched the working of
Mr. Hancock's new conveyance with more than passing
interest, uncertain, no doubt, whether, in the immediate
future, steam would not become a very formidable
opponent to the coaching business, which the two
proprietors abovenamed carried out on so vast a scale.
The experience of the day, however, must have caused

them to take heart, for although some of the critics foretold that in a very short time the steam-carriage would do the distance in less than five hours, the machine once more broke down a week or two later, when, after running between Stratford and London, it paid a second visit to Brighton. The mishap, however, seems to have occurred in Brighton, while the concern was, like Lord Dundreary's bird, "flocking by itself" through the streets of Brighton.

The "Infant" seems to have been anything but a noiseless machine, for it signalised its departure from Brighton by such snorting and puffing that it frightened a gentleman's horse, which broke away from the lad who was holding it, and dashed over a barrow containing some dozens of ginger-beer, "which were mostly broken." There was, indeed, as the local journals observed, "a sort of fatality" over these steam-carriages in their journeys to Brighton, as not one had succeeded in getting there and back without an accident of some kind.

Mr. Hancock, however, was not easily cast down; and, in spite of broken piston-rods, a failure of fuel, and frightened horses, he announced that he would soon run a steam-carriage between Brighton and Worthing. Meantime another steam vehicle, called the Autopsy, steamed down to Brighton early in October 1833. It appears to have been owned by some rival of Hancock's, and the proprietor of the opposition, taking advantage of the curiosity of the multitude, turned a few honest pence by carrying people round the town at a shilling a head.

One person there was who watched those steam-coaches with a keen, and a not altogether disinterested, eye—the hated Byers, the informer. In them he fancied he saw a source of probable gain, and hesitated not to avow his intention of laying information against

the proprietors of these machines for plying for hire
without having the Stamp Office plate attached to their
vehicles. He stated that he would proceed under the
Hackney Carriage Act, but I cannot discover that he
carried his threat into execution.

The summer of 1833 witnessed the usual amount of
opposition on the road; several new coaches were, as
in former years, put on for the busy season. One by
one, however, the " butterflies " were taken off as the
winter approached, and the road resumed its wonted
comparative quiet, as exemplified by about sixteen or
seventeen coaches. During the summer, however, the
Brighton magistrates attempted to read a wholesome
lesson to those men who set pace above everything, by
inflicting the penalty of £5 on James Bristow, coachman and part proprietor of the New Red Rover (an opposition coach to the Red Rover), for furious driving.

Here I must have recourse to the "Driving" volume
of the Badminton Library to enable me to fill in some
of the gaps in the local journals. Goodman's Times I
have already mentioned; and the Duke of Beaufort
relates that during this year (1833) his father, then
Marquis of Worcester, took a house in Brighton, but
having to attend to his parliamentary duties, was
obliged to travel often between Brighton and London.
Being a very fine coachman, and well known on several
roads, he was in the habit of driving the public coach
on whatever road he might happen to travel, and he
not unnaturally expected to drive between London and
Brighton. This, however, old Goodman, a fine coachman, but described by the Duke of Beaufort as "a
surly, cross-grained fellow," would not allow him to
do on the Times. The Marquis of Worcester was very
angry at this, and at once entered into negotiations
with Alexander, a coach contractor and livery stable-
keeper in the Borough, to start his opposition coaches.

Preliminaries were soon arranged, and the outcome was the establishment of the Wonder, a yellow coach which left Brighton at seven A.M., the same hour as the Early Times; and the Quicksilver, which opposed Goodman's "Four-o'clock Times." Both travelled between Brighton and the Elephant and Castle in four hours and three-quarters; Capps, either the proprietor of the booking-office or some relation of his, drove the Wonder, while Bob Pointer,[1] who had formerly been on the Oxford road, was on the Quicksilver. The latter coach appears to have made its first journey on the 10th July 1833, when, as the local papers tell us, "an unusually large crowd assembled in Castle Square and North Street, attracted by the departure of the Quicksilver coach, driven by the Marquis of Worcester. Most of the officers of the 1st Dragoon Guards, and many other fashionables, were among the assemblage." A fortnight later there was unhappily far less cause for congratulation.

---

[1] In Mr. Ward's book appears the following lecture delivered by Bob Pointer to a young Oxonian who chanced to be his box-seat passenger: "Soldiers and sailors may soon learn to fight; lawyers and parsons go to college, where they are crammed with all sorts of nonsense that all the nobs have read and wrote since Adam—of course very good if they like it; but to be a *coachman*, sir, you must go into the stable almost before you can run alone, and learn the nature of horses, and the difference between corn and chaff. Well can I remember the first time I went out with four horses. I never slept a wink all night. I got a little flurried coming out of the yard, and looking round on the envious chaps who were watching me—it was as bad as getting married—at least I should think so, never having been in that predicament myself. I have escaped that dilemma, for when a man is going backwards and forwards between two points, what is the use of a wife; a coachman could never be much more than half married. Now if the law—in the case of coachmen—allowed two wives, that would be quite another story, because he could then have the tea-things set out at both ends of the journey. Driving, sir, is very like life; it's all so smooth when

"All went swimmingly," says the Badminton Library, "till one evening, going out of Brighton, a young coachman, son of one of the large coach proprietors whose office was in Castle Square,[1] was driving the four thoroughbred chestnuts, as good and quick a 'Town-end team' as could be found, when, for some never-to-be-explained reason, they broke away from him, and he turned the coach over just opposite the New Steine Hotel. Several passengers were badly shaken, and two unfortunate ones were thrown on the spikes that surmount the railings of the New Steine. Happily in time they all recovered, but it cost some money to cure them."

In the *Brighton Gazette* of the 25th July 1833, there is a further account of the accident :—

"The melancholy coach accident which occurred here last Thursday has seldom been equalled as regards the number of sufferers, although it is now hoped that no fatal consequences will ensue. Almost the whole of the passengers, of whom there were no fewer than thirteen, the inside being full, were severely

---

you start with the best team, so well-behaved and handsome; but get on a bit, and you will find you have some hills to go up and down, with all sorts of horses, as they used to give us over the middle ground. Another thing, sir, never let your horses know you are driving them, or, like women, they may get restive. Don't pull and haul, and stick your elbows a-kimbo; keep your hands as though you were playing the piano; let every horse be at work, and don't get flurried; handle their mouths lightly; do all this, and you might even drive four young ladies without ever ruffling their feathers or their tempers." The Duke of Beaufort says that Pointer had one great failing. He could be depended upon to start at any hour perfectly sober; but it was necessary to have the stables at which the coach changed horses away from a public-house, or he would certainly have become intoxicated before he reached his journey's end.

[1] Young John Snow, a booking-clerk in the office, was driving.

DRAWING OF THE OLD ROADS AT HANE CROSS

hurt, some of them very dangerously, and in particular
Mr. Sugon, who is well known here as an annual visitor,
was so much injured that instant death was expected
to ensue. His right arm was dreadfully fractured,
several ribs were broken, and both jaws ; yet, to the
astonishment of his medical attendants, Messrs. Taylor
and Lawrence, as well as of all around him, he is not
only still alive, but, thanks to an excellent constitution,
hopes are even entertained of his recovery. Among
the other passengers were Mr. Pearson, the Common
Councilman ; Captain Hunter, Mr. Beale, a butcher at
Peckham, whose wife and child were inside, as well
as many others, were all more or less hurt. Mr. John
Snow, who drove the coach, sustained considerable
injury, and now lies very ill. The regular driver, Mr.
Halyar,[1] who was also on the coach, escaped with
some slight bruises. As usual on such occasions, all
sorts of stories are in circulation, some of which are
certainly groundless. It has been said, for instance,
that Mr. Snow was intoxicated ; but this we can state
to be untrue. All we know with certainty is that Mr.
Snow had undertaken, on the morning of Thursday
last, to drive one of the new coaches, the Quicksilver,
which leaves Brighton for London at five o'clock. The
horses became unmanageable soon after starting. When
they reached the sharp projecting corner in Marlborough
Place, beyond the King and Queen, a cart was standing near the lamp-post at that spot, and, in making a
sweep to avoid it, the coach was overturned : unfortunately the injury which such an accident must, under
any circumstances, have occasioned, was increased by
the passengers being thrown against the iron rails of
the North Steine, several of which were absolutely

---

[1] Presumably he drove the other side of the road to Bob Pointer,
mentioned above.

N

broken. From this spot the coach was dragged, after being upset, by the unmanageable horses a considerable distance before they could be stopped. The passengers were conveyed to the King and Queen, the Gloucester Hotel, &c., where surgical assistance was immediately obtained, and every assistance which care and skill could bestow was afforded. It has long been easy to foresee that, amongst so much competition and fast driving, some serious calamity would occur, and we have ourselves, by the expression of our apprehensions on this point, more than once sought to avert it; but the evil having arrived, we shall await the elucidation, which will no doubt be made, of the truth, and in the meantime only express our hope that the melancholy occurrence has put an end to the dangerous mania for 'fast driving' which some coach proprietors and drivers have recently been seeking to make fashionable. They may gratify by such means a few heedless persons; but must, at the same time, in so doing, cause dissatisfaction to others, while they incur a frightful risk of inflicting suffering on their passengers, to say nothing of the certain loss which must follow to themselves."

The strictures of the above writer on fast driving may have been deserved in a general way; but it must be remembered it was not every fast coach that came to grief at short intervals. The still living Mr. C. S. Ward, who has taught generations of amateur coachmen to drive, tells us in his book that, when only seventeen years old, he drove the Norwich and Ipswich mail between London and Colchester for nearly five years without an accident; and when he was promoted to the Quicksilver, a namesake of the ill-fated coach on the Brighton road, the like good fortune attended him, on the fastest coach at that time (about 1835 to 1842) out of London, for seven years. The Quicksilver, it need scarcely be said, was the Devonport coach ; while we may quote Mr. Ward once more as showing what fast driving there was on other roads.

A few years later this famous coachman was on the Exeter Telegraph, which subsequently became, owing to the railway opposition, a fast coach from Devonport to London, joining the railway at Bridgewater ; and later on, the coach went from Exeter to Plymouth only. " We did the fifty miles," says Mr. Ward, " several times in three hours and twenty-eight minutes (that is, at the average rate of a mile in four minutes nine seconds, including stoppages), and for months together we never exceeded four hours."

With reference to the Brighton Quicksilver accident, however, it is perhaps incorrect to say that intentional fast driving was in any sense the cause of the capsize. No coachman would start his horses at their best pace ; the horses broke away with Snow, who was going fast in spite of himself by the time the Steine was reached. At the close of the account of the Quicksilver accident there is a paragraph stating that the Blue Office Van, a vehicle which certainly did not run any risk by galloping, was capsized while going down a hill near St. John's Common, on which occasion the coachman and guard sustained but little injury, though the van was a great deal damaged.

At this time (1833) there was a sort of controversy on bearing-reins, a piece of harness the use of which has been disputed down to the present day. " Nimrod" was unquestionably at his best when writing upon hunting subjects, but he had a tolerably wide experience of the road ; and he boldly averred that the man was then unborn who could, without bearing-reins, drive the horses to be found in some coaches. " In the first place," he wrote, " there are many horses—sometimes whole teams—that will not face anything but

the cheek; and where is the arm that could bear the
weight of four horses leaning upon it for an hour or
more together, perhaps at full gallop?" "Nimrod,"
in short, was an advocate for the bearing-rein, a contrivance which, like many other things, is open to both
use and abuse; and the writer in one of the Sussex
papers would appear to have been of the same opinion,
for he wrote, "Persons acquainted with the art of driving
attribute the late stage-coach accidents to the novel
practice of discontinuing the use of bearing-reins. We
believe there are at this time upwards of fifty coaches
running between Brighton and London daily." Here,
however, I must for the present leave the knotty point
of bearing-reins, which the reader will find fully dis-
cussed in Nimrod's Essays, reprinted from the *Sporting
Magazine* in Captain Malet's " Annals of the Road."

The proprietors of the Quicksilver not unnaturally
came to the conclusion that the above-related accident
would render the coach unpopular with the public,
so they promptly repainted her brown, and, as the
Driving volume of the Badminton Library informs us,
she again took her place on the road re-named the
Criterion.

Everything appears to have gone well with the
Criterion, until one day in March in the following
year (1834), when the coachman, Bob Pointer aforesaid, appeared before the local bench of magistrates to
answer a charge of having contravened the Town Act.
The carriage belonging to a Mrs. Hoare was standing on
the Old Steine, when the Criterion, driven by Pointer,
collided with it, causing some damage. Harum-scarum
coachmen of all ages are very much alike, and Pointer
drove on without stopping to see what injury he had
caused, an unchivalrous line of conduct, which, however, stood him in good stead, for, as he could not be
identified, the summons was eventually dismissed.

Misfortunes, it is truly said, never come singly ; and three months later a terrible and fatal accident overtook the Criterion (late Quicksilver) coach, by which Sir William Cosway lost his life, and a Mr. Todhunter sustained a fracture of the thigh. The accounts in the papers are very lengthy, but the main features may be shortly summarised.

Driven by John Howchin, the Criterion left London with several passengers, and all went well till coming down the declivity on the Surrey side of London Bridge, where, a dray being in the way, and the driver making no effort to clear the road, the coachman of the Criterion had to pass the dray on the wrong, that is, on the near side. There being insufficient room, the dray struck the off fore-wheel of the Criterion, and the collision was of such violence as nearly to throw one of the outside passengers off his seat. This contretemps, in the opinion of the witnesses who gave evidence at the inquest held on Sir William Cosway, caused the pole to crack, though no one seems to have been aware of the fact at the time. Some little distance farther on, a horse ridden by a gentleman shied at a barrow which was covered with a white cloth, and ran in front of the leaders of the Criterion. Howchin, who seems to have been deservedly described as a skilful and careful coach-man, was equal to the occasion, and at very short notice stopped his horses at once, a feat which was supposed to have caused the complete fracture of the damaged pole at the futchells—"near the splinter bar," as one of the witnesses described it.

This sudden stoppage, though it seems to have vir-tually saved the gentleman on the shying horse, cost Sir William Cosway his life, as, soon after starting again, the broken portion of the pole dropped down, and struck the hind-legs of the wheel-horses, who thereupon became unmanageable. A porter in the

employ of Mr. Alexander, the nominal proprietor of the
Criterion, happened to be on the coach, and Howchin,
seeing what had happened, called to him to try and
skid the wheel.   This the man made every attempt to
do by climbing down the back of the coach and making
his way to the step; but he was not able to get the
wheel into the slipper.   The horses were, it is said,
further startled by a well-meaning pedestrian catching
hold of the reins.   A coach with a broken pole, however, is obviously a risky conveyance, and so thought
Sir William Cosway, who, on seeing the turn matters
had taken, attempted to clamber on his hands and
knees from the box-seat, which he was occupying, to
the roof, presumably with the intention of dropping off
the coach at the back; and a Mr. Stokes, a fellow-
passenger who gave evidence, prepared to follow this
example.   Before this intention could be carried into
effect by either passenger, the Criterion turned over.
The inside passengers, as was the case when the Quicksilver capsized, escaped injury; but, as already stated,
Mr. Todhunter broke his thigh, and Sir William Cosway fractured his skull.   The latter was picked up and
carried into the house of Mr. Lever, a surgeon of Bridge
House Place; and, in Mr. Lever's absence, a Mr. Stringer
attended, and remained with Sir William till he expired,
an hour and a half later.

After hearing a good deal of expert evidence, the
jury found that the coach was overturned in consequence
of the pole having been broken, and gave it as their
opinion that no blame attached to the coachman, who,
they thought, acted with the greatest propriety in the
difficult circumstances in which he was placed.

Mention has already been made of the opposition
which at intervals set in on the Brighton road, and
one of the incidents was that the coach-masters were
willing to make bargains for fares.   This practice occa-

sionally led to disputes, and shortly after Sir William
Cosway's lamentable death a Mr. Chamier brought an
action against Thomas Wilkins, the coachman of the
Echo, one of the recognised fast coaches, for "demanding
a larger sum of money for fare and luggage than he had
a right to do." According to Mr. Chamier's account,
he was induced to travel by the Echo by reason of
an advertisement ; and he stated that the bookkeeper at Hatchett's Hotel engaged that he should
travel down to Brighton as an inside passenger for the
sum of fourteen shillings. On the coach arriving at
Castle Square, Brighton, Wilkins, the coachman, demanded seven shillings more, saying that the inside
fare was a guinea. In vain did Mr. Chamier protest
that he made his bargain in London, as the coachman
and the Brighton bookkeeper said that they had nothing to do with him ; and on the part of the coachman
it was urged that he had no power to carry passengers
at lower fares, he being responsible to his proprietors
for the amount on the way-bill, and on this particular
way-bill Mr. Chamier was put down as a twenty-one
shillings passenger. The seven shillings were paid,
and the coachman was summoned.

The defence was that Mr. Chamier contracted with
an unauthorised person, and that he was mistaken
about the advertisement, the appearance of which, he
alleged, induced him to book himself. The advertisement stated that passengers would be carried inside
from Brighton to London for fourteen shillings, but
nothing was said about the same rate being charged
on the down-journey ; though it was admitted that, after
the coach had left the West End, it was not unusual to
make special terms with people, especially poor people,
who, anxious to get to Brighton, picked up the coach
on the Surrey side of the water. Eventually the magistrates, considering the case proved, fined Wilkins

twenty-five shillings and costs, whereupon Mr. Chamier, who had previously stated that he brought the case into court "to see if such knavery is to flourish," professed himself satisfied, and withdrew another charge against Wilkins for an overcharge on the luggage, for the carriage of which he was charged twenty-five shillings, after the bookkeeper had engaged that it should go free.

Coach proprietors, it would seem, were, in some respects, slow in learning lessons which considerations of safety would suggest. Many mishaps occurred, some of which have been recounted here, through having insufficient attendance for the horses on the arrival of the different coaches; and in the July of 1834 there was another instance of the folly of leaving horses unattended, as, after the arrival of the Union coach from London, the leaders, anxious no doubt to get to their stables, suddenly turned round, knocked down a man who was standing near, and trampled upon him. The victim chanced to be a post-boy from Sutton, and so not unaccustomed to the ways of horses. On finding himself, therefore, in the above dangerous predicament, he had the presence of mind to roll away from the wheels of the Union, which would otherwise have passed over him. As it was, he sustained injuries to his head, but was not otherwise seriously hurt.

CHAPTER XI.

FROM 1835 TO 1839.

IN the previous chapter I have mentioned the famous Age, started by the late Mr. Stevenson after he gave up the Coronet. "Well-born coachmen prevail on this road," wrote "Nimrod" in his *Quarterly Review* article. "A gentleman connected with the first families in Wales, and whose father long represented his native county in Parliament, horsed and drove one side of the ground with Mr. Stevenson." This gentleman was Mr. Sackville Frederick Gwynne, who, as will hereafter be seen, experienced his full share of ups and downs on life's road.

We are left rather in the dark as to the arrangements for carrying on the Age after Mr. Stevenson's death, though practically there can be no doubt that Mr. Gwynne, Mr. Capps, of the Brighton booking-office, and the people who horsed it at various stages, kept the coach going, with Mr. Capps as the man of money. On Christmas Day, 1834, however, the following announcement was published in the *Brighton Gazette* :—

AGE COACH.

The Public are respectfully informed that, in consequence of one of the late Proprietors of the Age having suddenly withdrawn his stock from the concern, the Coach has commenced running from Goodman's Office, No. 10 Castle Square, instead of what is called the Age Office. No alteration will take place at the London end, the Coach continuing to book at the same Offices it has hitherto done, and will leave the Bull and Mouth, Regent Circus, as usual, at twelve o'clock precisely.

JOHN JAMES WILLAN & Co.,
Proprietors.

201

Mr. J. J. Willan was a Hampshire man, who formerly lived at Preston Candover, and was a prominent member of the old Hambledon Cricket Club. He subsequently either let or sold his residence to Mr. John Truman Villebois, who was one of the ruling body of the Hampshire Hounds from 1802 to 1804, and sole master from that date to the time of his death in 1837.

An oft-told story is that Mr. Willan succeeded to the Age on the death of Mr. Stevenson, and the above advertisement would appear to be some confirmation of the commonly accepted version. But there were two Kings of Brentford, as on the same day (Christmas Day, 1834) the following advertisement appeared :—

AGE OFFICE, No. 5 CASTLE SQUARE, BRIGHTON.

NOTICE.—The Public is most respectfully informed that the Age Coach will continue running from the above Office as usual, daily at twelve o'clock, the late Proprietor, Sackville Frederick Gwynne, Esq., having assigned the same to Thomas Ward Capps; and having conducted the whole of the Age business ever since its commencement under the late Henry Stevenson, Esq., he throws himself on a generous Public for that patronage and support with which the Age Coach has for the last nine years been favoured.

N.B.—There being another Age now running, J. W. Capps begs to caution the Public that it has no connection with the Age from the Age Office, 5 Castle Square.

It will be observed that in the above advertisement Mr. Capps refers to the patronage extended to the Age " for the last nine years." This would mean that the Age was running in 1826 ; yet the name of this coach is missing from Cary's list of that year (see *ante*, p. 147). The Coronet, Mr. Stevenson's first coach, was then in existence, however, and possibly Mr. Capps may have regarded the Coronet, and its successor the Age, as one concern, just as the Quicksilver and the Criterion were practically one and the same coach,—a more likely explanation. However, the two above-quoted advertisements by no means settled the question, as on New Year's Day, 1835, Mr. Capps sought, in the columns of the local papers, to uphold his claim to the possession of the original Age; and he published these particulars :—

A CAUTION.

A Coach having commenced running from Mr. Goodman's Office, named the Age, in opposition to the one from the Age Office, and an advertisement having appeared leading the public to suppose that the Age Coach had been removed from the Age Office to that of Mr. Goodman, the present proprietor feels called upon to publish the following letter, which he has received from the late proprietor, Sackville Frederick Gwynne, Esq.

LONDON, *December* 23, 1834.

DEAR SIR,—I have been informed that an advertisement has appeared in the Brighton papers stating that the Age Coach had been removed from the Age Office to Mr. Goodman's, which may be detrimental to your Coach. I beg to say I have in no way assigned my interest to Messrs. Goodman & Willan, or anybody else, excepting yourself, and I consider the Coach going from Mr. Goodman's Office decidedly in opposition. You may make any use of this you think proper, and hoping that you may meet with the same liberal support that I did,—I remain, yours very truly,

S. F. GWYNNE.

To Mr. Capps, Age Office, Brighton.

Then follows a repetition of the advertisement of the 25th December 1834, put forth by Mr. Capps, who subjoins this notice :—

In consequence of an intrigue with the opposition Coach, the Proprietors are compelled (for the present) to alter their London Offices. The Age Coach now leaves as follows : The Gloucester Warehouse, corner of Park Street ; the Feathers Office, 336 Oxford Street ; and Mosse's Green Man and Still, Oxford Street, at half-past eleven o'clock ; the Spread Eagle Office, Regent's Circus ; British Coffee-House, Cockspur Street ; Hungerford Office, 16 Strand, and 71 Gracechurch Street, at 12 o'clock precisely.

T. W. CAPPS & CO., *Proprietors.*

The opposition, "J. J. Willan & Co.," lost no time in replying to Mr. Capps's statement, and, repeating the notice of the previous Christmas Day, added this explanation :—

Having inserted the first notice above, stating that I had removed the Age Coach, which I have been horsing and managing from London to Horley (28 miles) since the 3rd of last August, from Mr. Capps's office to Mr. Goodman's, my attention has been called to a contradiction from Mr. Capps, who states he has conducted the whole of the Age business since its commencement, and further adds a letter from Mr. Gwynne, stating that he has made over his interest in the Age entirely to Mr. Capps. Now, with respect to Mr. Capps having had the sole management of the Age since its commencement, the statement is a direct falsehood, he having been solely employed as a bookkeeper by the proprietors, and paid five guineas a month for his services. He has, however, I admit, had the direction and management of the Brighton end during the last three months, owing to Mr. Gwynne's stock having been seized by the Sheriff under an execution issued by Mr. David Lloyd Harries, solicitor, Llandovery, Carmarthenshire, and under which they were sold by Mr. Alexander on Tuesday, the 6th inst. (January).

Mr. Harries residing at a distance, assigned over the stock he had taken to Mr. Capps, who conducted for him his business from Brighton to Horley. On Saturday, December 13, I received the following letter from Mr. Capps, giving me notice Mr. Harries intended taking his stock off the Age that day week, and whether a week's notice is a handsome and sufficient one, I will leave all coachmasters and the public to decide.

AGE OFFICE, BRIGHTON, December 19, 1834.

SIR,—Mr. Harries has come to the determination to take his stock off the Age this day week (Saturday). An arrangement will be made to continue working the same without any delay, but when it is definitely settled I will write to you again immediately. Probably you can give me some information on the subject.—I am, sir, your obedient servant,

T. W. CAPPS.

J. J. Willan, Esq.

This shows how much interest Mr. Gwynne possessed in the coach, he not having had a horse at work on it during a period of three months. Upon the strength of this notice, not wishing to be left in the lurch, or obliged to draw the coach the whole way myself,

I applied to Mr. Goodman and his partners to take the ground from Horley to Brighton, which they immediately acceded to, viz., on Sunday the 14th. On Monday the 15th, Mr. Capps wrote to me (and both his letters are lying for any person's inspection at No. 10 Castle Square), to say that he himself intended horsing the coach to Horley (and Mr. Alexander *intended lending him horses* for the present to take it to Hand Cross). I sent him an answer stating that as I was drawing the coach twenty-eight miles, I considered I had a perfect right to choose my own partners; that I had already got the ground covered, and that I declined working with him. I stated at the same time that neither myself nor Mr. Goodman had any wish to remove the coach from his office, but would pay him as usual five guineas a month for booking, and would continue to do so, and that nothing but misconduct on his part would ever cause its removal. My letter he has, and may publish it if it will contradict what I assert. This he declined, and has joined Mr. Alexander, and they have altered the colour and name of the Surprise coach, which formerly started at ten and various other hours, to our time at twelve o'clock, and they now call it the Age.

Under these circumstances I had no alternative but to remove my coach to the Red Office, 10 Castle Square, and I will now leave the subject for ever, allowing the public to decide to whom the charge of putting on an opposition coach applies.

The best proof that this is the original Age is, that it books at the original offices in London, being the Globe, Baker Street and New Road; the Bull and Mouth, corner of Portman and Oxford Streets, and starts from the same office in London as before.

J. J. WILLAN.

Then came a counterblast from Mr. Capps, who repeated his earlier Age advertisement, and then devoted himself to the task of pulverising his rival, in these words :—

In consequence of the unfounded assertion inserted in the *Brighton Herald* of the 17th inst., and signed "J. J. Willan," I, Thomas Ward Capps, the present proprietor of the Age coach, feel myself called upon to state the simple facts.

Mr. John James Willan states that he horsed twenty-eight miles of the Age coach up to the 27th December last, viz : from London to Horley; and in consequence of a notice which he, Mr. Willan, received from me respecting the horses on the lower ground, from Horley to Brighton, that he was compelled to apply to Mr. Goodman and his partners to take the coach, and which they immediately

acceded to, not wishing (as he, Mr. Willan, says) to be left in the
lurch, or be obliged to draw the coach the whole way himself. Now
in reply to this I say, without fear of contradiction, that up to
Saturday, the 27th December last (as Mr. Willan and Mr. Goodman
and his partners started another Age coach in opposition to mine
on Monday, the 29th of December), Mr. Willan had not so much
as a single horse on it; but the twenty-eight miles Mr. John James
Willan represents himself as proprietor of, belonged to Major
Haddon, who, on Friday, the 26th, offered the horses for sale to
a coach proprietor (which I am prepared to prove), but on or about
the 27th Mr. Willan and his partners made an arrangement with
Major Haddon for his stock, in order that they might leave me, as
they supposed, unprepared to continue the coach.

Mr. Willan was in no way a proprietor on the 27th of December;
he was a mere servant acting in the capacity of coachman, for which
he received twelve shillings per week, the same being regularly paid
by me in the ordinary way as I pay the other coachmen from my
office.

As to my letter to Mr. Willan, of which he speaks, it was addressed to him as well from courtesy as from necessity, I not
knowing Major Haddon's address at the time, and being desirous
that Mr. Willan should communicate to Major Haddon the change
then about to take place. I regret being compelled to expose Mr.
Willan's real situation at the time a coalition took place between
him and Messrs. Goodman & Co. against mine, the "Age" coach,
on the 29th December, and but for the mean and cowardly attack
made upon his master, the late proprietor, by Mr. Willan, who
forgets that he himself was a short time ago the inmate of a prison,
I should not have considered his weak and unfounded assertion
worthy of notice.

To the above hard-hitting manifesto the worthy Capps
appended his name, and gave his opponents to understand that he had another shot in his locker by adding,
with perhaps more regard for the requirements of the
Latin tongue than he always displayed when dealing
with the King's English, *Plus, si necesse sit.* This
document he followed up by inserting in a local paper
for the 12th February 1835 :—

AGE OFFICE, 5 CASTLE SQUARE, BRIGHTON.

CAUTION.—Having seen an advertisement in the *Brighton Guardian* purporting to give a statement of facts concerning the Age

Coach, and having answered that statement fully and satisfactorily (*vide* the *Brighton Gazette*, Jan. 29, 1835), showing the false position of Messrs. Willan & Co., satisfying the public that the Age Coach still continues running as usual from the Age Office, 5 Castle Square, Mr. Goodman having promised me his garbled statement should not appear again, I find in the *Guardian* of yesterday (*i.e.*, Feb. 11, 1835) he still continues to deceive the public, and Thomas Ward Capps, the proprietor of the original Age Coach (having succeeded S. F. Gwynne, Esq.), begs to caution the public against a conveyance bearing the same name, running from the Red Coach Office. Thos. Ward Capps writes to acquaint the public he has no connexion whatever with that Office, it being decidedly an opposition coach.

BRIGHTON, *Feb.* 12, 1835.

As the Age is possibly the most notable of the old coaches on the Brighton road, it has been thought worth while to reproduce all these notices in connection with it, especially as, so far as I know, they are not to be found elsewhere than in the columns of the newspapers from which they have been extracted, and as the dispute between the rival proprietors is not generally known, the common idea being that Mr. Willan succeeded without let or hindrance to the Age, and disposed of it as easily as he became possessed of it. Owing to the difficulty of ascertaining exactly what took place after Mr. Stevenson's death, one cannot quite clearly see what led up to the dispute between Mr. Willan and Capps. There, however, seems to be no doubt that the original vehicle was that driven by Mr. Willan; and, as we shall presently see, the latter gentleman seems to have desired a way out of all difficulties. He, of course, had Goodman behind him, or the Age would then and there have become a past Age; while, had it not been for Capps's money, it would unquestionably have stopped before, as after the withdrawal of Mr. Stevenson's stock it must have been a work of some difficulty to keep the coach on the road.

The close of the year 1835 brings the name of

Shillibeer into the history of the Brighton road. We
of the present day associate the name with "black
work;" but before he turned his attention to the construction of a combined hearse and mourning-coach,
Mr. Shillibeer was connected with vehicles used for
more joyous occasions than going to funerals.

In the autumn of 1835, for instance, he advertised
his "distinguished conveyance to London by Reigate
and Cuckfield in six hours." Taking quite a pardonable pride in his invention, Mr. Shillibeer described his
diligence as "combining the comfort of a nobleman's
chariot with the usual convenience of a stage carriage,"
and expressing a hope that he might enjoy a large
portion of public patronage, assured those who might
travel by his conveyance that it was novel, excellent,
and had "an extraordinary interior." It left the Royal
Clarence Hotel, Brighton, at half-past ten every day,
and ran to 11 Charing Cross, London. Mr. Shillibeer,
however, soon found himself involved in a "horse
cause," the facts of which give us some insight into
the value of a coach-horse at this time. Shillibeer
bought of one Cussell, who seems to have been connected with the Tally-Ho, a brown gelding at the price
of £10. This inexpensive slave had, according to the
evidence of Cussell, been working eleven miles *per diem*
between Ditchling and Lindfield: he was admittedly
a roarer, but an "excellent goer," nevertheless, and,
had he been sound, £50 would not have bought him.
Three weeks after Shillibeer purchased him the horse
died, and a post-mortem revealed the fact that he
was, internally, "a mass of corruption," arising from a
disease of long standing. Shillibeer declined to pay
for him; but, as there was no warranty, the case went
against him.

In July 1836 we find that the original diligence
belonged to Boulton, Carpenter, & Co.; ran to London

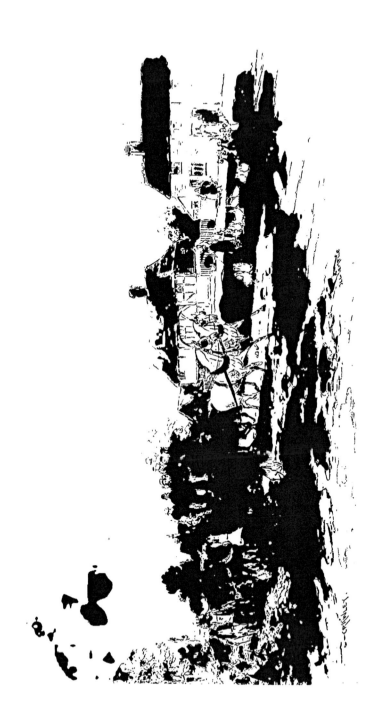

in five hours and a quarter. Passengers in the coach
paid sixteen shillings; those in the omnibus, twelve
shillings; while eight shillings was the outside fare.

During the year 1835 the following coaches were
running between London and Brighton :—

Depart from	Hour.	Coach.
Snow's Office, 18 Castle Sq.	6 a.m.	Dart.
,, ,,	10 a.m.	Comet.
,, ,,	11 a.m.	Magnet.
,, ,,	3 p.m.	Sovereign.
Red Office, Castle Square.	7 a.m.	Times.
,, ,,	9 a.m.	Royal Clarence.
,, ,,	10 a.m.	Regent.
,, ,,	12.0 noon.	Age (Willan's).
,, ,,	5 p.m.	Times.
Blue Office, Castle Square.	8 a.m.	Item.
,, ,,	9 a.m.	Royal William.
,, ,,	10 a.m.	True Blue.
,, ,,	11 a.m.	Royal George.
,, ,,	10.30 p.m.	Royal Mail.
Hine's Office, East Street.	9 a.m.	Alert.
,, ,,	11 a.m.	Union.
5 Castle Square.	10 a.m.	Emerald.
,,	12.0 noon.	Age (Capps's).
3 Castle Square.	10 a.m.	Telegraph.
,,	12.0 noon.	New Dart.
Clarence Hotel.	10.30 a.m.	The Diligence.

Of the above coaches the Item's London terminus
was the Boar and Castle, Oxford Street, whence it
left for Brighton at three o'clock, calling at Griffen's
Green Man and Still; Hatchett's White Horse Cellar;
Bull and Mouth, Regent Circus; British Office, Cockspur Street; Silver Cross, Charing Cross; Nos. 11 and
74 Charing Cross; the Half-Moon, Gracechurch Street;
and reached the Elephant and Castle at four o'clock;
but some of these offices were no doubt served by
branch coaches. This coach made the double journey
daily. Early in 1836 the times were so far changed
that the Item left Brighton at six o'clock on the

mornings of Monday and Tuesday, and at eight o'clock on other days, travelling both up and down *viâ* Cuckfield, Worth, Reigate, Sutton, and Clapham.

How long the two Ages continued in opposition I am unable to say; but in the spring of 1836 Mr. Willan appears to have sold his Age to Sir St. Vincent Cotton, of Madingley Park, about three miles and a half distant from Cambridge, Mr. Willan joining Mr. William Cripps, and one or two others, in the proprietorship of the Magnet, which had previously been taken off the road for a short time. The new owners assured their patrons that no expense would be spared in making the Magnet equal to any conveyance in the kingdom; and, as they had no intention of professing more than they could perform, they undertook to do the journey in six hours, leaving 18 Castle Square, Brighton, at eleven o'clock in the forenoon, and arriving at the Three Kings, Piccadilly, punctually at five o'clock in the afternoon. Immunity from accident, however, was more than the proprietary could guarantee, and, as they knew that mishaps would overtake the best coaches, they were wisely silent on this point in their advertisement. At any rate, the Magnet had not long been in the hands of Messrs. Cripps, Willan, & Co., ere the axle broke one Sunday afternoon when the coach was a short way from Brighton. Francis Vickers was driving; he was thrown off with great violence, and was much hurt, while an outside passenger who jumped off sustained somewhat severe injuries, but another who let himself down behind was unharmed; and two inside passengers were frightened only and not hurt; in fact, as I have before said, the inside of a coach appears to have always been the safer.

Messrs. Chaplin & Crunden appear for some time to have been more or less associated with Goodman, the proprietor of the Red Coach-Office, Castle Square, and of some of the coaches running therefrom. Subsequently they seem to have had business relations with Snow, of the Spread Eagle Office, and in the summer of 1836 they "most respectfully announced their acquisition of the whole of the Brighton establishment with which they were lately connected, and which they have in consequence entirely remodelled." This, from a man like Mr. Chaplin, who had upwards of seventeen hundred horses working on different roads, meant a good deal. The Spread Eagle Office was at 18 Castle Square.

To begin with, they put on the Vivid, a new and fast coach, leaving Brighton at six o'clock; the Comet (with barouche seats for families) ran in the same interest, and so did the Sovereign, this coach now travelling at an accelerated pace; while visitors and the public generally were assured that 18 Castle Square would be found a perfect bureau of information, where all would be treated with Chesterfield-like politeness, and would receive ready redress on any subject about which it might be considered necessary to complain. The Magnet afore-mentioned, and the Times likewise, started from the Spread Eagle Office, though Goodman had a proprietary interest in the latter, in conjunction with Horne, who, later on, joined Chaplin in founding the huge carrying firm, the name of which lives to this day.

Accidents, we know, occur quite as often through the *lâches* of others as through the fault of a coachman himself, and here are instances of each. A horse-keeper was leading some of the Age horses near Patcham, when two drunken fellows came along driving a horse and cart at a furious pace. The horse-keeper did his best to dodge the approaching vehicle; but, not being able to succeed, one of the coach-horses was killed on

the spot by the shaft of the cart being driven deep
into its chest.

The second case was that of Matthew Cussell, coachman of the Tally-Ho, and presumably some relation of
Edward Cussell, landlord of the Globe Inn, Brighton,
who appeared to an information charging him with
having been intoxicated while acting as the driver of a
stage-coach. This was a rather curious case, as the
man drove well enough from London to Croydon :
none of the passengers were called to say that he had
anything to drink at Croydon ; yet soon after leaving
that place the coach was twice driven off the road ; and
at Crawley Cussell was so drunk that he fell down as
soon as he attempted to descend from the box. A
stage-coachman under the influence of liquor is necessarily capable of causing a great amount of trouble, so,
in spite of appeals for leniency put forth by some of
the passengers who had given evidence, the magistrates
very properly imposed a fine of £3.

A perusal of the list of coaches leaving Brighton
will have shown that several of the conveyances started
for London at the same hour, the Magnet and the
Union being timed to depart at eleven o'clock. They
were thus in sight of one another for some time, and
one day, in the autumn of 1836, a curious coincidence
happened, which, had they been racing, would have
done a good turn to the Union, which chanced to be in
front. Close to Preston a large tree which the Union
had just passed was blown down in front of the
Magnet, thereby barring its further progress ; so there
was nothing left for the Magnet's coachman to do but
to turn round and drive up the Ditchling Road and
over the hills to Preston.

This brings me to the great snowstorm of 1836—a
storm almost without parallel in the annals of stage-
coaching. Though severe almost everywhere, it was

perhaps worse south of London than anywhere else.
It began a day or two before Christmas Day, the Times,
which left for London on Sunday, the 25th December,
being the first to feel the full violence of the storm.
She got through, however, as the coachman of the
outward mail passed her at Brixton; but the down-
coach had great difficulty in reaching Brighton. At
eleven o'clock at night all hopes of seeing her were
abandoned; but she arrived about half an hour later,
Dear, the coachman, having given the reins to some one
else, and mounted himself upon one of the leaders at
Pangdean; and even then a good many perils had to
be encountered before Brighton was reached. About
four miles from Brighton, Dear and his leaders tumbled
neck and heels over a snow-ridge, and the sudden
strain on the pole hook caused the pole to crack; but
as there was then no danger of the coach overrunning
the horses, or any temptation to travel quickly, the
remainder of the journey was accomplished at a slow
pace, with the pole in its damaged state.

The *Brighton Gazette* for the 29th of December gives
the following account of the storm :—

On Friday afternoon (*i.e.*, 23rd December) the wind changed
from S.S.W. to N.N.E., and on Saturday morning the ground was
covered with snow. The frost, however, was not very keen. During Saturday snow fell at intervals, but till Sunday afternoon the
fall was inconsiderable, when, as it grew dusk, the wind increased to
a gale, accompanied by sleet and snow. From six o'clock till ten
the snow had drifted so much that in some places it covered the
ground to the depth of a foot. About ten o'clock there was a slight
abatement, but shortly afterwards it was renewed with increased
force. The sentinels at the Palace were covered with snow in their
boxes, and large heaps of snow drifted on the pavement, until at
midnight it was breast high. At eleven o'clock the few flymen who
had ventured out were under the necessity of putting two horses to
their flys, and even then could only proceed at a walking pace.
One horse fell down exhausted opposite St. Peter's Church and died.
. . . Towards midnight the wind and snow increased, and, we
believe, did not abate till break of day, when such a scene presented

itself as was perhaps never witnessed in Brighton before within the
memory of man. Some of the streets were completely blocked up by
snow, and totally impassable; in others, where the snow drifted,
high ridges were formed at the side of the road from one end of the
street to the other, which were in most places four or five feet deep.
Hundreds of persons had to dig their way out of doors; large masses
of snow covered the tops of the houses; and, where the drift was
greatest, the windows were completely covered, presenting a most
singular appearance. In Gloucester Lane the snow was eight or
ten feet deep, and the streets at the back of Edward Street were
nearly filled. Near Mr. Colbatch's house, on Rose Hill, it was
about fifteen feet deep. Tracks were soon made on the pavements,
and it was a curious sight in some places to see persons walking
between the houses and these ridges, their heads just peeping above
the snow. Scarcely a shop was opened on Monday, and but few on
Tuesday; in short, business was to a great extent suspended ever
since.

It will readily be imagined that in such conditions
of weather the coach traffic of the south, and especially
around Brighton, was completely paralysed for a time,
yet the coachmen and guards made the most strenuous,
and in some instances absolutely heroic, attempts to
re-establish communication.

The Brighton mail leaving London on the Sunday,
the third day of the storm, had a somewhat varied
experience. It carried one solitary but plucky passenger, and when it stuck fast in the snow at four
o'clock on Monday morning at Clayton Hill, he and
the coachman made themselves as comfortable as
circumstances permitted inside the coach, while the
guard essayed to make the best of his way to Brighton
with the mail-bags on one of the horses. When day
broke, the coachman and the passenger contrived to
turn the coach, and get her back to Friars Oak; but
the miserable guard had a very sorry time of it. He
managed somehow to get upon the Downs, and several
times he, his horse, and the mail-bags were rolling
together in the snow. It was one o'clock on Monday
afternoon when he reached Brighton, in a state of

OFF THE ROAD, EARLSWOOD COMMON

exhaustion; and then he was taken to Ward's Baths, and afterwards put to bed. We must all sympathise with these officials in their hardships in travelling in bad weather; but, in connection with this snowstorm, we hear nothing about the horses and their sufferings. The coachman of the mail, by the way, reached Brighton at four o'clock on the afternoon of Tuesday.

Amongst other sufferers from the inclement weather was one of the King's cooks, named Querini, who travelled from London on the Sunday by the Times coach. At Bolney he dropped his stick, and somewhat imprudently got down from the coach to pick it up. The coachman left him behind, so the artist had to proceed on foot to the inn at Albourne, where he refreshed himself, and then left to make his way into Brighton. Soon after Mr. Querini had departed, the landlord began to entertain fears that he would lose his way, and perhaps perish from exposure, so he hurried on after his late guest, and it was perhaps fortunate that he did so, for he eventually came up with the cook, who was then seated on the snow, looking probably a very wretched edition of a *chaud-froid*. There was not much difficulty in persuading him to return to Albourne, where he tarried for the night; but at seven o'clock the next morning he resumed his journey, accompanied by a guide, and after five hours' hard work reached Mr. Hudson's house at Brighton, covered with snow from head to foot, both the cook and his guide being in a very exhausted state.

One cannot help admiring the zeal with which the Post-Office officials attempted to secure the transit of the mail-bags, be the weather what it might. On the Monday of the storm, *i.e.* Boxing Day, the bags were sent off from Brighton at one o'clock in the morning by men on horseback, and this mounted band took five hours in reaching Pyecombe, where they remained

all night. On Tuesday morning, at the same hour, one
o'clock, the London bags were intrusted to six men on
foot, and a track having been cut through the snow,
they found walking less difficult than riding. The
down-mail, which left London on the Monday night,
was snowed up; and the bags were taken on by men
on horseback, who reached the Brighton Post-Office
late on Tuesday afternoon; while the London papers,
which generally found their way into Brighton about
two on Monday afternoon, were not delivered till six
on the following evening.

The weather seems to have been at last too much
even for the Worthing mail-cart, for on the Tuesday
the letters for that place were sent by two men on
horseback, who rode nearly all the way along the
beach.

Meantime Goodman, the coach proprietor, waited
patiently at his farm at Albourne till the Tuesday,
when, after a difficult journey, he reached Brighton on
horseback, and immediately set about making arrangements for having the roads cleared.

The Sovereign coach was dug out of the snow twice
on the Monday, and with the greatest difficulty got as
far as Pangdean, where the passengers alighted, and
walked on into Brighton. On the Wednesday (28th
December) the London mail-bags were brought in by
men on horseback; six horses and a number of men
were sent off from the Blue Coach-Office to Clayton
Hill to try and get the mail out of the snow; while
the early and late Times and the Regent started for
London each with six horses. Some coaches were
snowed up at Cuckfield; while at Crawley, Henfield,
and other places were coaches which, through the
violence of the storm, could not complete their journey
either up or down. Altogether eight coaches left
Brighton for London on the Wednesday, most of them

with six horses; while no fewer than eighteen cart-
horses were required to drag the Gloucester mail out
of her difficulties; so for one reason and another the
Christmas of 1836 could not have been a very merry
one. For the first time for very many years the
Brighton mail was stopped for a full night within a
few miles of London, and all intercourse between town
and the southern shires was cut off for two days.

The year 1837 could scarcely have failed to bring
with it some sort of misgivings as to what kind of
opposition steam power would, in the near future, offer
to stage-coaches. It may have been that coach proprietors were mindful of this; but the fact remains
that scarcely had the snowstorm passed away ere
coaches were running at reduced fares. The New
Dart (Nelson & Wiggins proprietors) carried inside
passengers at eighteen shillings, and charged no more
than nine shillings as outside fare, and a week or two
later the figures were reduced to sixteen shillings and
six shillings, while previously existing arrangements as
regards the mails were so far altered that the mail now
left Brighton at eleven at night instead of half-past
ten.

Some of the older school of coaching men have made
great fun of the patent brake, oblivious, possibly, of
the fact that wood and asphalt offer less resistance to
wheels than did macadam and stone pitching. The
latter was, no doubt, desperately greasy at times, but
its unevenness gave some sort of foothold for the horses,
and saved the road from becoming the slide it often is
now that it is paved with wood.

At any rate, the merits of some sort of brake were
recognised so long ago as 1837—indeed, a "coach
retarder" had been invented twelve years before—
when the new mails had a piece of machinery attached
to the hinder part of the coach "for the purpose of

locking down the hills without the guard getting
down, or, in case of the horses running away down a
hill, of stopping the mail instantly. The contrivance
is very simple, and is done by the pressure of two
pieces of wood against the wheels; the connecting-rod,
going to the top of the coach, is turned by a screw,
and the effect on the wheels is immediate. This
'machinery' had always been used by the diligences
in France, and some astonishment was expressed that
it had never before been introduced into England."
Brakes of some sort, however, were known long before
this, and were, I think, first applied to some of the
trollies in the Northumberland pits.

Towards the close of the year 1837, Mr. Thomas
Crosweller, the proprietor, or one of the proprietors,
of the Blue Coach-Office, died at his residence, 71
Grand Parade, greatly lamented by the coaching fraternity at Brighton and elsewhere. When stage-coaching
was in its infancy, that is to say, at the dawning of the
present century, Mr. Crosweller was driving a coach
between Brighton and London, his whilom partner,
Mr. Hine, being in charge of another. Mr. Crosweller,
however, appears to have been an excellent man of
business, and when he gave up driving, about the
year 1818, he turned his attention to the booking-office,
and soon afterwards opened a livery and posting yard
at the Bedford Mews, King's Road; and, as his connection increased, he subsequently took the Albion
Mews, St. James's Street, and on his death both these
establishments were disposed of.

During this time Mr. Crosweller was largely engaged
in the coaching business. As already mentioned, he
was part proprietor of several of the coaches starting
from the Blue Office in Castle Square, and he horsed
most of them over some of their ground. The Blue
coaches were not surpassed by any running on the

London and Brighton road ; they were well built, well
horsed, and the firm employed as good coachmen as
they could get. The Blue coaches did not, however,
rank as the fastest. For some time a Mr. Blaber had
been Mr. Crosweller's partner, and, on the death of
the latter, Mr. Blaber announced, through the medium
of the Sussex papers, that he would carry on the business himself. He hoped for "a continuation of that
patronage," &c., and his prayer appears to have been
granted, as in March 1838, and therefore prior to the
summer arrangements coming into force, we find the
following coaches starting from the Blue Office for
London :[1]—

The Era, which, leaving Brighton at noon, ran
through Hickstead, Crawley, Reigate, and Sutton to
the Belle Sauvage and half a dozen other offices. The
Era left London at a quarter past eleven. This was
a new coach, of which the proprietors were Edmund
Strevens and John Wiggins of Brighton, Samuel Relf
of Reigate, and John Nelson of London.

The Item, at six o'clock on Monday and Tuesday,
and eight o'clock on the remaining four days. She did
not run on Sunday. The Item accomplished the
double journey in the day, leaving Oxford Street at
two in the afternoon, and ran through Cuckfield,
Worth, Horley, and Croydon.

The Optimus, a new four-o'clock coach, *vià* Hickstead, Crawley, Reigate, Sutton, and Clapham, reaching London in five hours.

The night-mail at 11 P.M., leaving the Blossoms
Inn, Cheapside, at 8 P.M.

The Royal Blue "safety barouche," at ten in the
morning, through Cuckfield and Croydon.

---

[1] In July 1838 the Blue Coach-Office was in course of rebuilding,
so the business was removed to the Blue Van Office in East Street,
whence the coaches for London and the provinces started.

In addition to the above, there were the Hero, to Oxford and Reading; the day-mail and Times, to Southampton; the Sovereign, to Windsor; the Royal Blue, to Tunbridge Wells, Maidstone, and Chatham; the Defiance, to Tunbridge Wells; the Hero and Rival, to Hastings; and the Optimus, to Worthing. These provincial coaches, however, are dealt with in subsequent chapters. Of all the above coaches, Messrs. Strevens, Wiggins, Relf, Nelson, and others forming this great confederacy, were the proprietors.

Vans, as usual, left London and Brighton every night for the transport of heavy luggage, the majority of the light parcels being carried by the coaches, which derived a great portion of their takings from this source; in fact, the passenger-fares alone would never have paid the proprietors.

On the arrival of the coaches at either end, preparations were made for delivering such parcels as had not been dropped along the route, this duty falling almost entirely to the porters, who were allowed a small commission for their trouble; but some of them sought to add to their income by dishonest means. The making up of dummy parcels was an industry so well known that many people were accustomed to give their servants directions not to pay the charges marked thereon until the contents of the parcels had been examined.

On the 1st February 1838, one John Chatfield, a porter from Hine's Coach-Office, called at 25 Oriental Place, Brighton, the residence of a Mr. M'Mullen, handed a parcel to the servant, and demanded eighteenpence for the carriage thereof. The consignee of this parcel was one of those who had presumably been taken in before, and prior to paying the charge the servant took the precaution of opening the package, which, though marked "to be kept dry," contained nothing but "a dirty knife-cloth and some pieces of cheese rind." The porter was therefore given into custody, and duly charged before the magistrates ; but the books and waybills having conclusively proved that the parcel was handed in at a West End Office in London, the case against Chatfield was dismissed.

In previous pages mention has been made of the various attempts to construct a safety-coach, and the idea of inventing a vehicle warranted to keep right side uppermost appears never to have been abandoned. In the *Brighton Gazette* of the 11th January 1838 we come across a notice of another new invention, though at the same time it is not very clear, at least to the mind of any one not a coachbuilder, in what the provisions for safety consisted. The inventor, rightly enough, stated that "the great desideratum is the safety of the coach from being overturned, however great the inequality of the road may be, or in the event of the wheels on one side being lifted from the road upon the pathway." In this particular vehicle, called the "Stafford" safety-coach, the body was said to be suspended on springs placed nearly at the top of the coach, and supported upon strong pieces of timber, forming almost an angle, which were, at the lower extremities, inserted in the axletrees of the front and hind wheels, by which means the body was under all circumstances kept in an upright position, and the centre of gravity thrown considerably lower than was the case in the coaches built upon the old plan. It was claimed for the "Stafford" that increased speed was unattended with risk, and the carriage was so far lighter that one horse power was saved in the draught. As we have already seen, it was once the fashion to make roads very high in the centre, a practice fraught with great danger to heavily laden coaches ; but the inventor of the "Stafford" declared

that his coach was as safe on a crowned road as on
a flat one. By way of experiment it carried a very
heavy load from Blackfriars to Hayes, and to test its
stability the coachman went down Notting Hill at an
estimated pace of sixteen miles an hour. "Nevertheless," says the report, "there was no rocking nor jolting.
The body preserved its equilibrium in the roughest
parts of the road, and fully answered the purpose for
which the patent has been granted."

By the time the summer of 1838 arrived, the Post-
master - General found it necessary to put on a day-
mail, which made its first journey from Brighton at
10.30 A.M. on Monday, July the 23rd, 1838, the route
being through Cuckfield, Crawley, Reigate, and Croydon. The mail from London reached Brighton at a
quarter past four, so the new arrangement permitted of
letters posted in London and Brighton in the morning
being delivered on the same day. This was, of course,
a great convenience to the commercial world; and it
may be noted that the first coachman of this day-mail
was the still living Mr. Charles Ward, the well-known
driving instructor and dealer of the Brompton Road.
This excellent coachman began his career by a five
years' spell at driving the Norwich and Ipswich mail
between London and Colchester. He was then promoted to the Quicksilver Devonport mail, which he
drove between London and Bagshot. Taking as my
authority Mr. Ward's own book, he appears to have
grown somewhat weary of this perpetual night-work,
so he applied to Mr. Chaplin, the well-known coach
proprietor and contractor, for a change. A man with
nearly two thousand horses engaged in coach work
must naturally have had some difficulty in finding
places for his coachmen and his cattle, and so he said
to Mr. Ward, "I can't find you all day coaches; besides,
who am I to get to drive your mail?" However, since

he had determined to horse the day-mail, Mr. Chaplin made Mr. Ward the offer to drive the whole distance between London and Brighton, and horse the coach for a stage, or, if he preferred it, he might drive without horsing it. Fired with a very natural ambition, he closed with the first offer, but the speculation, he tells us, did not prove to be a very profitable one, and so, as the railway was making great progress, he eventually sold his team to Mr. Richard Cooper, who succeeded him on the coach.

This Mr. Richard Cooper, before he took Mr. Ward's place, was coachman of the Rival, and in the month of August (1838) we find him appearing before the Brighton Bench to answer an information of having endangered the safety of the Rev. Mr. Pollen and others, by racing the Hero coach at Pyecombe. Even in those days a mass of contradictory evidence was characteristic of the running - down or racing - down cases, and this one was no exception to the rule. In the end, Cooper, who was a fine coachman, was fined in the mitigated penalty of twenty-five shillings and costs, the magistrates promising that in future they would inflict the maximum punishment.

At this period (1838) the time was not far distant when the railways were to cause the sudden downfall of the industry of stage-coaching which had been brought to such perfection. In some parts of England lines had already been opened, and compelled proprietors to take so many coaches off the road, or to convey them part of the distance by train, that great inconvenience was experienced by persons dwelling at intermediate points, which had formerly been well served by the coaches. The Brighton road, however, was still in full swing, though further afield the railways caused a great change in the Post-Office arrangements. The effect was to some extent felt at Brighton, for the

Western mail had changed its hours, and brought with
it some inconveniences to Brighton's residents.

In spite of the skill of the coachmen, the earlier
coaches continued to topple over with the greatest
regularity, and from causes which would seem to us
now to be insufficient. In September 1838, for
instance, Adams's London and Brighton coach, with
a full complement of passengers on board, and carrying besides a good deal of luggage, turned over near
Warnham Hill, about a mile out of Horsham. According to the account of an outside passenger, it seems
that the coach had been rocking for some time, and on
reaching an angle in the road the coachman had to
draw on one side to pass a waggon, the driver of
which, after the manner of his kind, did not give way.
Why this should have contributed to a capsize does
not plainly appear, for one would have thought that
the coachman would at least have slackened his pace
on passing the waggon, when probably the rocking
would have ceased. He seems, however, to have gone
on; and, as already stated, turned his coach over. It
was reported that three passengers were killed, but
this happily turned out to be untrue, though two ladies
who were inside were somewhat seriously injured, and
had it not been for the fact that the coach fell against
the hedge, the consequences might have been still worse.
The coach itself was too much damaged to proceed on
its journey, so some of the passengers were forwarded
in postchaises from the King's Head, Horsham, the
proprietors of which house were greatly praised for
their attention to those who had suffered by the accident; but the King's Head was an old coaching-house;
the London and Horsham coach started from the door,
and several others changed horses or called there.

In the November of this year (1838) Adams appears
to have sold his unlucky coach and stock to Goodman,

the proprietor of the Times Coach-Office, 10 Castle Square ; J. Egerton, one of the best coachmen at Brighton ; R. Howes, of the King's Head, Horsham ; W. Coomber, and W. Chaplin. They rechristened her the Royal Victoria, running her to London on Monday, Wednesday, and Friday, and down on the alternate days. It went by the long route through Henfield, Cowfold, Horsham, Capel, Dorking, Leather-head, Kingston, and Richmond.

Meantime the two Ages were running as they were when we took our leave of them at the end of the newspaper war in which the proprietors were engaged. Sir St. Vincent Cotton now drove what had been Willan's Age up to November 1838, when, partly owing to the ill-health of his mother, and partly to his own impaired resources, the Baronet gave up coach-ing, and went to reside at his place in Cambridgeshire, his successor being Mr. Charles Tyrwhitt Jones. Sir St. Vincent Cotton must have been a very fine coach-man from all accounts, since all the writers of his time award him unstinted praise both for strength, skill, and grace on the box; while Mr. Charles Jones, before having a turn on the Age, had horsed and driven the Monarch over some of its ground.

Meantime, the Optimus, one of the coaches running from the Blue Coach-Office, professed to have reduced its fares, though it is difficult to see to what extent, inasmuch as inside passengers paid £1, and outsides half that amount. The Optimus still kept on its old route by Hickstead, Crawley, Reigate, Sutton, and Clapham.

Pickett, who had formerly been the coachman of the Union fast coach, was now (1838) on the box of the Item ; and, while assisting at changing horses at Bal-combe, one of the leaders kicked him severely in the face, which disabled him from continuing his journey ;

P

so the horse-keeper at Balcombe was promoted to the box, and took the coach safely to London. In those days horse-keepers who showed any talent for driving frequently had an opportunity for taking a stage or two, when the regular coachman was either unable to drive or wanted a holiday, and not a few of the famous coachmen whose deeds we read of began their life in the more humble capacity of horse-keeper, and when they were raised to the bench they started with the advantage of knowing something about putting horses together. Moreover, their first experiences were with horses they knew; and, having seen the regular coachmen start them scores of times, they knew what to do first; while, if the professional happened to be on the coach, they were able to have proper instruction from the first, instead of contracting all sorts of bad habits, which would have to be unlearned afterwards.

The railway had already begun to make its influence felt in the coaching world, and there was by this time probably not a single soul connected with stage-coaching who did not feel sure that the days of the stage-coach were numbered. As this dawned by degrees upon proprietors, they began to wince afresh at the amount of the duties exacted from them by the Government. Coach proprietors had long grumbled in different parts of England; but the first step towards seeking for redress appears to have been taken in the North, where the coach proprietors and postmasters decided to petition Parliament, in 1838, to lessen the duties then payable, and so to place them upon an equal footing with railway companies. The remission of the mileage duty, and the duty of a shilling, and one and ninepence, for every horse let for hire to go no greater distance than eight miles from the place of letting, was demanded; and in lieu of the scale of duties then in force, a fresh tariff was suggested.

In the summer of 1839 the Brighton coach-masters began to bestir themselves, though it was rather late in the day. In a petition which it was resolved to present to the House of Commons, it was pointed out that the coaching industry was labouring under great depression, owing to the completion of the lightly taxed railroads, and the House was asked to take into consideration all surrounding circumstances; to repeal the duties then in force; and to grant such relief, by an equalisation of the duties, as might seem fit in accordance with the report of the Committee. In the course of the next month (August 1839) a "Stage-Carriage" Bill was before the House, and a clause was inserted therein to give coach proprietors the advantage of an additional passenger, and a reduction of a halfpenny per mile on the duty—a small favour for which the proprietors were properly grateful, seeing that in 1838 the mileage duty paid on stage-coaches in England showed those vehicles to have run 40,530,000 miles.

In a book not very often met with, the "Autobiography of a Stage-Coachman," by Thomas Cross, the author gives in his appendix the text of a petition presented to the House of Commons on his behalf by Lord Joscelyn in the year 1846. The petitioner saw with dismay the invention, and rapid increase, of railroads accomplishing the ruin of hundreds in the same calling as himself; and, after calling attention to the large amount of money invested in turnpike trusts, then nearly bankrupt in consequence of the railways supplanting stage-coach travelling, the petition proceeded to inform the House that the injury "had its ramifications from one end of the island to the other," threatening the depreciation of property to a ruinous extent; in proof of which Mr. Cross could point to every town in the kingdom which a railroad had approached, except two or three of the largest cities and

towns, and even to these possible exceptions he thought
the benefit would be questionable should inquiry be
made into the state of every class of their overcrowded
population. Mr. Cross was not unwilling to admit the
convenience, the luxury, " nay, even the safety and
importance, as regarded the speed of the new mode of
travelling ; " and he would, in the same spirit of justice, acknowledge the truth of the French philosopher's
axiom, that the quick communication of persons and
thoughts is the very perfection of civilisation ; but, he
urged, luxury is not happiness, any more than civilisation
is prosperity in a nation or in a family. The petition
included further indictments against the making of
railroads, and concluded thus : " Therefore, your petitioner lastly prays that, in passing any Bills having
reference to railroads, in some or one of them such
provision shall be made as shall prevent your petitioner
and his family from coming to the extreme of misery."

It used to be a saying that when a stage-coachman
was no longer able to perform his own duties, he was
not fit to do the work of any one else ; but when
railroads were an accomplished fact, the above statement was partially falsified, as a goodly number of
coachmen and guards found occupation in the service
of the different railway companies, while some took
to driving omnibuses. Many years ago there was a
service of white omnibuses which ran from the West
End to Richmond *via* Hammersmith Bridge and Barnes.
The coachmen wore gold bands to their hats, and were,
with scarcely an exception, elderly men. I have been
told that the majority of them had been stage-coachmen.

Nevertheless, it is beyond question that, when stage-
coaches were run off the road, penury overtook very
many men who had previously been engaged in the
business. Porters, booking-clerks, horse-keepers, coachmen, and others suddenly found their means of liveli-

hood taken away from them; while the inns and
posting-houses speedily came down to the level of
beer-shops, or at the very least suffered a sort of
diminutio capitis, and from this time (1839) the history of coaching on the Brighton road is but the
history of a waning industry.

Meantime Mr. Edmund Cussell, the proprietor of
the Globe coach, had died, and nineteen of the horses
which had worked in the coach, together with sundry
other effects, were sold on the premises on the 1st
February 1839; and at this date a heavy snowstorm
caused all the coaches to be late.

From various statements in these pages it will be
seen that not a few coach accidents were due to the
coachmen, presuming upon their skill and experience,
taking unwarrantable liberties with their horses on the
road. In similar fashion guards occasionally neglected
obvious precautions. They were naturally anxious to
prove themselves smart; to save the coachman from
pulling up more often than was necessary; and it appears to have been a favourite boast with many of them
that they could unskid without calling upon the coachman to stop. No more than a year or two ago I saw the
guard of one of the modern coaches do this. When the
moment arrived for the shoe to be taken off, he placed
one foot upon the spokes of the wheel, and throwing
all his weight upon that one foot, backed the wheel,
so to say, for an instant, and released the skid; but it
was easy to see that if anything had gone wrong a
serious accident would have occurred. On this occasion all went well, luckily; and the skid being released,
the guard lowered himself down to the step, picked
up the chain, and rehung the skid upon its hook. I,
for one, do not like to see men incur these needless
risks, though, at the same time, quite acknowledging
that an active guard has saved many a mishap.

A disregard of danger it was that caused the death of one of the most respected guards on the Brighton road, one Fisher, who was on the night-mail. The coach, which left Brighton at eleven o'clock at night, had gone down Clayton Hill, when Fisher got down to take off the skid. He shouted " All right," and the coachman proceeded, but, on looking over his shoulder, almost immediately afterwards, observed that the guard's seat was unoccupied. He at once pulled up, and on going a short way back, found the unfortunate Fisher lying on the road with his skull fractured, and one of his legs broken just above the ankle. The supposition was that, on getting on to the coach, he had put his foot on the wheel instead of on the step, and was thus thrown violently to the ground. The passengers on the mail took a gate from off its hinges, and on it conveyed the sufferer to the Friars Oak Inn. A doctor was sent for, but poor Fisher died a day or two later.

It will have been noticed, from what has been said before, that the Act of Parliament—it was unquestionably a wise Act—which forbade a coachman to carry more passengers than were allowed by the terms of his license, was sometimes very strictly enforced. As I have already pointed out, some limit to the number of passengers which the very natural greed of proprietor and coachman might crowd in and upon a coach was absolutely necessary, both for the safety of the concern and for the comfort of the men and women it carried. We of to-day grumble if we are compelled to ride for a short distance in a railway carriage into which more than the proper number of passengers have intruded themselves; but what must have been the discomfort of travelling between London and Brighton, even by a fast coach, with an extra person or two in the somewhat stuffy interior?

Some such considerations as these would appear to have occurred to a lady who took the law of Francis Vickers, a most excellent coachman, who drove the Wonder, one of the coaches put on the road by the Marquis of Worcester, and Israel Alexander of Southwark. The strict letter of the law was so far relaxed in practice that "half" a passenger, in the shape of a child, was permitted to be carried in addition to the four adults which the inside of a coach was supposed to accommodate; and one day, towards the latter end of August 1839, the Wonder pulled up at the Elephant and Castle on its way to Brighton with three grown-up people and a child inside. At the Elephant another passenger and child were picked up, and, in spite of the remonstrance of the aforesaid lady, were packed away in the Wonder's inside. In this instance, therefore, Vickers carried half a passenger more than he ought to have done, a contravention of the law, which was punished by a fine of twenty-five shillings and a sovereign for costs. This, however, was but the beginning of Vickers's troubles, as shortly afterwards we find him figuring in the London Bankruptcy Court.

During the year 1839 the Era fast coach continued to run daily at noon from Brighton to London ; but the proprietor ceased booking at the Spread Eagle Office, and ran instead from the Blue Office, under the proprietorship of Messrs. Nelson, Relf, Strevens, & Co. ; while a fast coach, called the Czar, started from the Blue Coach-Office, Brighton, every Sunday afternoon at two o'clock.

CHAPTER XII

WE are now, unfortunately, getting very near to the end of the history of coaching on the Brighton road ; in fact, before the chapter is brought to a conclusion, the early history of the Brighton railway will have been touched upon ; and, as the sequel shows, the coaches and the railroad could no more live together than can " crabbed age and youth." It scarcely needed very much argument to convince most people that steam would prove superior to horse-power from every point of view. A single engine would take more persons than could be carried on all the Brighton coaches put together—how many coaches would be needed to take the passengers by any of the morning trains up, or the afternoon trains down ?—while the amount of the coal bill would be far short of that of the corn bill for the conveyance of the same number. On the question of economy, the following calculations, which appeared in the *Brighton Gazette* for the 4th of June 1840, may not be without interest. It was estimated that while a dozen stage-coaches carrying fifteen passengers each and 1200 horses would be needed to carry 180 people 240 miles in twenty-four hours, at ten miles an hour, one locomotive would take that number, and perform two journeys in the same time, so that it would do the work of 2400 horses. Then again it would require thirty mail-coaches, carrying six passengers each, and 3000 horses, to take 180 passengers 240 miles in twenty-four hours, at the rate of ten miles an hour ; but one loco-

motive would take that number, make two journeys in
the same time, and so do the work of 6000 horses. The
proverbial odds of "a guinea to a gooseberry," therefore,
would not have been extravagant in favour of steam.

At the end of March 1840 a singular accident befell
the Times coach. The wheelers had just been put to
at the bottom of Middle Street, and the ostler was standing at their heads waiting for the leaders and the coachman, when, from some unexplained cause, the two
horses took fright and started towards the cliff. The
ostler clung to their heads as long as he could ; but, on
reaching the King's Road, he lost his hold, and the
wheels of the coach unhappily passed over his legs.
Nearly facing the bottom of Middle Street was the
Middle Street gap, a flight of steps leading to the beach.
with a couple of posts at the top of the steps. The
horses galloped straight for this gap ; the pole struck
one of the posts, and one of the horses having run
through the opening, remained suspended in mid-air by
the harness. The usual crowd collected immediately ;
some one unfastened the traces, and the horse was, after
a time, lowered to the beach. Neither coach nor horses
were injured ; in fact, half an hour later these same
horses proceeded on their journey. The poor ostler was
less fortunate. he was taken to the County Hospital,
where it was found necessary to amputate one of his
legs, the thigh having been fractured.

With the spring of the year (1840) came another
reminder of the improvements effected in the steam-
engine, in the shape of another steam-carriage which
arrived at Brighton from London on the 20th May,
after having had something of a race with the day-
mail, which reached Brighton nearly a quarter of an
hour in front of time, and a few minutes before the
steam-carriage. The latter left Camberwell at eleven
o'clock, and completed its journey at ten minutes past

four; but, as six stoppages of twenty minutes each
were made for the purpose of taking in water, the
actual journey took about three hours.   At the Pitt's
Head Inn, Handcross, which was one of the stopping
places, three gentlemen on horseback were in waiting,
and when the steam conveyance started they started
too.   The horses, we are told, went in front at first ;
but, on going up the next hill, described in the papers
as a "smart rise," the steam-coach took the lead of the
horses, running over the ground at great speed with
the utmost ease.   With which side victory ultimately
rested is not stated.

A few days later, the patentee of the steam-carriage
wrote a letter to the *Morning Post* correcting several
of the previously published statements, and explaining
that the journey from London to Brighton was accomplished in four hours and a half, including stoppages,
which took up one hour exactly.   The hills made no
difference to the working of the machinery; but the
mud, which was taken into the boiler along with the
water, was every now and then a source of difficulty,
causing the conveyance to come to a halt.   In spite of
this drawback, however, the machine ran at an average
pace of fifteen miles an hour, and attained its greatest
speed on a piece of level road, three miles being run
in seven minutes and a half.   On the return journey
there was again a race with the Brighton day-mail,
which, according to one account, was a long way
ahead at one period, but was eventually overtaken by
the steam-carriage.

When Hancock's carriage (*ante,* p. 186) was put
upon the road, the papers were loud in its praise ; but
this one, the invention of Mr. Hills, completely put out
of joint the nose of the more antiquated machine, to
which the new one was reputed to be far superior in
appearance.   The vehicle was said to resemble a gentle-

man's open carriage, but much larger; and a local paper
described it as being elegantly painted and fitted up,
and altogether far superior to Hancock's carriage, which
had been exhibited in Brighton some years before. Such
is fame. When Hancock's carriage was first seen, the
reporters went into ecstasies over it. "The boiler and
machinery," the account continues, "are placed behind
in a sort of second carriage, and the machinery is
almost entirely concealed. When in motion, no smoke
or steam is visible, and a small portion only of steam
issues from the boiler when the vehicle is standing
still." A condensing engine was employed, there was
"an absence of the thumping noise which is heard
from high-pressure engines, such as those used on
railroads." The fare was no more than five shillings.

And now to coaching proper.

There was at least one firm of coach proprietors who
were not inclined to knuckle under without a struggle
before the advancing railway. "A New Coach to
London in Five Hours" was the heading to an advertisement in the Brighton papers for the 25th June 1840,
"The Duke of Beaufort, for elegance, comfort, and
regularity unrivalled in all the world." Some of the
old coaching people would appear to have set at complete defiance the maxim about self-praise being no
recommendation. The Duke of Beaufort, however,
was put on by Alexander & Co., the "Co.," no doubt,
being the coach's namesake. The new undertaking
left J. Snow's office, 3 Castle Square, for London at
one o'clock every Monday, Wednesday, and Friday,
returning on the alternate days. The Duke of Beaufort
made its first journey on the 24th of June 1840, and
on the 1st July it became a two-end coach, leaving
London and Brighton daily. The local reporter was
in attendance, and declared that "the horses, harness,
and trappings were in perfect keeping with the splendour

of the coach." But this grand conveyance did not have
a very long life ; it did not, so far as can be ascertained,
run during the following winter; and, if it was put
upon the road in the next summer, it was for a short
season only.

Early in 1841 there was a slight attempt at humour
in the announcement that the Brighton day-mail had
come to be known as the "Conservative Mail, because
of the distinguished and honourable fare which it last
week conveyed to London." Who this distinguished
gentleman was there is no means of finding out;
but the next announcement in the papers of May 27,
1841, was veritably the beginning of the end of stage-
coaching. For some years previously the railroad had
been in course of construction, and on the above-
mentioned date there was in the papers an advertisement headed "The London and Brighton Railway
Company." It was addressed, "To coachmasters and
others," and must have filled many coachmen, guards,
helpers, innkeepers, and others with dismay. It was
nothing less than an announcement that the directors
of the railway company were desirous of receiving proposals for the conveyance of passengers from "Hayward Heath, near Cuckfield," to Brighton, a distance
of about fifteen miles, and from Brighton to Hayward's
Heath, in four-horse coaches and omnibuses, at a price
to be named per coach per journey, from and after
the 28th of June then next (1841). The proposals
were to be sent in on or before the 1st June to Mr.
Thomas Wood, the secretary of the Company, at 10
Angel Street, Throgmorton Street.

On reading the above advertisement, it will be
noticed that Hayward's Heath was described as being
near Cuckfield; for the former, being off the main
road, was not so well known ; and, before trains were
invented, to be off a main road was to be in com-

parative obscurity ; while to be off a branch road was to be out of the world altogether. There is an old coaching story that the inhabitants of a small Lanca-shire village were one day surprised to hear the church-bells ring out a merry peal. There was no great wedding that they knew of, and the simple rustics were at a loss to account for the ringing of the bells, so they sought information from the clergyman, and from him they learned that it was the anniversary of the battle of Waterloo : that was the first they had heard of Wellington's great victory, as no coach passed within some miles of the village ! Lord Macaulay said that in remote parts of Cornwall people did not hear of the death of Queen Elizabeth until London had left off its mourning for her. To-day Cuckfield, as a coaching place, has well-nigh faded out of memory ; the Comet does not run that road ; it is at the present time described as near Hayward's Heath, there being a large station at the latter place.

In July the railway was opened between London and Hayward's Heath, and nearly all the once-famous London and Brighton coaches came to an end. Here were the Times, Sovereign, Vivid, Royal Blue, and Rival coaches—coaches which had been regarded as expresses and which had been driven by consummate artists—engaged by the railway, their arch-enemy, and eking out a precarious temporary livelihood by carrying people between Brighton and Hayward's Heath. But coach proprietors, like other mortals, had to bow to the inevitable. Some of the other coaches found occupa-tion in running between Hayward's Heath and Lewes, Maresfield, Uckfield, and Eastbourne ; while branch coaches were started to other places contiguous to the line ; but it must have been a great come-down for Messrs. Strevens, Snow, & Goodman, who were the proprietors with whom the railway company chiefly

did business; while the Red, Blue, and Spread Eagle
Offices now called themselves "Coach and Railway
Offices."

A few coaches, however, were kept on the road
between London and Brighton, for there were still
some outlying places which were not served by the
rail; and there were also a certain number of old-
fashioned passengers who would not look kindly upon
the new-fangled trains. The Alert and Union coaches
continued to run *viâ* Cuckfield, Crawley, Reigate,
Sutton, Tooting, and Clapham, starting from Hine's
Office, 52 East Street, and going to the Bull, Holborn;
the Green Man and Still; Gloucester Coffee-House;
and Angel, Islington. Families could be picked up
anywhere in Brighton, and set down at their town
residence without change of coaches. In this way
did the few remaining proprietors seek to ward off the
evil day; but the end came, and in December (1842)
Pickett's Union, a very old-established coach, was finally
taken off the road, leaving only one or two to ply
between London and Brighton, and one of these ran
the long road by Horsham and Dorking, in order to
pick up what trade there was at places not yet upon
the line of railroad.

Mail-coaches had been running since 1784, and from
that time up to 1842 the guards had been paid a
miserable wage of about ten or twelve shillings a week,
depending upon tips to bring their money up to a
sum sufficient to keep them and their families; but
now that the entire supercession of coaches, mail and
stage, was within measurable distance, we actually find
the Government of the day making fresh arrangements
with their guards. For fifty-seven years they had been
getting tips, and now the Post-Office raised the salaries
of guards to sums varying from £70 to £120 a year,
according to length of service, prohibiting them at the

same time, under pain of dismissal, from taking presents
from passengers. This was remarkably like shutting
the stable-door after the stealing of the steed.

Meantime the Rival coach appears to have been kept
running, and the report of a law case seems to show
the straits to which coachmen and proprietors were
put in order to make both ends meet. A Mrs. Cox
had, a short time before, gone with her three children
from Brighton to Brixton by the Coronet coach, the
coachman, Poole, having taken them to town for eight
shillings, that is to say, for two shillings a head. Having been carried on such very favourable terms, Mrs.
Cox thought that she could not do better than return
by the same vehicle, and accordingly waited with her
children in the Brixton Road for the Coronet to pass.

The Rival, however, came by first, and the coachman
asked Mrs. Cox if she wanted to go to Brighton; she
replied that she did, but was waiting for the Coronet,
Poole having engaged to take the party back for eight
shillings. The Rival's coachman offered to carry them
for the same money, so they elected to go by it. At
Reigate, a fresh coachman (Seymour) took the coach
on to Brighton, and Mrs. Cox, who seems to have been
a tolerably experienced traveller, at once drew Seymour's
attention to the fact that she and her party were travelling at a special rate, the answer being that he knew all
about it. On the coach arriving at Brighton, the sum
of sixteen shillings was demanded. Glennie, the coachman who drove from London to Reigate, denied having
agreed to carry Mrs. Cox and her children for the eight
shillings, and was promptly told by the Bench that they
did not believe him. Ultimately, Seymour, against whom
the charge was that he demanded more than the sum
agreed upon, was fined twenty-five shillings, and two
pounds for costs. A day or two afterwards Glennie
was summoned for having carried on the Rival more

passengers than were allowed by the Act of Parliament ;
but the summons was dismissed. This case is note-
worthy from the fact that Glennie was defended by
" Mr. Lewis of Ely Place," an uncle, probably, of Sir
George Lewis.

The remainder of the line from Hayward's Heath to
Brighton was opened on Tuesday, the 21st September
1841, and the form of the advertisements in local papers
underwent a complete change. We read nothing more
of going to London in five hours, proprietors no longer
sang the praises of their fast coaches ; nor does the
familiar woodcut of the coach-and-four any more appear.
Instead of the old order of things, we find Mr. Strevens,
of the " Blue Coach and Railway Office," announcing
that he had started several new omnibuses and flys for
the conveyance of passengers between the Brighton terminus and various parts of the town, including Kemp
Town, Brunswick Square and Terrace, and the hotels.
A coach ran between Brighton and Lewes to bring
people in from the latter place to catch the express
train for London ; and an omnibus brought the Worthing folk to Shoreham, whence they came by train to
Brighton, proceeding thence to London.

The day-mail ran between London and Brighton
till October 1841 ; but the presence in the town
of Mr. Johnson, the Post-Office surveyor, portended
a change, and this came to pass when the mails
were carried by train, with the result that the Brightonians had their London letters delivered earlier than
before.

The few items of coaching news that can be gleaned
from the papers in the autumn of 1841 are one and all
couched in a melancholy sort of strain befitting the
occasion. The wheels of one of the few coaches left
on the London and Brighton took fire near Albourne,
and, with somewhat hasty judgment, most of the pas-

STAGE COACHMEN AT THE GOLDEN

sengers, doubtless drawing in their own minds com-
parisons unfavourable to coaching, at once started for
Brighton, some in whatever vehicles they could procure,
and some on foot, while others wisely stuck by the coach,
which, after fresh wheels had been procured, proceeded
on its way, arriving at Brighton six hours late—that is
to say, at two o'clock the next morning. During the
month of November 1841 the London road appears
to have been in such a bad state that the few coaches
which still kept on running were, in some places, obliged
to proceed at a walking pace ; one fairly stuck in the
mud, and was two hours late ; while a "fast" coach took
seven hours to complete its journey. The Brighton
night-mail was still on the road, but in the form of a
pair-horse coach, as I gather from an account of a mishap which overtook her in January 1842. She was
passing through Preston, on her way to Brighton, at
three o'clock in the morning, when one of the horses
was seized with the megrims and fell, owing to which
the other horse and the coach were drawn against a
cottage and upset. The coach was a good deal damaged, and the coachman was seriously injured through
being thrown from his seat ; but the guard was unhurt
—the guards in the great majority of accidents did
somehow or other contrive to fall upon their feet. The
prevailing dulness which had overspread the coaching
world appears to have been not without its effect on a
horse-keeper at Storrington. He had been heard to
lament the decay of coaching, and then came to the
conclusion that he had something growing inside him.
Both these matters preyed upon his mind ; and one day,
after harnessing his horses, he went and hanged himself ; while Mrs. Hine, the widow of the well-known
Brighton coach proprietor, advertised in the *Brighton
Gazette* that, having had to give up the road business
in consequence of the opening of the Brighton Railway,

Q

she had " commenced in the stationery and perfumery line at her ' office,' 52 East Street, Brighton, where she respectfully solicited patronage and support." The few proprietors, however, who still kept running do not invariably appear to have gone to work in a manner best calculated to attract whatever custom remained for the road, as we find a gentleman signing himself " Viator" complaining that, after booking two inside places by the half-past nine Times, he was charged thirteen shillings for the carriage of an amount of luggage only very slightly in excess of that which, in the more remunerative days of coaching, had always been carried free.

Over the appearance of Brighton itself a great change had come. The flickering embers of the road were indeed fanned by the coaches running to provincial towns, and the two or three that still ran to London; but the gilt was rubbed off, and some of the short coaches were neither horsed nor kept up as they had been. As in London, so it was in Brighton: at the coaching inns, or at some favourite hostel close at hand, there had been a room devoted to the use of coachmen, and in Brighton the coachmen foregathered at the Golden Fleece; but now these little reunions were broken up, for the company was lacking. In lieu of the well-appointed vehicles the Brightonians had been accustomed to see, the Brighton streets, like those of London, were full of cabs, flys, and omnibuses; "and," said the *Brighton Gazette* of the 13th October 1842, "a thriving trade they seem to carry on. These omnibuses are found, both by inhabitants and visitors, extremely convenient and economical vehicles. Throughout the day they are to be met with in every part of the town; and, though their principal object is to convey passengers to and from the terminus, other parties also find their use highly advantageous." The curious thing is that to-day there is no railway station, London or provincial, which has a poorer omnibus service than that at Brighton.

Mr. Capps, in his capacity of coach proprietor, was nothing if not thorough: from the very first his coaches were horsed in capital style; even the *Sporting Magazine* critics admitted that his vehicles were of the best and newest make, and his coachmen as good as he could find them. When at last brought face to face with the most formidable opposition he had ever been called upon to contend against, he would not strike his colours without a struggle; and so, perhaps, thinking that some measure of success might attend upon a plucky endeavour to avert entire failure, he gathered himself together for a final effort, which took the form of establishing a coach called the Rail Road, and the publication of a facetious leaflet headed—

THE RAIL ROAD.

Considerable disappointment having been expressed by the Public in consequence of the delay and difficulties in deciding on a Line of Rail Road for Brighton, T. W. CAPPS & Co., anxious to meet the wishes of their friends, have established a "RAIL ROAD" for their accommodation free from all the objections urged against the other Lines. They have dispensed with the tedious and expensive form of carrying a Bill through the House of Commons; and the necessary arrangements having been completed, it is now ready for the conveyance of travellers.

The advocates of Sir John Rennie's Line are informed that this is the most Direct that the circumstances will admit of; and those who are opposed to Sir John, are assured that Capps's Line is entirely free from tunnels and cuttings: and as the original "Age" Office, No. 5 Castle Square, was formerly associated with the name of Stevenson, it is presumed that no objection will be offered by the supporters of the Shoreham Line; while the opposers of that route will be pleased to hear that no foggy districts or unhealthy marshes will be passed through; that no gentleman's pleasure-ground will be cut up, and that the prosperity of Brighton is not likely to be compromised by digression to Worthing.

The curves and gradients have been reduced as much as possible ; and, in order to meet the wishes of all parties, the Termini will be neither at Nine Elms, London Bridge, Rose Hill, nor the Antheum. The London Terminus is at "The Globe" Tavern, Baker Street, and the Brighton Terminus at the "Age" Office, No. 5 Castle Square, whence the Rail Road starts every day at two o'clock upon the usual estimated fares.

N.B.—Passengers will not be troubled with "smoke," excepting over their tea at Merstham.

Even this brilliant production did not suffice to attract very much custom. For a short time there were a certain number of persons who patronised the worthy Capps when they could ; but, even then, people became more or less matter of fact, forsaking the old manner of travelling for the new; and, before the railway had been opened for a year, the spirited Capps was almost the only man in Brighton to own a coach and four horses ; and so long as there was the chance of paying the corn-bill, Capps's Victoria coach continued to run to London by the long road through Dorking and Horsham. The last coach to run by the nearest route, *via* Hickstead and Crawley, was Capps's "Age;" while the opening of the Lewes line in the month of June 1846 caused the proprietors of the coaches which ran thence to London to make speedy arrangements for the cessation of their business. The last coach from Lewes to London ran on the 12th July 1846.

Now, indeed, it was all over with stage-coaching on the Brighton road—not even the shouting remained. As some one wrote, "The *days*, nay, the very *nights* of those who have so 'long *reined*' supreme over the Nonpareils, the Brilliants, the Telegraphs and the Stars, the Magnets and the Emeralds, are nearly at an end, and the final waybill of the 'total Eclipse is made up.' The coachmen were 'regularly booked,' and their places taken by one who shows no disposition to

make way for them. In a few days everything connected with coaching was destined to vanish,

And, like the baseless fabric of a vision,
Leave not a *trace* behind.

No, not even a buckle nor an inch of whip-cord ; and
if, some years hence, a petrified whipple-tree or the
skeleton of a coachman should be turned up, they will
be hung up side by side with rusty armour and the
geological gleanings of our antediluvian ancestors."

The race of what "Nimrod" called "gentlemen
coachmen" had quite died out on the Brighton road.
Mention has been made of some, but there were others
whose names have not been mentioned in any of the
Sussex newspapers, and concerning whose doings no
details are to be found. Mr. Brackenbury, for instance,
was for some time on the Age while Mr. Willan was
proprietor, and the Hon. Frank Jerningham drove one
end of the day-mail. There were two Brackenburys,
Richard and Robert ; one drove the Windsor Taglioni,
that flash coach which was horsed with so many piebalds and skewbalds, and had a portrait of the famous
danseuse on the hind-boot ; but which of the two
brothers drove to Windsor, and which to Brighton, I
cannot quite make out. Lord Chesterfield, too, the
founder of the Richmond Driving Club, often drove on
the Brighton road. "Nimrod" says that Mr. Charles
Jones, of the Age, had a coach called the Pearl on the
Brighton road, which he horsed and drove himself.
No mention can be found in the papers of this coach ;
but there was a Pearl on the London and Bognor road,
which belonged, it is believed, to the brothers Walker :
possibly "Nimrod" has mixed up the two.

In making mention of Mr. Sackville Gwynne's connection with the Brighton Age, I omitted to give a few
particulars concerning him. He was the son of Colonel

Gwynne, who possessed estates in Carmarthenshire; but, in consequence, it is said, of some dispute about the disposition of the property, Mr. Sackville Gwynne quarrelled with his family, and withdrew himself from Wales, subsequently becoming a professional coachman on some other road before taking a share in the Brighton Age. After his compulsory severance from that undertaking he disappeared for a time, but was some time afterwards found driving a cab in Liverpool; and, when any of the local jobmasters were in want of some one to drive four horses to a bean-feast or race-meeting, his services were frequently secured. By his fellow-cabmen he was much liked, and he continued to drive his cab almost up to the day of his death, which occurred in 1874, Mr. Gwynne being then seventy-three years of age.

The Brighton papers, too, each in its own fashion, lamented the downfall of the road; and probably the Brighton compositors set up more "Ichabods" than they had ever, in their whole lives, been called upon to do before. Castle Square without a cad or a coach! a once bustling locality now deserted like the dreary halls; this was a change indeed. Yet beneath all this lamentation was a trace of the *Le roi est mort, vive le roi* doctrine. Coaches and coachmen were, to be sure, disestablished and disendowed, but more visitors than ever would come to Brighton by train; and, if coach proprietors suffered, the ordinary tradesman might take heart and look forward to times the like of which he had never known before. Time has shown that the death of stage-coaching was by no means synonymous with the dissolution of Brighton, which can now be reached in the old style and the new; but the Brighton road in modern times must form the subject of a new chapter.

THE CHEQUERS HORLEY

CHAPTER XIII.

THE BRIGHTON ROAD IN MODERN TIMES.

PRIOR to the dawning of the coaching revival, in 1866, there had been a sort of coaching middle age on the long road between London and Brighton; but that period perhaps belongs rather to the new than to the old régime, for it was in itself in the nature of a revival. The old coaches had been off the road for about six or seven years, when James Adlam, who, as the Duke of Beaufort tells us in the "Driving" volume of the Badminton Library, had driven the Bath York House coach from London to Marlborough, being then out of harness, started a coach to run between London and Brighton. This must have been about the year 1848. I rather think that Adlam first went by way of Tunbridge Wells and Lewes, but he subsequently changed to the Horsham route. Adlam, however, was not a success; and after about four or five years he gave up his coach, whereupon George Clark put on the Age, in the maintenance of which he was greatly assisted by the present Duke of Beaufort. This concern did pretty well for a time; but, in 1862, it finally stopped—it had been nearly doing so in 1858—and then for four years all the Brighton roads were absolutely coachless.

There was, however, in existence the present Four-in-Hand Driving Club, founded in 1856, and it served to prevent the driving of four horses from becoming quite a lost art, and then, in 1866, the love for stage-coaching once more cropped up, thanks to the late Captain

Haworth, a Queen's messenger, the author of " Road Scrapings," and subsequently the manager of a carriage factory somewhere in Pimlico. The Captain had for a year or two been desirous of reviving the Brighton road; and, in 1866, sought the co-operation of the Duke of Beaufort, Colonel Armytage, Mr. Charles Lawrie, Mr. Chandos Pole, Lord H. Thynne, and two or three others who fell in with the proposal, the outcome being the Old Times, a little yellow coach. which ran to Brighton on alternate days. Of course, money was lost over the coach; but not much came out of each pocket, as there were a good many to share the deficiency. In 1867 two new coaches were built by Holland & Holland, so that there was a coach each way daily. The professionals were William Pratt (on the Old Times in 1866) and Alfred Tedder; the guards, George Dackombe and Phillips; while the proprietors were the Duke of Beaufort, Mr. Chandos Pole, and Mr. Angell. The route was through Cuckfield, both coaches meeting for luncheon at Horley, in which respect the then arrangement differed from that of after years, when the down-coach arrived first, and was off before the up-coach came in. That old-fashioned inn, the Chequers, has not altered for many years, and those who see it to-day view it very much as it was in our grandfathers' time. When the summer (1867) season had run its course, Mr. Chandos Pole was the only partner who did not sell his horses, and he and his brother, Mr. Pole Gell, determined to run a winter coach, their vehicle being one of the old patent mails, while Tedder and Dackombe remained as coachman and guard.

The Duke of Beaufort left the road in 1868, bequeathing it to Mr. Chandos Pole and Mr. Pole Gell, who, however, were joined in mid-season by Mr. G. Meek. The confederacy was increased in 1869 by Colonel Stracey

Clitherow and Lord Londesborough, but one coach
only was used; and except that Lord Londesborough
had no share in the coach, very similar arrangements
prevailed in 1870, 1871, and 1872, by which time
Mr. Cooper and Mr. Smith were connected with the
road.

Nearly all those who had hitherto been connected
with the Brighton coach remembered coaching as it was
before the introduction of railways; but, in 1873, the
road for the third or fourth time collapsed, and from
that day to this it has been worked by men of a younger
generation, always excepting Colonel Stracey Clitherow,
who is still (1893) one of the proprietors. At one
time it appeared as though there would be no Brighton
coach at all; but at the last moment an American
gentleman, Mr. Tiffany, was found to have the ambition
to become a coach proprietor, and in his hands the
road was very well done. Then, in 1874, Brighton
would probably have been coachless, had not Captain
Haworth, who started the season by going to Rochester,
become sick of the road, and changed to Brighton.

We now come to 1875, in which year Mr. Stewart
Freeman, who has accepted the dedication of this
book, began his connection with the Brighton road.
For three years, that is to say, to 1877 inclusive, he
ran the Age single-handed; in 1878 he was joined by
Colonel Stracey Clitherow; in 1879 Mr. Chandos Pole,
son of the former proprietor, and now Master of the
Cattistock Hounds, took a share; and in the following
year Lord Algernon Lennox and Mr. Craven were associated with Mr. Freeman and Colonel Stracey Clitherow.
John Thorogood became Mr. Freeman's coachman in
his first season, having succeeded Pope soon after the
coach was put upon the road, and he kept his post
till the end of the season of 1889, when Alexander
Pennington, who had been driving the Brighton Parcel

Mail, succeeded him. In 1890 William Wragg replaced
Pennington. Mr. Freeman did not run to Brighton
in 1881, 1884, 1885, or 1886 ; in the last-mentioned
year, however, he put on a coach to Windsor; while in
1881, Edwin Fownes, sen., put on the Brighton road
a coach which revived the memory of the Age.

William Wragg, who, since his appointment three
years ago, has continued to drive the Comet, has a
sort of hereditary connection with the Brighton road.
He is the sixth of his line to be engaged in stage-
coaching, and his father, the late Mr. Francis Wragg,
who died at Walthamstow in 1891, at the age of eighty-
five, for many years owned and drove the coach which
ran between Walthamstow and London, as his father,
grandfather, great-grandfather, and great-great-grand-
father had done before him. When the Vivid was
first put on the Brighton road in 1836, the proprietors
wanted a coachman, and so Bob Snow, who was said
to have "more coachmanship in his little finger than
his brother had in his whole body," knowing the Wraggs,
betook himself to Walthamstow, saw " Young Frank,"
as he was then, and expressed his desire to engage him
for the Vivid, though curiously enough young Frank's
father was doubtful about his son's ability to drive one
of the crack fast coaches. Snow, however, judged for
himself; Wragg turned out a great success, and Snow,
with pardonable pride in his own powers of discern-
ment, was accustomed to point to his latest importa-
tion and say, " I have found a coachman." On the Vivid
Frank Wragg continued till 1841, when the railway
caused it to be taken off the road. It is, therefore, in
the fitness of things that his son, who learned driving
in a good school, should now be on the Comet.

With the possible exception of a year or two, Colonel
Stracey Clitherow has been a partner in the coach all
through, and since 1881 others have been included in

the list of proprietors: Baron Oppenheim in 1882;
Messrs. M'Adam and Beckett in 1887; Lord Wiltshire
and Mr. M'Calmont in 1888; Mr. Wemyss in 1889;
and Sir J. D. Poynder for a year or two. When the
coach has been doubled, as it was in 1880, Harry Ward,
formerly on the Exeter road, and brother to Charles
Ward, also a famous coachman on the Western road,
drove the other side of the road; but in 1882 Edwin
Fownes was Thorogood's partner, Pennington driving
the second coach in 1889, Arthur Woodland helping
Wragg in 1890. The regular Brighton coach has, with
one exception, run by one of the direct roads through
Cuckfield or Hickstead; but Mr. Tiffany elected to go
through Reigate; and in 1880 Mr. Carlton Blythe, who
was fond of long journeys, revived the memory of the
original road to Brighton, and carried us back to the
days of the early proprietors, by running through Tunbridge Wells, Uckfield, and Lewes, using three leaders
abreast over the three stages from Tunbridge Wells to
Lewes. During the summer of 1888 there was a sort
of mild opposition on the Brighton road, as the late
James Selby somewhat unwisely put on the Old Times,
and did the double journey in a day once or twice a
week. When the summer season was over, both Mr.
Freeman and Selby resolved to run during the winter;
but the 7th of December was the last day Selby ever
drove. He took the Old Times to Brighton, but complained of a cold; and just one week later—that is to
say, the 14th of December 1888—he died from bronchitis
and disease of the heart. In fact, before he undertook
his drive against time to Brighton and back, he was
strenuously warned by his doctor that he should be very
careful of himself, as he was suffering from heart-disease.

So far as can be seen at present, the Brighton road
seems likely to retain that favour which from very early
time has been bestowed upon it. Assuredly none of

the old coaches could have been turned out in better style, none of them were better horsed, than the Comet has been since Mr. Freeman, assisted by Mr. Henry Goodbun, has taken to buying his horses instead of contracting for them, as for several years his practice was. Strict punctuality is observed; in fact, everything is done that can be done to make it a business-like stage-coach.

In Brighton it so happens that, after a lapse of years, the Old Ship once more finds itself a coaching house. While the Comet has been running to Brighton, there have been other coaches from that place to Arundel, Worthing, and Eastbourne, and the number has been further augmented by one or two started by Mr. Jackson, a Brighton livery stable-keeper. When, therefore, there have been two, three, or four coaches a day from the Old Ship, we have had a kind of miniature revival of Castle Square in the olden days. Let us be thankful, however, that stage-coaching survives in any form; while those who would be unwilling to experience the discomforts of a by-gone time may find a cause for gladness in the fact, that railway travelling has been brought to a pitch of speed and luxury of which those who watched the first Brighton trains in and out of the station could never have dreamed. If the weather be bad, there is the Pullman car at their service; if it be fine, there is the "fast and well-appointed" four-horse coach, the Comet, to bear them through some typical Sussex scenery, and to land them in London or Brighton with an appetite begotten of fresh air and a change from the common mode of travelling.

CHAPTER XIV.

BRIGHTON'S CROSS-COUNTRY COACHES.

THE foregoing chapters will have given some idea of the magnitude of the stage-coach business between London and Brighton. It will have been seen that, when coaching was at its best, there were between forty and fifty coaches on the main road. Most of them started from, or called at, one or more of the numerous offices in Castle Square; while, with the single exception of the office in St. James's Street, the whole of the business of the coaches was transacted either in Castle Square itself, or at offices in East and North Streets, immediately adjoining the Square.

In the year 1822 there were no fewer than sixty-two coaches running between Brighton, London, Hastings, Tunbridge Wells, Oxford, Portsmouth, and the intermediate places; but this number was afterwards added to. The sixty-two were made up thus :—

To and from London	.	.	. . .	39
,, ,, Portsmouth	.	.	. .	2
,, ,, Southampton	.	.	. .	2
,, ,, Lewes	.	.	. .	6
To Hastings .	.	.	. . .	2
,, Tunbridge Wells and Maidstone.			. . .	1
,, Oxford	.	.	. . .	1
,, Windsor .	.	.	. . .	1
To and from Worthing .		.	. .	8
		Total	. .	62

Subsequently coaches ran with greater frequency from Brighton to Lewes and Worthing; opposition set

in on the Hastings road; new coaches were started to
Southampton, Bristol, and Bath; and more than one
proprietor ran to Bognor, Littlehampton, Chichester,
Portsmouth, and Arundel. Nearly all these provincial
coaches started from Castle Square, and perhaps the
Blue Office was the headquarters of the majority; but
Snow, who had an office of his own, was interested in
some of the ventures. The illustration on the opposite
page represents the Blue Coach-Office as it was in the
time of Crosweller, and altogether this was the busiest
office of the three in and around this bustling centre.
It will of course be remembered that Castle Square was
not then as we see it at the present day. The Blue
Office, however, stood where we now find the establishment of Messrs. Treacher; and from the time that
the six-o'clock morning coaches left, there was one
continued bustle in the Square and neighbouring
streets with coaches arriving and departing, people
coming to book seats in advance, and men starting
out to deliver the small parcels brought in by the
different coaches. It has not been thought worth
while to trace the history of the provincial roads with
the same detail as that of the main road, but enough
has been said, it is hoped, to give some idea of the
means by which communication was carried on with
other places.

TO LEWES, EASTBOURNE, AND HASTINGS.

It has already been mentioned that Lewes was, in
very early times, better off than Brighton with respect
to coach and waggon communication; but this is not
to be wondered at, for Lewes was a market town when
her now fashionable neighbour was no more than a
mean fishing-village. Lewes, moreover, was the conduit pipe, as it were, by which Brighton was fed, for

CASTLE SQUARE BRIGHTON.

the Brighton waggons and coaches passed through
Lewes, transporting to the former place the London
fashions and various articles of merchandise, and bearing away whatever fish the fish-carts could not take.
Batchelor, Tubb, Davis, and Brawne no doubt in their
day opened out communication with Brighton ; in fact,
in announcing the death of Robert Davis, the *Sussex
Advertiser* for the 26th April 1790 says that he had
been for *many years* driver and proprietor of the
Lewes and Brighton stage-coach.

Shortly before this, however, a Mr. Smart started a
stage waggon to Brighton. It left Lewes every Monday
morning, and returned from Brighton at three in the
afternoon, to which place it set out again at eleven
o'clock at night, departing for Lewes at seven o'clock on
Tuesday morning. Eight o'clock on Wednesday morning saw the stage again starting for Brighton, and it returned thence at seven in the evening ; on Friday two
journeys each way were accomplished ; while on Thursday and Saturday both man and horses must have been
thankful for the rest which they seem to have obtained.
Smart's coach ran for several years, while from about
1782 Thomas Fuller, of Eastbourne, ran a coach to
Lewes during the summer months, connecting with
Smart's, and so giving communication with Brighton.
For about five-and-twenty years Fuller advertised his
arrangements with the greatest regularity. He went
in for no high-falutin notifications ; but in March or
April he just put in a modest little advertisement to
say that Fuller's Eastbourne coach would run till
further notice ; and then in November came another
advertisement to say that it would stop till further
notice.

In 1804 we first hear of a coach, or rather a diligence, running through from Eastbourne. It was put
on the road by Fuller, above mentioned, in competition

with Allen, Crosweller, & Co., of Brighton, and left
Fuller's house, the New Inn, Eastbourne, at nine o'clock
on the mornings of Monday, Wednesday, and Friday,
returning from the Blue Coach-Office, 44 East Street,
on the alternate days. Other proprietors between
Brighton and Lewes were Soper & Penfold (whose
coach left the Crown Inn, Lewes, at nine o'clock in
the morning, and returned from the King and Queen,
Brighton, at six in the evening), and Kendal and
Quartermaine, who worked the reverse way—that is
to say, they ran at ten in the morning from the Star
and Garter, Brighton, to the Bear Inn at Lewes, making
the return journey at six in the evening; but further
communication was afforded by the London coach of
Tilt, Hicks, Baulcombe, Boulton, & Co., which, as we
have seen (*ante*, p. 60), ran from Lewes to London
by way of Brighton. Baulcombe died in 1810, and his
share in the undertaking came into the market.

In April 1807 a conveyance, bearing the modest
description of "a new light caravan," was put upon
the road between Brighton and Hastings by William
Durden. It left the Blue Coach-Office, 44 East Street,
Brighton, on Mondays and Fridays at ten o'clock, returning from Eastbourne at the same hour on Tuesday and
Saturday, the route being through Rottingdean, Newhaven, Seaford, Eastbourne, Pevensey, and Bexhill.
In the next year (1808) J. Crosweller and J. Attree
are found running a new light coach between the same
places, and by the same route, the only difference being
that it started at seven in the morning instead of at
ten. The energetic firm of Crosweller & Co. may have
bought up Durden's concern, or, after the manner of
more powerful combinations, they may have started an
opposition coach. Whichever it was, the coach was
named the Royal Charlotte, and it took ten hours to
go to Hastings.

The old coachmen who had the luck to drive along the coast turned a more or less dishonest penny by standing in with the smugglers, and conveying contraband goods to their customers. Nor, indeed, was the practice confined to the uneducated coachmen of that date; for nothing was more common than for some of the gentry and farmers in places near the sea to aid and abet smugglers in getting rid of their contraband articles. From a paragraph in the *Brighton Herald* of the 17th August 1811, it would appear that the coachman of the Eastbourne and Hastings coach was one of those obliging persons who sometimes get themselves into trouble through their good-nature, for on the coach being stopped by some of the coast-guard men, packages of contraband goods addressed to a tradesman at " South Born" were discovered.

The next few years were somewhat barren of incident. Coaches ran under the same arrangements as formerly, and in sufficient numbers to satisfy the requirements of the Brighton and Hastings people, as well as those of the dwellers at intermediate places. In 1816, however, the supply was in excess of the demand; for a local paper was informed that the coaches were doomed to travel almost without passengers, and both in Brighton and Hastings " To be Lets" were many. Mr. D. Patterson enrolled himself in the list of coach proprietors in 1818, his speculation being the Telegraph between Brighton and Hastings. At half-past eight on the mornings of Tuesday, Thursday, and Sunday, the Telegraph left 9 Castle Square for the Crown and Cutter Inn, Hastings, the journey being accomplished in seven hours.

So far as can be gathered, there were at this time two ways of getting to Eastbourne and Hastings by road. One route lay through Rottingdean, Seaford, and Newhaven, and the other through Lewes and

R

Uckfield. For some time, now that coaches were growing in number, it had been seen that a short cut after leaving Lewes would be of the greatest service to Eastbourne and Hastings travellers ; but, though the utility was admitted, the project hung fire till 1818, when some energetic people bestirred themselves, collected £8000 out of the £10,000 the new cutting was likely to cost, and busied themselves about carrying the improvement into execution, the ultimate result being the road along which the Item travelled in 1892 and previous years.

The year 1820 brought with it the planning of what was one of the long-distance runs from Brighton. Crosweller, who was a Chaplin on a smaller scale, and was ever ready to invest capital in any road likely to pay its way, joined Smith & Co., of Hastings, and Chitty, Back, & Co., of Deal, and these three firms put on the Union line of coaches between Brighton and Margate, a distance of 114 miles. These vehicles, which left both ends daily, had double routes : on one day they passed through (counting from Margate) Ramsgate, Sandwich, Deal, Folkestone, Hythe, Romney, Rye, Winchelsea, Hastings, Battle, Catsfield, Ninfield, Hurstmonceux, Horsebridge, and Lewes ; on the next day they travelled from Hastings viâ Bexhill, Eastbourne, Seaford, and Newhaven—thus accommodating a double set of patrons, though not effecting a saving in horse-flesh. The Unions left Margate at six o'clock every morning, and in twelve hours reached Hastings, where they rested for the night, setting out again at eight the next morning for Brighton, which was reached at four in the afternoon. The time of departure from Brighton was eight in the morning, instead of six ; and as the coach was at Hastings by four o'clock in the afternoon, passengers had some time in which to amuse themselves ; as the journey was not resumed till seven o'clock the next morning.

The above announcement reads as though one coach ran through this pleasant coast route all the way from end to end ; but a subsequent advertisement rather leads one to the conclusion that the coaches which carried the Folkestone, Deal, and Margate passengers from Brighton were not extra ones, as the first advertisement might imply, but were merely the ordinary Hastings coaches timed to work in with those running from Hastings to Margate.

In 1822 Newman ran a coach to Hastings on the mornings of Tuesday, Thursday, and Sunday ; and then we find the light-coach question cropping up again, Messrs. Ade, of Lewes, stating that they ran from Lewes to Brighton a very convenient low double-bodied light stage-coach on six springs (weight of coach 13½ cwt.) The first advantage claimed for this feather-weight affair was that the greatest weight was placed low in front ; that the high fore-wheels gave a more powerful leverage and caused less friction than the low fore-wheels ; while the weight being nearer the horses, the coach would follow more lightly than when the greater weight in the form of outside passengers was placed behind. Secondly, the six springs gave the coach, it was claimed, steadiness and firmness, and did away with the rolling motion of the long coaches ; while one horse out of four would be saved. Thirdly, as coachman, coach, and passengers were so near to the ground, and as the luggage was underneath the coach, a capsize was rendered all the more difficult of accomplishment.

In May 1825, "John Hoare, proprietor of the Magnet coach," came out with a displayed advertisement, headed by a woodcut of a coach-and-four, announcing that his coach would leave Ball's Coach-Office, High

Street, Lewes, at nine in the morning and three in
the afternoon for Horton's Coach-Office, East Street,
Brighton, whence it set out for Lewes at eleven in
the forenoon and seven in the evening. He assured
his friends that he had spared " neither pains nor
expense to procure the best of horses, and a coach
upon the most improved principles of safety (manu-
factured by Messrs. Ade, of Lewes). As a proof, the
coach, since it has been his property, has regularly
performed the journey a full half-hour earlier than
it was in the habit of doing. J. H., in consequence
of an opposition, *unsuspected as undeserved* in the
quarter from which it sprang, will carry his passengers
at the same price as they offer, viz., 2s. 6d. inside, and
1s. 6d. out; but still, at the same time, he cannot but
state to the public that his former charges for modera-
tion will bear a comparison with any coach in the
country with coach and horses of the same quality;
and, further, that no passenger has been delayed, to
his knowledge, from want of room, since he has been
the proprietor of the concern."

"The opposition, unsuspected as undeserved," came
from no other quarter than Mr. Durrant Ade, to whom
Hoare had given a friendly little puff in stating that
Ade was the builder of the Lewes and Brighton Magnet. Ade's advertisement, headed " Superior and Improved," announced that " a commodious low safety
Brighton coach will start every morning at ten o'clock
from Mr. Hammond's, 42 High Street, Lewes, opposite
the Old Bank, to 5 Castle Square, Brighton, and returns
in the evening at six o'clock ;" but, having discovered
that Hoare (who returned at seven) carried more passengers on the Magnet than he did on his patent low
safety, advertised that, having proved six o'clock to be
too early for his coach to leave Brighton, he had determined, " for the better accommodation of the public "

-he says nothing about the hope of increased receipts
-that his coach should in future leave Brighton at a
quarter before seven, that is to say, a quarter of an
hour before his rival's Magnet. The local reporter was,
of course, present to see Ade's coach make its first
journey, and stated that "as the starting of the new
venture had caused considerable speculative opinions,"
a greater degree of interest was excited than is usual
on such occasions. "We never saw," wrote this appre-
ciative gentleman, "a better turn out; the coach is
truly handsome, the cattle good, and the harness corresponding, forming altogether one of the most respectable things of the kind upon this or any other road.
However injurious opposition may be to individuals
(if this may be considered an opposition), the public
generally derive some benefit, as in this case, for it has
the effect of reducing the fares to their usual and long
standing prices." It would appear, therefore, that by
virtue of his superior turn-out Mr. Hoare had put up
his prices.

By this time there were eighteen or nineteen vehicles
of one sort or another running between Brighton and
Lewes, and this great increase in the traffic appears to
have aroused the trustees of the road to improve it; so
they set to work near Ashcombe Gate, and made a new
cutting to avoid the sharp rise; and this, in the
opinion of the authorities, made the road as nearly
level as possible, with the exception of two small
hills.

Meantime, the energetic John Hoare had bought of
Patterson the Sussex, Brighton and Hastings, coach.
He got together a whole stud of fresh horses, ordered
a new coach, and prepared to do the thing in style,
arranging for the Sussex to leave Hastings at half-past
one on Mondays, Wednesdays, and Fridays, and to return
at the same hour on the alternate days; but, during

the winter (1825–26), it ran but twice a week, that is
to say, from Genn's Coach-Office, 135 North Street,
Brighton, on Tuesday and Saturday, and from the
Crown Coach-Office, Hastings, on Monday and Friday,
the route being Lewes, Horsebridge, and Battle; but
the first week in April 1826 saw the summer arrangements once more in force, except that the Sussex started
at nine instead of half-past eight.   Although there were
now upwards of twenty conveyances—coaches, diligences, and passenger vans—between Brighton and
Lewes, there was a rumour that another proprietor was
about to try his fortune on the road, the coachmen on
which had a very uncomfortable time in November.
Some very heavy rain made some of the roads almost
impassable, and most of the Brighton coachmen feared
that they had got off the road on finding their horses
more than knee-deep in the water, while the School
Hill, Lewes, at the foot of which the water collected
to a depth of more than three feet, must have almost
presented the appearance of a waterfall.

Just as John Hoare had established his connection,
and was apparently doing well with both his coaches,
he died suddenly, either at the close of the year 1826
or early in January 1827, as the preliminary advertisement announcing the sale of his stock appeared in the
Brighton Gazette for the 27th January 1827.   The two
coaches are said to have been a source of great profit to
the spirited proprietor, who was at any rate not over-
horsed, seeing that he worked the Brighton and Hastings coach (39 miles) with sixteen horses, and the
Lewes and Brighton coach (8¼ miles) with five horses.
Inasmuch as the advertisement stated that there were
three sets of harness belonging to the Hastings concern,
we may conclude that Hoare did the thirty-nine miles
with three teams, which would leave him four rest
horses.   His stages would thus average about thirteen

miles; but then his horses worked once a day only.
The Brighton coach may have been drawn by a pair of
horses. For the Hastings coach, harness, and horses
£650 was asked, and for the Lewes and Brighton concern, £270. What became of the Lewes and Brighton
coach the advertisements do not say, but the Hastings
Sussex passed into the hands of John Egerton, who, if
I mistake not, was one of the best coachmen on the
London and Brighton road. Egerton made the hour
of departure ten o'clock at both ends, but in other
respects he kept to Hoare's arrangements.

Fuller, of the New Inn, Eastbourne, appears to have
been so successful with his house and his London
and Brighton coaches, that in 1827 he refurnished his
inn, and made some structural alterations, the better to
adapt it to the requirements of his business, in making
arrangements for his summer coach to London. Fuller
determined to send her by way of Uckfield instead of
by Lewes; but soon after she had been put upon the
road, his old patrons clamoured for their accustomed
convenience, so he put on a second coach, and business
appears to have prospered with him. Meantime Hastings, like Eastbourne, was growing, and the primitive
arrangements of conveying the mails which had hitherto
prevailed were felt to be inadequate to the wants of the
place, for as yet there was no mail-coach to Hastings
either from London or from Brighton. So far as can
be made out, the mails from Brighton were left at
Battle, where they remained till well into the next
day; and as this delay gave rise to a good deal of
grumbling, a mail-cart, which made its journey from
Brighton during the night, was substituted for the post-
boy on horseback. It was not till early in August
1836 that a mail-coach was put on the road between
London and Hastings; but when once "some gentlemen connected with the Post-Office" came down to

make arrangements, no time was lost in carrying the proposal into effect, and in two or three weeks the mail duly made its appearance, to the great convenience of dwellers in Eastbourne and Hastings.

Between the time that John Egerton bought the Hastings Sussex coach from the executors of the late John Hoare, other coach proprietors appear to have entertained the opinion that as Hastings was growing in favour as a watering-place, there was room for more coaches ; so presently the Hero was put on by Croswel- ler & Co., to run from the Blue Coach-Office, Brighton, to Hastings, on Mondays, Wednesdays, and Fridays, through Newhaven, Seaford, Eastbourne, Pevensey, and Bexhill ; on the alternate days it ran from Hastings to Brighton, the hour of starting at each end being nine o'clock in the morning. The local papers stated that both the Sussex and the Hero were well turned out in every respect ; yet business was anything but brisk ; the fares were reduced, yet passengers came not ; and when, a couple of years later (1830), the Wonder joined in the competition, the latter carried passengers for a shilling a head, while the Hero took them gratis ! What had become of Egerton's Sussex at this time cannot be discovered ; but the presumption is that she was still on the road, as mention is made of three coaches daily between Hastings and Brighton. About 1834, however, the Wonder and Hero were both run by Crosweller & Co. ; and while one ran to Hastings on Monday, Wednesday, and Friday, the other went on Tuesday, Thursday, and Saturday. They ran, however, by different routes, for whereas the Hero travelled by way of Lewes, Firle, Wellingdon, Eastbourne, Peven- sey, and Bexhill, the Wonder ran through Lewes, Horsebridge, Gardener's Street, and Battle. An "N.B." to the advertisement informs us that, taking advantage of the Brighton connection for the places on the other

side, there were from Hastings and St. Leonards
coaches to Dover, Ramsgate, and Margate; coaches
to London three times a day, and the royal mail at
night; also to Chichester, Portsmouth, Southampton,
Salisbury, Bath, Bristol, Guildford, Windsor, Tunbridge
Wells, Maidstone, and Chatham, all of them starting
from the Blue Coach-Office.

In April 1839 yet another new coach was started
between Brighton and Hastings from the Red Office,
10 Castle Square, Brighton, under the proprietorship of
Samuel Goodman (of the London and Brighton Times),
Charles Pope Hutchings, Henry Peter Hutchings,
William Laurence Yates, and James Ballard. This
new concern ran the same route and on the same days
as the Wonder; but as the paper stated that there
were three coaches between Brighton and Hastings,
either the Sussex or the Wonder must have been taken
off. It was not the Hero, we know; because just afterwards John Boxall, the coachman of that vehicle, had
to pay thirty shillings for driving the Hero in an
improper manner. Goodman's coaches running from
Brighton to London were by common consent allowed
to be horsed and turned out generally in faultless style;
and neither "Nimrod" nor "Viator Junior," the latter
a *Sporting Magazine* scribe, ventured to pick holes in
Goodman's horses.

Whatever else we learn about stage-coaching between
Hastings, Eastbourne, and Brighton is merely frag-
mentary and unimportant until the year 1842, when
coaching was on the decline owing to the impending
opening of the railway. The first note of warning
was struck in April 1842, when the local papers
announced that, "from indisputable authority," they
were able to state that final arrangements had been
made between the proprietors of the South-Eastern
Railway and the coach proprietors of Hastings and

St. Leonards. The line was to be opened as far as
Tunbridge on the 16th May (1842), after which date
there would be one coach only from Hastings and
Eastbourne to London, and three to the railway station.
By the 9th of June (1842) final arrangements had
been made; and these were to the effect that what had
hitherto been one of the London and Eastbourne
coaches (and which had formerly been conveyed by
train from Hayward's Heath to Croydon, from which
place it went by road to London) left Eastbourne every
Monday, Wednesday, and Friday at ten o'clock, and
travelling *via* Wellingdon, Wilmington, Firle, and
Lewes, reached Brighton in time to enable passengers to
catch the half-past one train to London. On Tuesday,
Thursday, and Saturday the coach returned after the
arrival of the train leaving London at a quarter to
twelve. The coach called at Streven's booking-office
after leaving Brighton Station; and, after the death of
Henry Strevens, who had been coachman between
Lewes and London, and for a time between Brighton
and Tunbridge Wells, his widow, Mrs. Mary Strevens,
was appointed female turnkey at Lewes prison "for a
month upon trial."

Before finally closing this chapter, reference may
shortly be made to one or two incidents in connection
with the Lewes and Brighton road. Going so far back
as December 1826, the *Brighton Gazette* tells us that
a man slipped off a bank on the Lewes road and put
out his knee-cap. The coach from Brighton happened
to pass at the time, while the poor fellow was in great
pain, but the coachman said that his coach was too
full to take the man on to Lewes; so he was left to
take his chance of assistance. The good Samaritan,
however, appeared in the shape of a deformed and
crippled tramp, who somehow or other contrived to
assist the sufferer to Lewes.

The next item of gossip (February 5) is of a somewhat different nature. It has been already mentioned, in connection with the main road, that the making up of dummy parcels was an industry sometimes affected by coach-porters as a means of adding to their income; and it appears to have dawned upon the shoeblack at the White Hart, at Lewes, that he might earn at least the price of a parcel charge by a trick of the same kind. He obtained some corn, probably without the preliminary formality of paying for it; the next step was to provide sample bags, and these he obtained by cutting out his pockets. Having addressed the corn samples to various merchants in Lewes, he delivered the bags and demanded " carriage-money " for them. One is scarcely surprised to hear that the fraud was discovered, and that the ingenious shoeblack was taken before a magistrate, who committed the delinquent to the sessions, after which he retired for a short time to the Lewes prison.

The coach traveller of old, like the railway passenger of to-day, had sometimes to put up with the vagaries of a drunken man; and at Christmas 1828 a Mr. Shotter would appear, during a visit to Lewes, to have kept the festive season in true old-fashioned style—that is to say, he was so very overtaken by the time the Lewes coach started for Brighton, that, unable to sit up, he laid himself down on some trunks on the roof of the coach. But when the wine is in, not only the wit, but also the art of balancing, is out, and the coach had not proceeded far before the festive Mr. Shotter began to roll about, and finally rolled off the top. Luckily for him, a couple of the passengers grasped the situation and Mr. Shotter's cloak, and there he hung, "like a spread eagle," as the paper says, until he was let down, and finally packed inside.

On the cross-roads, as on the main road between

London and Brighton, collisions were of common occurrence, and nearly all of the Lewes coachmen, one would
think from the number of reported cases, must have
been "pulled" at one time or another. Joseph Monk,
a man who, at any rate, could not plead inexperience,
was in May 1836 charged under a local Act with furiously driving one of Simcock's coaches in Brighton
and running against Reid's Hastings van, whereby the
lives of the passengers in the latter were placed in great
danger, and some received great injury. Mr. Monk
wriggled out of punishment in a manner which, though
technically a victory, was in reality a defeat. He com-
pensated the injured parties to the extent of about
five pounds each, and undertook to repair the van ; so,
upon the strength of this, his solicitor asked that the
information might be withdrawn. To this the chairman of the Bench, Sir David Scott, assented, but
explained that he would not have countenanced such
an arrangement had it not been that the amount
he had voluntarily offered to pay exceeded the sum
he could have been fined under the local Act of
Parliament.

The name of Simcock had for a long time been
known in connection with the Lewes coaches, some of
them having been owned by the family for a long
period ; and, like that of other members of their calling,
the lives of the Simcocks had been chequered by such
incidents as collisions, capsizes, being proceeded against
for furious driving, and being asked to pay damages for
hurt to persons or property. William Simcock, one of
the three brothers, had once been coachman on the
Brighton and Tunbridge Wells coach ; but one day early
in April 1843 he was on the Maidstone coach driven by
Baker, who pulled up about two miles out of Lewes to
set down a passenger. Thereupon Simcock climbed on
to the roof to adjust the luggage ; but, on the sudden

breaking of a strap, at which he was pulling with all his might, he fell backwards into the road, injured his spine, and died shortly afterwards ; while no more than two years previously (May 1841), William Simcock's brother Thomas died suddenly in the streets of London. One evening he was found opposite the Admiralty, sitting on the pavement and leaning against the railings. The first supposition was—it generally is in similar cases—that Thomas Simcock was intoxicated ; but a police constable who appears to have been born before his time examined the unfortunate man, deemed him to be seriously ill, obtained assistance, and took the sufferer to a surgeon's, where he died in a few seconds. Mr. Tayleure, one of the overseers of the parish of St. Martin's-in-the-Fields, attended the inquest, and stated that Simcock bore an excellent character, and had become in reduced circumstances through no fault of his own. In his more fortunate days Simcock was coachman and part proprietor of one of the Brighton and Lewes coaches, and was possibly one of the victims to the railway opposition ; for it used to be said that when a coachman could no longer do his own work, his bringing up as often as not unfitted him to do that of any one else ; and in many instances the saying proved to be true, though, happily for themselves, some of the more handy were able to take service under the hated railway companies, and to undertake other duties.

BRIGHTON TO TUNBRIDGE WELLS AND MAIDSTONE.

When roads were bad and locomotion slow between important places, it may not be supposed that there were any great facilities for travel between

provincial towns. Whatever other means of communication, however, may have been available between
Brighton and Tunbridge Wells in the year 1800, there
was at any rate a stage-cart, the driver of which, a man
named Edwards, was stopped "at the two mile-stone"
—presumably two miles from Tunbridge Wells—by
two footpads, one of whom was in military uniform.
Edwards was robbed of more than £10, and his dog,
who came to his assistance, sustained what was said to
have been a bayonet wound; and it is unsatisfactory
to read that the men escaped.

There had been, however, for some few years at
least, regular communication between Brighton and
Tunbridge Wells by means of a post-coach, which
left the General Office, North Street, Brighton, every
Monday and Thursday morning, and ran by way of
Lewes and Uckfield to the Sussex and Angel Inns.
Tunbridge Wells; while in the summer of 1802 "a
new carriage, called the Maidstone, Tunbridge, and
Tunbridge Wells, New Caravan," was put upon the
road. Like the above-mentioned post-coach, its starting-point at Brighton was the North Street Office,
and it must have left Brighton somewhat early in the
morning, seeing that it reached Tunbridge Wells at
eleven in the forenoon, and Maidstone at six in the
evening. It returned from Maidstone at six o'clock
in the morning, on "Monday and Wednesday during
the season." Little or nothing is heard about this
road until the summer of 1810, when a Mr. A.
Humphrey put on a "new and elegant light post-
coach" from the Gun Inn (now Harrison's Hotel)
to the New Inn, Tunbridge Wells. On Mondays,
Wednesdays, and Fridays it left Brighton at eight
in the morning, returning at nine on the alternate
days. In another two years this coach appears to
have passed into the hands of the insatiable Crosweller,

who had for partners W. Pattenden, John Allen, and
J. Green. The coach continued to leave Brighton at
eight in the morning three days a week, ran through
Lewes, Uckfield, Tunbridge, and Tunbridge Wells,
and now ran through to Maidstone ; but the same firm
soon afterwards put on a daily coach to Tunbridge
Wells, but which, for some reason or other, ran from
the Seven Stars in Ship Street, though the advertisement is headed from the Blue Coach - Office.
Meantime, in 1818, a Tunbridge Wells man named
Woods started a coach to Brighton ; but as it ran
up on the days on which Crosweller's vehicle performed the down-journey, the practical effect was a
daily coach between the two places. The coach
left the Swan Inn, Tunbridge Wells, on Mondays, Wednesdays, and Fridays, and ran *via* Lewes
and Uckfield to the Greyhound, East Street,
Brighton.

Crosweller's coaches ran so regularly for so long, that
it is unnecessary to mention them year by year ; it will
suffice, therefore, to say that, for the purpose of working the road from Brighton to the border, Crosweller
was, in course of time, associated with Fleet and Monk,
both of whom were coachmen. In 1822 the Maidstone
coach was extended to Chatham, the route being
through Rochester after leaving Maidstone. During
the winter months the coach made but two journeys a week, though a few years later it ran thrice a
week, and the Maidstone coach made the journey
daily.

Just before Christmas 1825, a correspondent signing
himself " Fair Play," writing to the *Brighton Gazette*,
complained in no measured terms of the condition
of the road between Brighton and Tunbridge Wells.
An "Inhabitant of Uckfield"—there is room for
much doubt whether he ever lived there—and an

"Inhabitant of Tunbridge Wells," and others, soon joined in the controversy, and between them there was quite a wordy war. As, however, the letters largely deal with points the gist of which is now quite lost, there is no occasion here to reproduce the correspondence *in extenso;* but, by way of showing some of the incidents of stage-coach travel in earlier days, it may be worth while to make an extract from one of the contributions. "The road," says the correspondent in question, writing to the *Gazette* of the 5th of January 1826, "is in a most shameful and dangerous state. I cannot assert it to be impassable, as I was, on Friday last, carried *through* (I cannot say *over*) the whole of it by the Brighton coach, and most certainly the *persons* of the passengers (to say nothing of our Christmas finery) were in the most imminent danger. The road is a complete slab of that admirable consistence as to flow into and fill the deep ruts, rendering them impervious to the eye, and it is not till too late that the extent of the danger is discovered. This was the case on Friday. No one can deny the merit of Fleet as a careful driver, but in one moment the wheel was sunk in a rut to the very axle, the coach was actually falling over, and but for the great adroitness of Mr. Fleet, the whole concern must have been deposited in that delectable compound of filth. Fleet, the coachman, declares that for a considerable time he has not expected to complete the journey without accident, and for that reason dare not take a day's rest with his family, even at this season, lest, by intrusting his coach to a servant, he should, in the event of an accident, be accused of sending a careless coachman ; 'and besides,' added he, 'you see the poor horses are tearing themselves to pieces.' As to the gentry and visitants of this place (Tunbridge Wells) attempting to ride or drive on such a road, it is out of the question. On

A CLOSE SHAVE.

Saturday last a gentleman, being too late for the coach, hired a light carriage with an exceedingly good horse ; he left Tunbridge Wells at three in the afternoon, but was not able to reach Lewes till after nine at night."

These statements were, in the main, corroborated by the Editor of the *Brighton Gazette*, who declared that Fleet had told him how fearful he was of meeting with an accident whenever his coach was at all heavily laden. Poor Fleet's prognostications of evil were unhappily destined to be realised, though not quite in the manner he expected. In June 1827 he was driving his coach from Tunbridge Wells, when, in the words of the local paper, one of the leaders became unmanageable. What a stereotyped phrase this was in the old newspapers ! What particular form of unmanageableness this leader indulged in we are not told ; but Fleet adopted the somewhat unusual course of descending from his box to quiet him. While engaged in so doing, one of the " hinder " horses—the writer of the paragraph was, perhaps, not very well up in coaching terms, and so may have given a somewhat incorrect version—made a sudden spring, and knocked down Fleet, over whose legs both wheels of the coach passed. Almost by a miracle, as it would seem, neither of his limbs was broken, though both of course were bruised and lacerated : luckily there chanced to be some one on the coach who could drive, so the vehicle reached Brighton in safety.

Possibly the slightly improved state of the road— for the Commissioners appear to have been roused to some sort of a sense of duty—contributed towards an increase of traffic between Brighton and Tunbridge Wells. At any rate, Crosweller, Fleet, & Smith, as the firm now was, put on a second coach in 1819, and ran three times a week, instead of twice, in the winter.

S

Poor Fleet, however, did not live long to enjoy the increased business, as he was killed by the overturning of his coach on the 19th of February 1832. The inquest was held at the Corn-Market House; and, from the evidence, it appeared that the coach had proceeded from Brighton having two ladies inside, with Fleet's niece and a sailor as outside passengers. The only person who could relate how the fatality occurred was Charles Bunker, a coach-porter, who had gone, as he was in the habit of doing, to meet the coach at the George Inn, where he jumped upon the vehicle. According to this man's evidence, Fleet did not put on the skid when going down the steep hill by Vale Royal; the horses broke into a gallop, and Fleet could not steady them; but in order, perhaps, to keep the coach in the road, he hit the off wheeler, and this just finished the work. The horses were completely out of his hand; he handed the whip to his box-seat passenger, and tried his best to stop, but returned no answer to Bunker, who asked if he should get down and try to put the skid on. Just as he was about to turn into the lower road, by Vale Royal, the coach went over, Fleet being thrown off with such violence that he broke a post against which he fell. The porter declared that Fleet had not skidded down the hill for the past three months. He was taken to the Kentish Hotel, put to bed, and everything was done to save his life, but he died from severe injuries to his head at half-past ten o'clock, before his wife, who had been sent for, could arrive.

Stockdale, a Tunbridge Wells coachman, happened to be on the jury, and had a good deal to say about the badness of the roads, and the dangerous state of the turning where the accident happened. It seems, however, perfectly clear, and the jury thought so too, that the immediate cause of the accident was, not the badness of the roads, but Fleet's unfortunate omission to put the skid on going down the steep hill; and it was not a little curious that the poor man, who had for years expressed himself as dreading an accident owing to the dangerous condition of the roads, should at last have met his death through an accident to which he himself materially contributed. The jury, by the way, returned a verdict of "Accidental Death," with a deodand of twenty shillings against the coach.

In the summer of 1832, "Crosweller & Co." put on a new coach called the Star; it left Brighton (the Blue Office) at four o'clock, and returned at eleven next morning. Fleet's successor was Henry Strevens, a member of a well-known coaching family; but, like Fleet, he was killed (in October 1834) by the over-turning of his coach. This fatality occurred near Lewes, Strevens being the only person outside the coach : the real cause of the accident was never ascertained ; but it was conjectured that the pole broke, and that the coach ran up against the bank at the roadside. The ill-luck which appeared to overtake the coachmen on the Brighton to Tunbridge Wells road nearly claimed as a victim William Boxall, who drove the Royal Blue —the coach from which Fleet and Strevens were killed. Boxall was returning to Tunbridge from Frant in a one-horse chaise between eight and nine o'clock at night, when he met a horse and cart travelling at a fairly brisk pace. It being dark, neither of the drivers appears to have seen the other; so, on the vehicles coming into collision, Boxall's chaise, being the lighter of the two, turned over, Boxall himself being somewhat hurt, though in a few weeks he had sufficiently recovered to drive the Royal Blue again. Boxall's horse, kicking itself clear of the body of the chaise, started off at full gallop, with the shafts dangling about its heels, and

ran with such violence against a shut turnpike gate as
to break it.

Just before the happening of this occurrence—that is
to say, just after Christmas 1836—so much snow fell
around Tunbridge Wells that by neither of the two
roads could the coaches proceed to Brighton. The
snow had, in some places, drifted to a depth of eight
or ten feet; and, curiously enough, there had been a
very violent snowstorm on the corresponding day (the
27th December) of the previous year. For several days
the London coaches had to go out with eight horses,
and about a week elapsed before they could travel with
fewer than six.

In the year 1839 the Tunbridge Wells and Maidstone
coaches running from the Blue Office, which was still
in Crosweller's name, were the Royal Blue and Defiance,
each running three days a week, the former through
Lewes, Maresfield, Uckfield, Groombridge, Tunbridge
Wells, and Tunbridge town; and the latter through
Lewes, Uckfield, and Crowborough to Tunbridge
Wells, whence a light omnibus ran to Tunbridge
town. Both coaches reached Maidstone in time to
enable passengers to catch coaches for Chatham,
Rochester, Sittingbourne, Ashford, and Canterbury.
In 1840 the Blue Office became the property of
Strevens; and in July of the same year Tunbridge
Wells was visited, apparently for the first time, by
one of the steam-carriages, which had given rise, as
we have already seen, to so great an amount of curio-
sity at Brighton. It ran to the Calverley Park Hotel,
ascending the hills with apparent ease, and left for
London in the afternoon. Shortly after this—that is
to say, on the 26th of May 1842—the South-Eastern
Railway was opened as far as Tunbridge, and at once
threw out of gear all the stage-coaching arrangements.
All the coach advertisements underwent a great change,

being henceforth confined, at least for a short time, to the coaches and other conveyances which brought passengers from Tunbridge Wells, Maidstone, Hastings, St. Leonards, Rye, Tenterden, and Cranbrook, to catch the rail at Tunbridge.

CHAPTER XV.

BRIGHTON'S CROSS-COUNTRY COACHES CONTINUED.

BRIGHTON TO WORTHING, CHICHESTER, PORTSMOUTH, BATH, AND BRISTOL.

IN early days, when Worthing was a comparatively unknown place, it must have been the scene of no little coaching bustle. It had a coach of its own to London, there were one or two from Brighton quite early in the century, while coaches to and from the places mentioned at the head of this chapter passed daily through it. As time went on, extra coaches were established to run to Worthing, until at last there were half a dozen or more in commission, exclusive of the coaches to Portsmouth and Arundel.

In 1807 the new road, by Lower Lancing, was planned, and its opening at the end of 1808 shortened the distance by two miles. Scarcely was it available for traffic, however, than a severe frost set in, and this being followed by a sudden thaw early in January 1809, the newly laid road was rendered almost impassable, and so the old road was opened up again. But this had for a considerable distance been dug out, the metal being taken to the new road; consequently, according to the *Brighton Herald* of January 7, 1809, the mail-coach and other vehicles had to drive over the turf, "which was also in a bad state."

The following year (1810) we come across an early instance of racing between two of the Worthing coaches. A Mr. Coles's coach left Worthing ten minutes before its proper time, and on getting to the

Sussex Pad the coachman drew his vehicle across the road so as to avoid being passed by the other; but, as he stopped to water at Shoreham, he lost the advantage, and both coaches then went along at a pace described as having been eleven or twelve miles an hour. A passenger persuaded the rival coachman to let Coles go by, which he did, but informed the passenger that he had received orders to get in first, even though he should lose a horse! Coles's coach, having cleared the other at a gallop, turned over at the corner at Buckingham Farm-house. Coles had both his legs broken, and was in other ways so seriously injured that he died on the next day, and at the inquest the jury gave a deodand of £30 against the coach and horses.

Nothing more of importance appears to have been chronicled, except that, in 1806, there was a royal mail, with a guard, running between Brighton and Chichester. It set out from the Blue Coach-Office, 44 East Street, every morning at seven o'clock precisely, reaching Chichester in five hours, but in after years this distance (thirty miles) was comfortably covered in three hours.

The first Portsmouth coach of which I can find mention was running in 1791, and it took two days to accomplish the journey. This road appears in many ways to have been a somewhat unlucky one, as in 1807 one of the Portsmouth coaches turned over; the coachman was killed on the spot, and some of the passengers were very severely injured; while only a few months later the Portsmouth and London mails collided. The man who was driving the London mail into the yard was thrown from the box and very seriously injured.

At seven o'clock in the morning the Portsmouth coach, passing through Shoreham, Worthing, Arundel, and Chichester, left Crosweller's Blue Office; and, on reaching Portsmouth, connected with coaches for Southampton, Salisbury, Bath, and Bristol, and for some

years apparently there was no rival vehicle. It may
here be incidentally mentioned that the journey from
Portsmouth to Bath was done in twenty-four hours,
and that the fare to Bristol was £3 inside and £2
outside.

In 1809 there was rather a novel race on the Portsmouth road, a man named Birch undertaking, for a
wager of five guineas, to run against the mail from
Brighton to Haresfoot Hill, between Arundel and
Chichester, a distance of twenty-three miles, and, to
the surprise of many people, the pedestrian beat the
coach by twenty minutes ; but possibly the value of
this performance may be somewhat discounted by
remembering that the mail went no faster than six
miles an hour. It would seem, however, that this
mail did not give entire satisfaction, as in the spring
of 1812 advertisements appeared in the county papers
announcing that persons willing to contract for the
conveyance of His Majesty's mails on horseback, or in
a light cart, from Portsmouth and Brighton to Chichester, through Shoreham, Worthing, and Arundel,
at the rate of six miles an hour, stoppages included,
might communicate with Anthony Scott, the District
Surveyor of the General Post-Office ; or it may have
been that the Post-Office were desirous of establishing
a second mail.

A little later on a somewhat awkward accident happened to one of the inside passengers of Crosweller's
coach. The inside passengers consisted of a man, a
lady, and her child. According to the local paper, the
man was " seized with insanity," and bit the lady in a
most shocking manner about the face and arms. The
coachman and the outside passengers, hearing the
screams, got down and secured the maniac, and the
papers, a few days later, seemed a good deal relieved
at discovering that the madman's victim was—his wife ;

on the assumption, one may suppose, that a man may do what he likes with his own.

A year or two later, Thomas Cross, of Portsmouth, who was either the writer of "The Autobiography of a Stage-Coachman" or the writer's father, joined Crosweller and others in the proprietorship of the Portsmouth coach; but, whatever their takings were, the proceedings which took place about the middle of August must, one would imagine, have turned a possible profit into a certain loss. On one day Cross and his partners were fined £97 for carrying more than the proper number of passengers outside the coach, while a day or two later penalties amounting to £75 were inflicted on the same firm. This information was not laid by a professional informer, but by an official who had been ordered to direct the magistrates' attention to the frequent breach of the law. He also said that he had warned all the coachmasters that he should look out, and take proceedings if the statutes were infringed.

For the third or fourth time this coach of Crosweller's turned over in 1815, owing to the breaking of an axle; but, although she was fully loaded, nobody appears to have been hurt; and only a day or two afterwards, a coachman, who was presumably on one of Crosweller's coaches, and who was described as being as bold, if not as discreet, as Blücher, was called upon to answer the twofold charge of having unmercifully whipped one of his horses, and driving his coach against a gig, for which he had to pay the sum of forty shillings and costs. Then a couple of years later, Crosweller's Portsmouth coach again came to grief. So far as can be gathered from the rather meagre account, the water seems to have been out and to have flooded the road, and while going through the water it was that the coach capsized, precipitating the nine outside passengers into the flood : " they were, however, all rescued," says the newspaper.

The Swan Inn at Chichester was for a long time a well-known coaching house, one of its apartments being, in fact, the coach-office; but it was a very old building, and very much out of repair. Early in January 1817 a chimney was blown down, the débris falling on the Swan : some of it crashed through the roof of the coach-office, and did damage to other portions of the structure. This accident had the effect of hastening on the repairs which were so urgently needed, and about eighteen months later it was reopened, having been entirely rebuilt.

The other coaching house in Chichester was the Dolphin, and here it was, in May 1820, that the passengers by the Western mail had a narrow escape from an accident. The coachman had pulled up to change horses, and the passengers took advantage of the halt to get some refreshment. Barely, however, had the last one gained the ground than the leaders suddenly sprang away, the coach being turned over by coming into collision with a cart.

During the summer of 1821 an increase of traffic appears to have warranted Crosweller in putting on a second coach to Portsmouth, and also a light post-coach to Southampton direct; while, in the following year, the Portsmouth Defiance was put on, to run from Genn's Office, 135 North Street, and 3 Castle Square, to Portsmouth in six hours. It left Brighton every day at noon, and returned at eight in the morning; while Orton & Herbert started the accommodation coach between Brighton and Chichester, doing the distance in four hours, the offices being the Swan at Chichester, and 53 East Street, Brighton.

Meantime Snow was working the short road to Worthing with considerable energy. The Eclipse left the Spread Eagle Office, 18 Castle Square, for Worthing at a quarter to ten in the morning, the Magnet leaving at six at night; and as there was still room for another coach, it made its appearance in the form of the New Magnet. The arrangement was that the Magnet left Worthing for Brighton at half-past eight in the morning, and returned from Brighton (as already stated) at six in the evening. The New Magnet, on the other hand, left Brighton at half-past ten and returned at three; while the Eclipse, which left Brighton for Worthing at half-past nine, returned from Worthing at six.

The provincial roads about this time were being very greatly patronised; and, in 1825, Mr. John Walker, of Michel Grove, and John Snow started a new coach, called the Champion, from Brighton to Chichester, taking the coast route *viâ* Worthing, Littlehampton, and Bognor.

Mr. John Walker, who was known as "The Squire," was a well-known hunting man in Sussex, and he also ran a coach from Bognor to London, which was put on under somewhat peculiar circumstances. The story is told in a little book called "Reminiscences of Old Coaching Days," written by Mr. James Town, himself an old coachman, but described on the cover of this work (which, by the way, costs but a penny, and a most excellent pennyworth it is)[1] as "job and posting master to the late Queen Amelia," Royal Mews and Steyne Mews, Worthing.

Before Squire Walker started the Bognor coach, he sent word to his groom in London to send a horse called "Rollin" to be sold at Tattersall's. It chanced, however, that in the stud was also a valuable horse called "Robin," and the groom, misreading the letter, promptly sent the valuable Robin to Tattersall's, leaving

---

[1] Published by Walter Paine, Worthing.

the worthless Rollin at home.   Shortly afterwards Mr.
Walker went to town, and, in going through the stables,
missed the peerless Robin, after whom he promptly
inquired, only to be told by his servant, "You sent
word to me to sell him."

"No, no," replied Mr. Walker, "nothing of the
kind; I told you to sell Rollin.   Why, I would not have
taken any money for Robin."

He then inquired who bought the horse, and on
learning that it was Mr. George Cross, the Littlehampton coach proprietor, the Squire became somewhat
pacified, believing that from his neighbour he could
easily get the horse back, and so lost no time in going
to Littlehampton.

"Mr. Cross," said he, "I hear you bought my horse
at Tattersall's?"

"Yes, Squire, I did," replied Cross.

"Well, then," rejoined Mr. Walker, "I must have
him back again; I didn't mean my groom to sell him."

"Oh no, you can't have him back, sir," said Cross
very decidedly.

This denial put Mr. Walker in a towering rage, and
he took his departure threatening to ruin Cross; and,
by way of carrying his threat into execution, he started
coaches from Bognor to London in opposition to
those run by Cross.   The latter's coaches used to
run through Arundel, down Berry Hill, through Pul-
borough and Clemsfold, striking the Worthing road at
Bear Green.   Mr. Walker, however, in order the more
effectually to carry into execution the ruination of the
obstinate Cross, went to the expense of making a road
by Long Furlong out by the kennels at Findon, so that
he could get to London before Cross.   The coach was
horsed in capital style, and nearly always had matched
teams.   The four blacks were succeeded by four
greys; but when it came to piebalds, Mr. Walker could

only find three; so to complete the team he bought a white-grey, and had him painted so that he should match the others. His brother, Mr. Richard Walker, horsed the coach on the other side of the road; but the two brothers had separate stables, and different changes on the road.

They may be called the pioneers of comfortable coaching, for the outside seats had nice soft cushions, and the backs of the seats and the roof-irons were padded, so that the passengers might sit and lean in greater comfort. All this, however, could not make the coaches paying concerns. It used to be said in old days that no man saw his money back if he gave more than £40 for a coach-horse, because the horse did not last long enough to work it out; and as the brothers Walker sometimes gave as much as sixty guineas for a horse they liked, it required, as " Nimrod " remarked, sixpences to be turned into ninepences to make the thing a success.

Mr. Walker's first coachman was little Phil Butcher, an exceedingly good performer, and he had a great reputation in Sussex. This coach, however, did not last more than two years, by which time Mr. Walker appears to have got rid of his money. He then sold Michel Grove to the present Duke of Norfolk's great-grandfather; the house was pulled down, and the park cut up into farms. The clock-tower, I believe, stands on the hill now, but the clock itself was given to Steyning, and a few years ago could be seen in the High Street.

Meantime Cross flourished and kept to the road, until, like other proprietors, he was driven off by the railway. The Champion coach, it may be mentioned, left the Spread Eagle Office, 18 Castle Square, at four o'clock in the afternoon for the Anchor Inn, Chichester, whence it returned every morning at eight. It reached

Worthing in an hour and a half—that is to say, at half-past five—and an hour later had left Littlehampton. The *Brighton Gazette* lost no time in patting the new venture on the back; but on Mr. Walker's other coach—that is to say, the one running between Bognor and London—being capsized while coming from town, so heavily laden as to require six horses to draw it, it gently chided the coachman, and expressed a hope that the mishap might prove a warning to fast drivers.

In 1826 Thomas Cross—presumably Mr. Walker's old enemy—appears to have joined hands with John Snow, and the two together started a new coach called the Earl of Arran to Bognor, the route being over the new ferry at Littlehampton. She left the Spread Eagle Office, 18 Castle Square, every morning at nine, running through Shoreham, Worthing, Angmering, and Littlehampton, returning at five o'clock. The proprietors, no doubt, did well in striking out these new routes. The novelty of crossing the river Arun, and the picturesque scenery there observed, could not fail to make this an " interesting excursion," the word " excursion " sounding rather strangely as applied to coaching in the old days.

Working on the stage between Chichester and Arundel in 1827 was a rather notable steed—that is to say, the roan horse which took Weare and his murderer, Thurtell, on their memorable expedition; while on the Petworth and Brighton road was the horse which, while running leader in the Exeter mail, was, in 1816, attacked on Salisbury Plain by the lioness which had escaped from a menagerie. This was a thoroughbred horse called Pomegranate, by Sir Solomon out of Fantail. He was foaled in 1809, and was bred by Lord Scarborough. From time to time we hear of horses with more or less of a history attaching to them earning their living in coaches on the Brighton, as well as other roads. The man who horsed a coach had no fancies; he took everything that could be bought at his price; so, for the middle ground, ex-racers, hunters, and harness horses all came to him, many of them, of course, because, by reason of vice or some other infirmity, they were useless to every one else.

It is difficult to account for all the accidents to coaches caused by the horses taking fright before everything was ready for a start. Nearly every coach would appear to have come more or less to grief from this cause; and we find the horses of one of the Worthing coaches emulating the famous steed "Hercules" at Laverock Wells. The team started out of the yard, and, galloping down Market Street and across High Street, dashed through the window of a tailor's shop. The horse-keeper, a man named Sandal, did his best to stop the horses, but was thrown under the wheels and had both his legs broken. Two little girls, who were going to have a ride from the yard to the office, were unhurt; but the horses were a good deal cut with the broken glass. "We will not attempt," says a contributor to a local paper, "to describe the consternation produced in the tailor's shop by the crash." Of blind horses there were plenty on all coach roads in England; nor were they disliked by coachmen, for they were seldom guilty of any vagaries, and, as a rule, trusted implicitly to the honour of their driver, who had, of course, to remember that he was driving a blind horse or horses. I think it is either Mr. Birch Reynardson or Captain Malet who tells the story of an old coachman who, after driving over a narrow and awkward bridge, turned to his box-seat passenger with the remark, "Well over that, sir; only one eye amongst us." The one eye was his own; his horses were all blind. A blind horse, however, which drew the Chichester

mail-cart was an exception to the general rule. While
waiting for the bags at the Post-Office in West Street,
he suddenly bolted, and ran with such violence against
Dr. M'Carogher's door as to smash it in pieces and to
kill itself.

If we may place implicit credit in the *Brighton
Gazette*, there was, after all, something in the safety
coaches. The Independent Chichester coach was delayed for some time owing to one of the wheels having
become " deranged." No one was hurt, nor was the
coach upset; and then the writer of the paragraph in
question somewhat hastily jumps to the conclusion
that the coach must have turned over but for the
superior principle upon which the patent wheels on
which the coach ran were constructed. An ordinary
coach, however, one of Nelson's, which was unprovided
with safety appliances, was turned over just afterwards
through the axle breaking; but happily none of the
passengers were injured.

Inquiry is often made as to the derivation of the
word "cad;" but without going into that question,
it is sufficient to mention that the word frequently
appears in the newspapers of this (1829) and of an anterior date in connection with coaches. On this coach
of Nelson's, for instance, turning over, "some cads"
were sent to take the coach home; but, instead of
leading the horses, they mounted the coach, and, with
the courage begotten of ignorance, attempted to have
a free drive. On turning a corner, the coach was a
second time overturned, and one of the "cads," less
fortunate than the passengers, had his thigh fractured,
while two others were severely injured.

Snow's Defiance continued to run to Portsmouth
from the Spread Eagle Office, 18 Castle Square; and
in November 1830 the Nimrod, a new fast coach,
doing the journey in six hours, was put on, and started

from Orton's Coach-Office, East Street, Brighton, on
Mondays, Wednesdays, and Fridays; while from Crosweller's Blue Office ran another post-coach to Portsmouth every afternoon at three o'clock.

For some time coaches had run from Brighton to
Bath and Bristol; but, in the spring of 1831, the Red
Rover, a coach turned out in the best style, was put
on the road to do the journey in sixteen hours; but so
few passengers did it carry for the first few weeks of
its career, that it was generally voted a very losing affair.
It took no more than three hours to go from Brighton
to Chichester, thirty miles, and travelled over the
remainder of the road at a like pace. It had not,
however, long been started before a lady, an inside
passenger, had a somewhat narrow escape. The coach
was being driven round a sharp corner at Titchfield,
when the pole of a gentleman's carriage came through
the window, and struck the lady on the temple. She
was fortunately able to get out of the way, but the
blow was sufficiently severe to cause the coach to delay
for an hour. The Red Rover ran through Southampton,
as did the other Bristol coach, and these, together with
other concerns going to or through the same place,
gave rise to such keen competition, that, for upwards
of a week, passengers were carried the whole way, from
Brighton to Southampton, at five shillings a head.

The Red Rover, in spite of its poor beginning,
appears to have afterwards met with better patronage,
as in the summer of 1832 the Little Red Rover started
from the Clarence Hotel, Brighton, to run daily to
Bath and Bristol in opposition, and both seem to have
carried plenty of passengers. Then the enterprising
J. Snow & Co. determined to accelerate the Red Rover,
so she ran the journey in fifteen hours, the distance
being 138 miles; but in 1836 the coach was advertised
as belonging to Crosweller. In January of the last-

T

named year the Red Rover met with an accident which
might have been attended with very serious results. One
of the horses jibbing at the top of a hill, the coach was,
in some curious way, drawn under a tree the branches
of which drew the coachman from his seat as the
coach passed beneath them. The jibber gave up his
jibbing, and all four horses ran at a great pace without
a coachman for a couple of miles, when they showed
how great is the horse "intelligence," which some
people can so readily discern, by turning into a hedge.
They fell all of a heap, and one of them was killed.
On finding that the horses had "gone," the guard
slipped down behind the coach, and hung on by the
rail till the coach was stopped, when he let out the
inside passengers, who were in complete ignorance of
what had happened ; while on the next day the coachman of one of the Chichester and Portsmouth coaches,
while in the act of getting off the coach to alter some
part of the harness, fell to the ground with sufficient force
to break one of the bones in his foot.   Early in June
1832 the Defiance Portsmouth coach was upset at
Lancing, on its way to Brighton ; but although there
were sixteen inside and outside passengers, no one was
seriously hurt, and, after a delay of three hours, a mail-
coach arrived from Brighton to take the people on,
while one of the leaders in the Red Rover fell dead
just as the coach had started from the Swan Inn,
Chichester.

It was no more than a few years before that the Brighton folk were congratulating themselves on the excellence of their mail arrangements ; but, owing to some
newly started plan, the letters to and from places on the
Portsmouth road were so much delayed that they were
not, in 1836, delivered until the second day ; but this
state of things was partially remedied by the putting
on of a new Gloucester mail by way of Southampton

and Salisbury, by which the communication with the
western portion of the country and beyond Portsmouth
was much facilitated, and places as far away as Dorking
and Dulwich derived no little benefit from the fresh
arrangement. All went well till the time of the snowstorm, to which, so far as the main road is concerned,
reference has been made at page 212.

The account of how the Gloucester mail-bags were
eventually brought to Brighton reads more like an
extract from the journal of an Arctic expedition than a
narrative of anything in connection with the English
Post-Office, with the scene laid within a few miles of
our most fashionable watering-place.

The Manchester and Liverpool mails were so long
delayed by stress of weather, that the Brighton mail
was three hours late in leaving Gloucester. The
coachman made fairly good travelling till about a
mile before reaching Worthing, and then the snow
fell so thickly that both coachman and guard thought
they would be unable to proceed. Taylor, the guard,
then got down, and, finding a finger-post near at
hand, was enabled to turn the horses' heads the
right way.

With the utmost difficulty the mail struggled on to
Shoreham, and on reaching the bonding pond, on
the Brighton side of the last-named place, the leaders
tumbled over a bank, but, luckily for the welfare of
the whole concern, the main bar snapped, and let the
leaders free, or the coach would have been upset to
a certainty. As luck had it, a pedestrian who was
making his way through the snow at this point
volunteered his services, and with his aid the coach
was righted; while, as he was going on to Shoreham, he
was asked to send some guides back to the coach.
Two men came on in answer to the appeal for aid;
but so terrible in its force was the storm, that, after

accompanying the coach for a short distance, their hearts failed them, and they returned whence they came.

With praiseworthy pluck, however, coachman and guard fought against what must have seemed overwhelming odds, and reached the Schooner public-house, between Copperas Gap and Southwick, where six feet of snow were found on the near side of the road. Here further aid offered itself, the *deus ex machinâ* in this case being the Worthing mail-cart on its way to Brighton. The mail-man took on the bags, and so lightened the coach and the minds of coachman and guard, who thought that they would have no difficulty in keeping the mail-cart in sight or of following in its track. The snow, however, drove in their faces with such violence, that they soon lost all traces of the cart, and one only wonders how that vehicle managed to get along so well; but mail-men, even the modern ones, have a knack of their own in accomplishing their journeys.

The British sailor, in the form of Lieutenant Stephens (of the coastguard) and one of his men, next came to the rescue, conducting the coach as far towards Brighton as their district extended, after which Lieutenant Franklin not only took the mail in tow and acted as guide as far as Hove, but took coachman and guard into his house and refreshed them. By this time the guard was greatly exhausted, having been up for twenty-four hours—guards invariably travelled longer distances than did coachmen. At length, thanks to the services of the coastguard, the mail-coach arrived at the Brighton Post-Office, and even then poor Taylor had no little difficulty in getting to his house in Middle Street.

Instances of coach-horses starting away by themselves, and running for several miles without bringing

the coach to harm, are common enough; and the
Times Southampton coach is only one of the many
examples given. The coachman got down to deliver
a parcel, and handed the reins to a gentleman while
he got down. The horses ran off, but the gentleman
was, as the *Brighton Gazette* pointed out, " no jarvey,"
as in a short time one of the wheel horses had broken
his bit, the other had got rid of his bridle, and one
of the leaders managed to break the reins. In these
circumstances the gentleman who held the reins could
have had little to do with guiding the horses; but,
to the infinite joy of the coachman, who had followed
on horseback, they pulled up as usual at the next
changing place, having brought about no further
damage than the breaking of the harness already
mentioned.

The papers for February 1840 contain accounts of
a sad accident which overtook the Brighton and
Southampton coach, and resulted in the death of the
coachman, Upfold, a man who was much respected.
As he was the victim of a strange run of ill-luck,
it may not be uninteresting, before relating how he
met his death, to give a slight sketch of his previous
career.

At the time of his death, Upfold was fifty-four years
of age, and had been driving a coach for about thirty-
five years. Like most other coachmen, he had had his
accidents and his narrow escapes; but, about the spring
of 1831, there commenced a series of mishaps which
eight years later culminated in his death. In the
above-mentioned year his coach turned over, and
Upfold broke his leg. Scarcely had he resumed his
duties on the box than the fore-axle of the coach
broke, and an upset was the result; and though there
were a dozen passengers, none of them appear to
have been hurt; but two or three fell upon the unlucky

Upfold, and he sustained some rather severe injuries. On the 5th of January 1832 he pulled up at Bosham Pond, about three miles from Chichester, and went into the inn leaving the reins in the hands of the box-seat passenger, the only person with him on the coach. No sooner, however, had Upfold crossed the threshold of the house than the passenger quietly dropped the reins and entered the inn too. The former, knowing that his horses were unlikely to stand still if left unattended, rushed out of the house just in time to see the team moving off. In his efforts to stop them, one of them kicked or struck him so severely in the calf of the leg that the limb was laid open. The kick caused Upfold to fall between the wheels, and the hind ones passing over him, broke the other leg. The horses then galloped off, and were not stopped until they reached Chichester.

This brings us to the year 1840, when Upfold's career was cut short by the accident before mentioned. The coach was on its way to Brighton, and about a mile beyond Broadwater there were two right-angled turns on hilly ground, which, says the report, had always been looked upon as dangerous. According to the account in the papers, the accident was caused neither by the corners nor by the hills, but simply because the coachman "inadvertently pulled the wrong rein;" and this version is borne out by the evidence of Mr. Pasco, of Chichester, who was on the box-seat. That gentleman deposed that Upfold was perfectly sober, and that all went well till the time came to make the first of the two right-angled turns above mentioned; and this turn was so badly made as to call forth a protest from Mr. Pasco, who said, "Upfold, what are you at with the horses?" His reply was, "I have pulled the wrong rein." Thereupon Mr. Pasco remarked, "Mind what you are about, and pull

the right one this time." The coach turned over
directly afterwards, and both Mr. Pasco and Upfold
were firmly caught by it. The rail of the box-seat appears to have pressed upon Upfold, who, being a very
stout man, undoubtedly kept the weight of the vehicle
off Mr. Pasco, though he too was caught by the legs
and was unable to extricate himself. A newsman
named Farrant, who was riding on the coach, rendered
valuable assistance, and when aid arrived and Mr.
Pasco was recovered, Upfold was found to be quite
dead. On this fatal occasion Upfold was driving a
unicorn team, and both Mr. Pasco and Farrant, the
newsman, agreed that Upfold pulled the wrong rein,
and did not appear to have the least control over
his single leader while going round the corners. The
evidence given at the inquest is fully set out in the
Brighton papers, but the accident is not satisfactorily
explained; for surely a man who had been driving
the same road for five-and-thirty years ought, humanly
speaking, to be safe on any road, and at any corners
round which it was possible to drive a coach. But
after Upfold's death bad luck continued to attend
the Times Southampton coach, for scarcely had Holds-
worth, Upfold's successor, fairly settled down to work
than the fore-axle broke, though happily no one was
injured; and a month or two later the coach overturned through a wheel coming off.

In 1841 omnibuses and trains play an important
part in the advertisements of the cross-country coaches,
just as in the case of those on the main road to
London. Snow's and other offices were shut up at
Shoreham and Worthing, everything pointing to
the speedy dissolution of the coaching business.
Proprietors were, however, on the look-out to make
hay so long as there was any sunshine at all; so
Strevens, of the Blue Coach-Office, hit upon the ex-

pedient of running to Portsmouth a daily coach by way
of Littlehampton Ferry and Bognor. The Brighton
end of the coach was put on the railway at nine
o'clock, and travelled by train to Shoreham, whence
it went by road; and the other coach returned to
Brighton by train from Shoreham; while new coaches
were started from Bognor, Littlehampton, and Arundel
for Shoreham, at which point the passengers could
take the train for Brighton. It was of course now
merely a question of time before the line of railway opened farther and farther, and drove all the
branch coaches off the road. This was not long in
coming, and, so far as Brighton is concerned, there
was but one coach running in and out of the place
after 1844, and that was Capps's Victoria, already
mentioned.[1]

THE WINDSOR, READING, AND OXFORD ROADS.

So far as can be ascertained, there was but little connection between Brighton, Windsor, and Oxford in the
early part of the present century; and the chances are
that a coach did not run direct between Brighton and
Windsor before the time of the Regency, when there
was necessarily a somewhat close connection between
the two places. For our present purpose, it is sufficient
to say that in 1822 the Hero coach ran from Hine's
Office, 52 East Street, at six o'clock on Tuesdays,
Thursdays, and Saturdays, to the Star and Angel Hotels,
Oxford, by way of Henfield, Horsham, Guildford,
Farnham, Odiham, Reading, and Wallingford; and
from Oxford coach communication could be obtained
with the West of England and North and South
Wales: the proprietors were Hine, Costar. Howe,

---

[1] Page 244.

Monk, & Co. In the same year there ran from Crosweller's Blue Coach-Office, at nine o'clock on Mondays,
Wednesdays, and Fridays, a coach to Windsor through
Henfield, Horsham, Guildford, Ripley, and Chertsey.
Except that the hours of departure from Brighton
became later, there was no material change in these
arrangements for the next few years.

It has been my good fortune to make the acquaintance of one of the few surviving coachmen who drove
in and out of Brighton in the thirties, and who was
more particularly concerned with this Windsor and
Oxford road.

Mr. John Millis, born in 1809, and now resident
in Brighton, comes of a family of coachmen.   His
father drove on the Rochester road so long ago at
least as 1813, and five or six of his relations worked
in and out of Brighton.   His uncle drove the Irresistible (see page 106), and afterwards drove Crosweller's True Blue, which ran to the Boar and Castle,
Oxford Street ; and when the regular coachman was unable, or was indisposed, to make the journey to London,
his deputy, as often as not, was Mr. John Millis above
mentioned.   Mr. Millis's own road, however, was from
Brighton to Windsor, his coach being the Royal Sovereign ; and, as illustrating the ups and downs of coaching, he told me that on more than one occasion he has
had a waybill showing upwards of seventeen pounds
as the result of a single journey between Windsor
and Brighton.   But, as my informant explained, "there
was no opposition ; we carried everything ; " and tre-
mendous loads the coach carried.   In the summer
the coach was doubled, another member of the family
driving on the other side of the road.   As a set-off,
however, to these remunerative waybills, Mr. Millis
came from Windsor to Brighton one Christmas Day
without a single passenger.   He had no guard, and

so was absolutely by himself; while a single shilling, paid for the carriage of a small parcel, represented the whole of the coach's earnings on that eventful day, when the snow lay deep, and the journey could not have been a pleasant one.

The Oxford coach, the Hero, ran, as I have already said, in 1822 and the following year, from Hine's Office, 52 East Street; but in 1826 it was advertised to start from the Blue Office, and this arrangement prevailed down to 1833, when it went to Hine's Office again, starting at seven in the morning, and reaching Oxford at eight in the evening. Appended to the advertisement was the notice that the Hero was the only coach direct from Brighton to Oxford, the reason being that Crosweller had started an opposition Oxford coach, called the Protector, as far as Farnham, and to this concern Mr. J. Millis was appointed coachman; but the curious thing is that a year or two later—that is to say, in 1835—the Hero is once more advertised to start from the Blue Coach-Office, and is described as being the property of Hone & Co., and not as Crosweller's; while an advertisement to the same effect appears in the papers for 1837. By 1838 Crosweller was dead, and the firm then appeared as Strevens, Hone, & Co. Strevens had been a booking-clerk in the office, but during the period of Crosweller's illness Strevens had managed the large business, and now figured as senior partner.

While Mr. Millis was driving the opposition Oxford coach to Farnham (by Guildford) he had a narrow escape from a bad accident. Mr. Lacoste, of Guildford, who horsed one of the London coaches, had a pulling, head-strong horse, of which the London coachman did not approve, so Lacoste said, " Put him in the Brighton, and let him run the fifteen-mile stage;" when, therefore, Millis reached Guildford on his way to Brighton—he was on a new coach which had been sent out from the factory on the previous day—he found this pulling horse running as his near leader. Those were the days of those abominations the head-terrets—that is to say, the leaders' reins passed through the terrets on the top of the wheelers' heads. The more the leader caught hold, the more uncomfortable did the near wheeler become, until at last he was relieved by the near leading rein breaking close to the head-terret. Both leaders then swerved, and carried the wheelers with them, and the pole broke—the new pole. A footman out of place, who happened to be in the inn near which the accident took place, ran to the leaders' heads, and a capsize was narrowly averted. A new pole and new reins were procured from Guildford, whither a second journey had to be made to obtain the services of a man to do something to the futchells ; but eventually the journey was resumed.

The year 1841 brought with it a change in the route of Strevens's Oxford coach, as in the April of that year the public were informed that the coach left the Blue Office on Tuesday, Thursday, and Saturday mornings at eight, running through Henfield, Horsham, Guildford, Farnham, Odiham, and Reading, *via* the Great Western Railway from Reading to Steventon, whence the coach ran by road to Oxford. In 1842 the Hero had passed into the hands of Capps, Hambleton, & Co., and seems to have run to Reading only, the remainder of the journey being accomplished by train.

Chapter XVI.

THE GROWTH OF COACHMANSHIP.

IN the foregoing pages an effort has been made to trace the growth of stage-coaching so far as it is connected with the Brighton road, while what has been said incidentally indicates the progress on other roads. I have tried to show how in early times the slow and heavy broad-wheeled stage-waggon was the only public means of conveyance; it will also have been noticed how comparatively slow was the growth towards completion. Then came a period of rapid advance, and between, say 1825 and 1836, stage-coaching had risen to a pitch of perfection in its organisation, and in its development, which the boldest would never have ventured to predict for it forty years before. Its rapid downfall, owing to the introduction of the railway, is a matter of history. But the curious thing is that, although we hear, not only on the Brighton, but on all other roads, of new coaches, of Acts of Parliament governing them, and the manners and customs of those who conducted the coaches, and, to a certain extent, of those who travelled by them, we hear simply nothing about the origin or growth of the coachman's art.

To begin at the beginning, as the story-tellers phrase it, I believe I am correct in saying that in the reign of William III. an Act of Parliament was passed providing that all horses in teams should go one behind the other, and not be yoked two abreast;

and it is to the agricultural community that we owe
the repeal of this law, which, upon the face of it,
tells that there could have been no such thing as
coachmanship in those days. Then, if we take a
jump to what may be called the carrier period—which,
for our present purpose, may be taken to be between
1700 and 1760—we are forbidden to think that what
we now designate as coachmanship was even in its
infancy; to my mind it was simply unborn. It was
incumbent upon the man who conducted the lumbering van, even so late as the time when, whether the
horses were two or four in number, they were driven
in hand, to possess a certain amount of skill, but his
skill was rather that of the carter who drives a farm-
cart over a rutted track.

To skip hastily on, we can scarcely think that the
coachmen who took two and three days to get their
horses between London and Brighton were coachmen as we understand the term nowadays. Indeed,
there is every reason to believe that the early coaches
were drawn by two horses only, and that when leaders
were first added they were managed by a postillion.
Yet it seems tolerably certain that some advance
must have been made in the art between the years
1780 and 1800, when the journey between London
and Brighton was accomplished in one day; and here
we must stop for a moment to remark that, so far as I
know, it cannot be discovered who first invented a
pole-hook, or who first devised the convenient arrangement of main and leading bars. I have seen some
woodcuts in old newspapers and on broad-sheets
which would lead one to suppose that when leaders
were first added they drew from the tugs of the
wheelers, just as the leader in a tandem does when
the bar is dispensed with. Then, when bars were
introduced, early pictures would seem to suggest that

the leaders had but one long bar between them.
Yet one cannot discover who planned even this
preliminary step. The invention of the coupling rein,
too, languishes in undeserved obscurity. Nor, again,
can we find out when, or by whom, it was ordered
that the draught rein should be outside, and the
coupling rein inside. Nor are we able to thank
by name the man who first told us how to hold our
reins when driving four horses; while for ancient
driving hints we may search in vain.

This is all the more curious, because in bygone
days the details of horsemanship came in for considerably more disquisition and discussion than at
present, and we have no lack of treatises upon the
art of equitation. For all practical purposes, we may
say that nothing was ever written upon driving until
"Nimrod" penned in the *Sporting Magazine* his
articles which have been reprinted in Captain Malet's
"Annals of the Road." We may remember that the
Benson Driving Club was founded as long ago as
1807, and that the next year saw the foundation of
a similar society, the Four-Horse Club. That association, as one of its members said, broke down
because they had not enough "in hand." It is clear,
therefore, that even at that time a large number of
amateurs drove four-in-hand, for the two clubs
comprised the names of many members, and those
coachmen must have learned the art from some one.
It is, of course, a short answer to say that coachmanship grew by degrees; that one man found out one
thing, and another discovered something else; but
in the days gone by the short wheel-rein, which lay
over the fingers, materially simplified, up to a certain
point, the coachman's labours, though, as "Nimrod"
points out, when going down-hill the coachman
practically drove with the long wheel-rein, inasmuch

as he had to draw the short rein back through his hand to hold his horses.

The chances are, too, that the early coachmen drove with what we should now call a full hand—that is to say, with a finger between each rein—until it was eventually found that the little finger was more useful to press down on the rein in the hand than it was for the purpose of driving or supporting the weight of a rein, as it would have to do with a full hand. The science or art of bitting we may the more easily understand, because a great deal had been written about it, and its importance was well established at the time of the publication of the treatises on horsemanship; but the art of putting horses together could not have made much progress till comparatively fast work was the rule rather than the exception. Any one, however, who reads "Nimrod's" essays will at once understand that all the minutiæ of coachmanship were well understood in his early days, and apparently had been so for some time previously.

And now we come to the use of the whip. In the pages of the *Sporting Magazine* there is a description of the old coachman—an overbearing, drunken, bloated sort of person, who mounted his box in the morning with a dozen whip-points in his buttonhole, and these were no more than sufficient to last him through the day. What sort of whips they had in those days we are unable to tell, for I have never yet been able to come across a genuine specimen of a whip in use a hundred years ago or more. Mr. Schomberg, the well-known whipmaker, tells me that in his opinion ancient whips were strengthened with iron or steel where we now find the quill, and it needs no very great stretch of imagination to come to the conclusion that the ancient whip was a very unfinished article, and one it was

scarcely possible to wield with ease, not to mention
grace.

Then, if we come to later times, there is every
reason for thinking that what we call "catching"
or "folding" a whip was a trouble kept in store for
latter-day coachmen. Let me give an extract from
"Nimrod's" writings. "There are," he says, "as many
ways of whipping a coach-horse as there are horses
on the coach, and as there is a right and a wrong
way of doing most things, a young beginner may
observe the following directions. We will begin with
the wheel horses. Before a coachman hits a wheel
horse he should twist his thong three times round
the crop of the whip, holding the crop at that moment somewhat horizontally, by which means the
thong will twist towards the thin end of the crop,
when the thong being doubled will not exceed the
length of a pair-horse thong, and in some measure
resembles it."

Now, if the thong had been already caught, there
would have been no necessity to take the three turns
to bring the thong "towards the thin end of the crop."
The reason of this, I take it to be, is that when horses
were bad, and whipping was a necessity, the coachman
would have been everlastingly catching and undoing
his whip, had catching it then been in fashion; but
as it was so often required in early days, it could never
have occurred to the greatest coaching genius to devise
a system by which the whip should have been rendered practically useless for at any rate some seconds
at a time.

Nimrod, too, wrote, in the late twenties—"There is
not a tenth part of the punishment administered to
horses in coaches that was to be seen when I first began
to travel with them. At that time the roads were bad,
which destroyed the vigour and courage of the horses

and they were not of so good and well-bred a sort as
we now make use of in coaches. At the time I am
alluding to, no sooner was a coachman on his box and
had started his coach, than he began to show off to
his passengers, by a display of neat strokes with his
whip, whether his horses required punishment or not.
I am ready to admit that some of these old hands
exhibited great execution in this part of their profession, and that, from the comparatively little use that
has been lately made of it, the expert management
of the whip is now rarely to be met with. Amongst
London coachmen I have most particularly noticed a
deficiency here.   I could name a score who are excellent performers as far as fingers go, but when they come
to hit a near-side leader the blow falls powerless, and
brings to one's mind the old joke of the flea biting the
lobster." This was written about sixty-five years ago.

We hear at times a good deal of rubbish talked
about the punishment men could inflict on their
leaders, and on this point, too, let me once more quote
"Nimrod." "It is," he says, "quite a mistaken notion
to suppose that it is in the power of a coachman to
punish a leader with the single, as he can a wheel
horse with the doubled thong. I have heard of those
men who could cut a horse's leg off, and all that; who
could lift him from the ground when before the bar;
but I have never seen the coachman who could mark a
horse with the point of his thong. No doubt the blow
from the single falls very sharp, as it falls on a tender
part—the inside of the thigh." Yet "Nimrod" lived
in the old punishment days.

On the part of one who does not remember the
old school of coaching, and who does not claim to be
a credit to the new, any remarks upon driving, either
ancient or modern, may be deemed presumptuous;
but, at the risk of being thought so, I may be permitted

U

to discuss one or two points which have always somewhat puzzled me.

In the foregoing pages mention has been made of
several accidents, but I have inserted scarcely a tithe
of those I have found reported in the various newspapers. Week after week one reads of the carriage
of a respectable gentleman standing at the door of
an equally respectable tradesman. One of the London
coaches comes down the road, and, as often as not,
collides with the respectable gentleman's carriage. I
have mentioned how a coach was upset on the Pavilion
Parade through the coachman turning so sharply, when
there was no need for him to do so, as to get the coach
on the lock. It may also be seen how men met their
deaths—poor Fleet, for instance, of the Tunbridge
Wells road—by neglecting to skid down a steep hill.
Upfold, the coachman of the Southampton Times, was
killed because, in the dusk of evening, he pulled the
wrong rein in going round a corner; while of coaches
upset by reason of going round corners, hitting or
running into banks, hitting posts, bridges—in fact,
everything that could be run against, one might have
compiled a most imposing list.

Now, with all deference to the heroes of old, I
venture to submit that all these frequent accidents
show that there was something wrong somewhere.
Even a "fresh catched" subscriber to a modern coach
would probably have his cheque returned to him with
thanks if he could not drive down a street without
running into a carriage which might be drawn up at
the kerb, or if he went off the crown of a hill at such
a pace as to prevent him from stopping his horses, even
without the aid of his patent brake; or, in fact, if he did
many other things of which not a few of the Brighton
coachmen (both amateur and professional) were very
frequently guilty of.

Danger, I take it, comes to men and vehicles from all and very many unexpected sources. A man may be so bad a coachman as morally not to be safe with everything in his favour ; but if a man possessed of infinite skill presume upon that skill, and deliberately expose himself and his passengers to needless risks, I fail to see that it is much safer to be driven by him than by the muff who has all his work cut out to drive a made team along the quietest of country roads ; and, in my humble judgment, a man who presumes upon his powers, and thereby brings danger to the coach, is every bit as blamable as a proprietor would be who put up a man who could not drive under favourable circumstances.

It is said, and with perfect truth, that coaching now and coaching in the thirties are two very different things. Be it so. The coachman of old had to drive heavily laden coaches, drawn by, in many cases, inferior horses, over roads which were bad. That they overcame these disadvantages is doubtless creditable to them ; but what was the price paid ? Why, that a horse on a fast coach rarely lasted more than two or three years. But, so far as I can see, there is no reason why our present race of coachmen should not be able to do the same sort of thing with a reasonable amount of practice.

One of the Worthing coachmen was pulled up for furious driving, and it came out in evidence that he had been told by his proprietor to get in before an opposition concern, "even though he should lose a horse." It is said, too, that Mrs. Ann Nelson, on one of her coachmen excusing himself, on the ground of a heavy load and bad roads, for having been beaten by a rival coach, replied, "Never you mind ; I find horses, you find whip-cord." I very much question whether that excellent woman of business ever said anything

of the kind, because, although early coach proprietors
were slow in learning the lesson, it came at last to be
acknowledged that there was no profit in driving a
horse to death. At the same time there is not the
least doubt that, in the fast coaches, horses did not last
long; they, as a rule, cost but little money, and beyond a certain point a proprietor could no more afford
to coddle his coach-horses than can the railway and
steamship companies afford to keep their engines for
ever at half-speed.

Nowadays the coach-horse has more serious claims
on his owner than had the coach-horse of old. They
cost a good deal more than formerly, and almost every
modern proprietor hopes to have a good sale at the
season's end, in order to compensate, in some degree,
for the difference between the amount of passenger
fares and the amount of the expenses. He, therefore,
who knocked his horses about would be defeating his
own ends. Consequently, when it is urged against
the modern coachman that he does not have to keep
time with inferior cattle, heavy loads, and over bad
roads, the statement does not appear to prove that
many of them could not do so if they tried.

Many, at least, of the coachmen of old did what
was required of them, and they did it well; but, in all
fairness, may not the same be said of some modern
performers? The men who habitually drive in and
out of London, through an amount of traffic the like
of which was certainly never beheld by any of the
coachmen of a past era, may surely be credited with
a certain amount of skill. Some coachmen now, as
was the case in days that are past, are better than
others; and, though I do not propose to be guilty of
the impertinence of criticising contemporary coachmen,
amateur or professional, the opinion may be ventured
that there are some of both kinds who would not have

disgraced the box even in the days of Henry Stevenson
and "the Baronet."

"Viator Junior," to whose writings in the *Sporting
Magazine* I have before referred, started a somewhat
curious theory with respect to the race of Brighton
coachmen. He declared that the road between
London and Brighton had been made so good as to
have completely done away with the finished performers; and either he or somebody else wrote that
"anybody could tool a team on a road like that to
Brighton in the style of a Stevenson or 'the Baronet.'"
Nonsense on the face of it, surely, not to mention
the fact that we are told over and over again what fine
coachmen Stevenson and Sir St. Vincent Cotton were.
Our friend "Viator Junior," after having delivered
himself of his sweeping condemnation of Brighton
coachmen, proceeds to bestow the most unsparing
criticism on men who were then at work. He mentioned several by name, and promised to show up
all the remainder, unless an improvement took place.
I do not pretend to dogmatise on these matters; but
for the life of me I cannot understand why a man
should be a bad coachman merely because his road
does not happen to be indented here and there with
two-foot ruts, or because there is not a Lynton Hill
in his route.

The true state of the case probably is that really
first-class men in any calling are, and have always
been, comparatively scarce, and if we could see all
the old Brighton coachmen to-morrow, we should
probably discover that, taken as a body, they were
neither better nor worse than those on any other
road.

To return more particularly to the growth of coachmanship: it would be interesting if we could find
out by whom the different rules for driving were

first framed, and by what school of coachmen they were first adopted.

A year or two ago, under the signature of " Soft Soap," I wrote to the *Field* a letter, wherein was set forth all the contradictory directions to be found on certain points in connection with the driving of four horses, the object being to elicit from coachmen of experience whether there was any one recognised way of doing certain things, and, secondly, what that way might be. The points specially mentioned were—1, the correct position for the left hand; 2, the admissibility of two-handed driving; and 3, the proper way to catch the whip.

Now first with regard to the proper position of the left hand. Some of the writers quoted in the *Field* letter laid it down that the left hand should be kept well up; some others voted for a straight arm, and, rightly or wrongly, a goodly number of the older professionals were of the same opinion, or, to speak more correctly, they were in favour of keeping the hand low. A few years ago I saw at Canterbury the late Mr. Clements, then ninety years of age, and who for many years drove the Eagle between London and Canterbury; in 1892 I saw the late Mr. Glover, of Worthing, who drove the Oxford Retaliator; and a day or two before these lines were written I talked on the subject to Mr. Millis, of whom mention is made in the chapter on the Oxford road. To these I may add the late Tim Carter; and one and all of these experts favoured the low position, without going the length of advocating the straight arm—that is, letting the left arm hang down by the side, as recommended by Colonel Corbett, the author of " An Old Coachman's Chatter." Mr. Millis said, " In my day we used to get our hands down on to the knee; then we had power over our horses." On the other hand, such famous coachmen as Mr. Charles Ward and Mr. E. Fownes advocate keeping the hand up ; and where such authorities differ, who shall decide ?

Now although no one can afford to overlook the importance of small matters in driving or in anything else, it is nevertheless quite possible to make too much of them.

The position of the hand would be unimportant, were it not that rules for position in riding, driving, cricket, rowing, singing, playing a musical instrument— in connection with everything, in short—are laid down, not out of mere arbitrariness, but because, by adopting the best position, there is a gain in power, and other faults are avoided. From this point of view, therefore, the position of the hand becomes of some importance. Now nearly all the older school of coachmen with whom I have talked favour a low position. Nearly twenty years ago, Goodwin, who was for a long time guard on one of the Exeter mails, told me that in his time the coachmen held their hands low. A Devon man named Stone, who was upwards of seventy years of age in 1870, held the same opinion ; and so did the late Paul Collings, of Exeter, who was taught by his father, a coachman on the Exeter and Plymouth road.

Now, if I may venture to express, not an opinion as to which position is to be preferred, but an explanation of directions apparently contradictory, it is this : It is possible that none of those who have given written directions have carefully measured their distances, or been at the pains to note accurately where the hand actually falls when driving. When the upper arm is pressed to the side, it will be found that the joint of the elbow is just over the hip-bone, and consequently at a lower level than either the top of the trousers, the heart, or the watch-pocket, three points which have been mentioned as landmarks for the hand ; and to keep the latter at either one or the other would involve driving with the hand higher than the joint of the elbow—that is to say, the forearm would have to slant upwards from the elbow. Now, I have carefully watched every coachman, amateur and professional, beside whom I have sat, and cannot call to mind one who has driven in this position. In the "Driving" volume of the Badminton Library the Duke of Beaufort tells the reader to keep his hand about the height of the top of his trousers; but in my letter to the *Field* I ventured to point out that on turning to the frontis-piece of the book, a representation of the Duke on the box—and one must assume that the drawing had his Grace's approval—the Duke was not acting up to his written instructions, for the hand is considerably below the top of the trousers; it is lower, indeed, than the joint of the elbow.

Nor, again, have I ever seen a coachman driving with the perfectly straight arm recommended by Colonel Corbett. In the first place, it is not easy to keep the arm straight; and, secondly, if it were kept so, the left hand would be quite out of reach of the right, so that in avoiding other vehicles or turning corners one of two things would have to happen—the coachman would either have to lean forward in order to touch the reins with the right hand, and that would be to fall into an ungraceful attitude, and to indulge in some of those "ungainly clawings" against which the *Sporting Maga-zine* writer protested, or else the left hand must be brought up to where the right hand can reach the reins.

My own idea, in short, is, that though there are two distinct sets of directions—in print—for the position of the left hand, there is really very little difference in practice. Whatever the theory may be, the hand, in practice, is very little above the legs. I have been given to understand that in the old coaching days the driving-seat was more sloping than is now found expedient; consequently it was possible to get the hand lower than is now practicable, if the coachman desired to do so; but, with the present arrangement, the hand, unless it be allowed to drop down outside the left leg, cannot go very low; while, as I said just now, a very little above the leg is the level at which hands find themselves.

This naturally leads on to the question of two-handed driving. Mr. Birch Reynardson and others, whatever may be the meaning of certain passages, would appear to lay down the principle that the right hand should never touch the reins. Modern coachmen are rebuked for pulling up with two hands, and for wanting a second hand to the reins at all. But what is a coachman to do if he find himself behind a strong team? or why, in the event of his having to do a long journey, should he throw all the labour of driving on to one hand, while the other has an idle time? In the afore-mentioned letter to the *Field* I sought to obtain information on this point; but a few answers only were forthcoming, one of them from a gentleman who ridiculed *in toto* the idea of two-handed riding or driving at all, and stated that somewhere abroad he had seen, in a driving competition, coachmen drive six and eight horses, and do sharp turns, with one hand alone to the reins. The fact, however, remains that no one has ever yet seen any coachman drive from Northumberland Avenue to Hyde Park Corner without placing his right hand on the reins; yet, according to some writers, he ought to do so. Pulling the reins out of the left hand with the right, and so using two hands, is of course quite a different matter, as when the right hand is then taken away the coachman finds himself with a lot of slack rein, and his horses at once go away to the left. This is of course altogether wrong, and may possibly be the kind of two-handed driving against which the several authorities protest; but if so, they do not make their meaning quite clear.

Then, again, there is the question of shortening the reins. Probably most people have heard the story of some one asking a coachman how he shortened his reins, and receiving the answer, "Sir, I never shorten them; as I start so I finish." The perfection of driving, truly, but a standard to which some of us can never hope to attain. In practice reins do need shortening, and when one is *out* of practice the occasions are too many in number: how, then, shall the operation be performed? The writers in the Badminton book say, Push them back though the fingers of the left hand; and most of the teachers of to-day tell one the same. But on asking Mr. Millis how it was done in his time, he said, "Why, from behind, of course. Your left hand lay on your knee, and what was easier than to draw back the rein that required shortening? I never saw it done in any other way." Mr. Glover, whose name has already been mentioned, was of the same opinion. I then told Mr. Millis what the present fashion was, whereupon he observed, "Some tailor, I'll be bound, invented that; while you're shortening one rein in front, you'll let the others slip."

After all, *quot homines tot sententiæ* would seem to hold good in driving as in other matters. I have tried to find out something about the development of the coachman's art; but beyond discovering that it did develop, I have been unable to trace to their source the various ways of doing things. The chances are that there never was any universal method of driving. There were, no doubt, certain fundamental principles and some broad rules; but in matters of

detail men no doubt pleased themselves, just as they
do in the manner in which they hold a pen.

And now this, my little coach, is off the road.   In
dealing with a multiplicity of facts of which I have no
personal knowledge, it is possible that I may, with
the clumsiness attributed to modern coachmen, have
turned her over by running against some of Time's
landmarks ; but I hope that she may be held to have
finished her journey right end upwards, and that some
few, at least of the younger generation of coaching
men, may have found this sketch of the old Brighton
road not very unpleasant.

APPENDIX

Page 13.—"Sixteen-String Jack" was hanged at Tyburn. The last execution at Tyburn took place on the 7th November 1783.

Page 13.—Sir John Lade's coachmanship was well known; but in after years Sir Felix Agar accomplished a feat which brought him great renown. He made a bet that he would drive his own four-horses up Grosvenor Place, down the passage into Tattersall's Yard (the famous repository was then at Hyde Park Corner), around the pillar which stood in the centre of it, and back again into Grosvenor Place, without either of his horses going at a slower pace than a trot.

Page 35.—"Children 'in lap' and outside passengers paid half price." In very early times the inside of a coach was the place of honour, whereas to-day no one would dream of going inside if there were room on the roof. De Quincey says that the roof of a coach was by some weak men called the attics or garrets, but was really the drawing-room, in which the box was the chief ottoman or sofa, while the inside, "which had been traditionally regarded as the only room tenantable by gentlemen, was, in fact, the coal-cellar in disguise." The essayist continues: "Great wits jump. The very same idea had not long before struck the celestial intellect of China. Amongst the presents carried out by our first embassy to that country was a state coach. It had been personally selected as a personal gift by George III.; but the exact mode of using it was an intense mystery to Pekin. The ambassador, indeed (Lord Macartney), had made some imperfect explanation upon this point; but, as his Excellency communicated these in a diplomatic whisper, at the very moment of his departure, the celestial intellect was very feebly illuminated, and it became necessary to call a Cabinet Council on the grand state question, 'Where was the Emperor to sit?' The hammer-cloth happened to be unusually gorgeous; and partly on that consideration, but partly also because the box offered the most elevated seat, was

318 APPENDIX

nearest to the moon, and undeniably went foremost, it was resolved by acclamation that the box was the imperial throne, and, for the scoundrel who drove, he might sit where he could find a perch. The horses, therefore, being harnessed, solemnly his imperial majesty ascended his English throne under a flourish of trumpets, having the First Lord of the Treasury on his right hand, and the Chief Jester on his left. Pekin gloried in the spectacle; and in the whole flowery people, consecutively present, there was but one discontented person, and *that* was the coachman. This mutinous individual audaciously shouted, 'Where am I to sit?' But the privy council, incensed by his disloyalty, opened the door, and kicked him into the inside. He had all the inside places to himself; but such is the rapacity of ambition, that he was still dissatisfied. 'I say,' he cried out in an extempore petition, addressed to the Emperor through the window—'I say, how am I to catch hold of the reins?' 'Anyhow,' was the imperial answer; 'don't trouble *me*, man, in my glory. How catch the reins? Why, through the windows, through the keyholes—anyhow.' Finally this contumacious coachman lengthened the check-strings into a sort of jury-reins communicating with the horses, and with these he drove as steadily as Pekin had any right to expect. The Emperor returned after the briefest of circuits; he descended in great pomp from his throne, with the severest resolution never to remount it."

Page 82.—The Four Horse Club was occasionally, though erroneously, called the Whip Club, and the Barouche Club. It was really started as a kind of overflow club, to accommodate those who, for various reasons, could not get elected to the slightly older and very much more select club. There appears to have always been a certain amount of chaff going on in connection with the Four Horse Club. Here, for instance, is an extract from a Brighton paper of 1810: "THE WHIP CLUB.—An inquiry is to be instituted before the next meeting of the Club in order to try a member on various charges, intending to prove him an incorrigible gentleman and no coachman. One of the charges is for blowing his nose in a pocket-handkerchief, instead of wiping it on the sleeve of the box-coat, contrary to the 47th article of the institution. Lord —— has hitherto been looked upon as a most correct disciplinarian; his Lordship has a most shrill, sharp whistle, and can squirt the quid fluid from the corner of his mouth three yards farther than any whip on the road." In later times one or two enthusiastic amateurs had their front teeth filed in imitation of a professional the natural growth of whose teeth so greatly facilitated expectoration.

Page 92. —" Cheap and expeditious travelling" by the Prince Regent coach. This may have been a cheap and at times an expeditious vehicle, but it was not invariably a safe one. It made its first journey on a Sunday; it capsized that day week at Merstham; and a few days later turned over again near Cuckfield, the performance being repeated in less than a week after the second accident.

Page 195.—In connection with fast driving, it may not be out of place to mention that on May Day 1830 the Independent Tally-Ho, in travelling against time, ran from London to Birmingham, a distance of 109 miles, in 7 hours 39 minutes. The following is the correct account of the time it took to perform the distances horsed by the various proprietors : —

Mr. Horne, from London to Colney, $17\frac{1}{4}$ miles, in 1 hour 6 minutes.

Mr. Bowman, from Colney to Redburn, $17\frac{1}{2}$ miles, in 1 hour 26 minutes (6 minutes for breakfast).

Mr. Morrell, Redburn to Hockliffe, $12\frac{1}{4}$ miles, in 1 hour 4 minutes.

Mr. Warden, Hockliffe to Shenley, 11 miles, in 47 minutes.

Mr. May, Shenley to Daventry, 24 miles, in 1 hour 49 minutes.

Mr. Garner, Daventry to Coventry, $19\frac{1}{4}$ miles, in 1 hour 12 minutes; Coventry to Birmingham, $17\frac{3}{4}$ miles, in 1 hour 15 minutes.

The original Tally-Ho performed the same distance in 7 hours 50 minutes.

On May Day 1838 the Shrewsbury Greyhound, with no passengers except a friend or two of the proprietor, accomplished the journey from London at the rate of 12 miles an hour, including stoppages. (From Captain Malet's " Annals of the Road.")

Page 208.—In Letts's " Diary of Events," a useful book written by Mr. Charles Ashton, I find, under July 4th, the following in connection with omnibuses introduced by Shillibeer : " In *Saunders's News Letter* of July 10, 1829, it is stated that on Saturday (the 4th) the new vehicle, called the *Omnibus*, commenced running from Paddington to the City, and excited considerable notice, both from the novel form of the carriage, and the elegance with which it is fitted out. It is capable of accommodating sixteen or eighteen persons, all inside ; and we apprehend it would be almost impossible to make it overturn, owing to the great width of the carriage. It was drawn by three beautiful bays, abreast, after the French fashion. The *Omnibus* is a handsome machine, in the shape of a van, with windows on each side, and one at the end. The width the horses occupy will render the vehicle rather inconvenient to be turned or driven through some of the streets of London."

It was introduced by Mr. Shillibeer, a contractor for funeral equipages, hearses, and carriages, who had been a coach-builder in Paris.

In giving evidence before the Board of Health on the general scheme for extra-mural sepulture, he incidentally mentioned that on the 4th July 1829 he started the first pair of omnibuses in the metropolis, from the Bank to the Yorkshire Stingo, at the Paddington end of the New Road, and that they were copied from those in Paris, where M. Lafitte, the banker, had established them in 1819.

The omnibuses carried twenty-two persons, and the fare to or from the Bank was one shilling, and half the journey was sixpence. As the ride took a long time (for the roads were very bad, and the machine very heavy), for some little time after their first starting light periodical reading was provided for the passengers. The conductors wore velveteen liveries. Omnibuses rapidly became favourites with the public, and were soon multiplied, even the Post-Office adopting them at once; for in an account of the opening of the new building in St. Martin's-le-Grand, 23rd September 1829, is the following: "In the course of the morning four vehicles were stationed within the railings at the back of the post-office, built after the manner of the omnibus. In these the letter-carriers having to deliver letters at the west and north-western parts of the metropolis took their seats about half past eight o'clock, two of the carriages proceeding up the Strand, and the other two up Holborn. There were about fourteen letter-carriers in each."

Page 223.—The Brighton Day-Mail. There were, I believe, no more than three or four places to which a day-mail ran from London, and Brighton was one of them. The Post-Office authorities were influenced by two considerations in putting on day-mails—the place to be served had to be of sufficient size and importance to warrant the authorities in subsidising the coach; and, secondly, the place must not be more than a six or eight hours' journey from London.

Page 248.—The Chequers at Horley. In a Sussex paper the story is told that a commercial traveller once baited his horse there. There was a fresh horse-keeper at work, and in the hurry in getting the change horses ready put the leading harness on the traveller's horse, which went very well in the coach. When the owner of the gig came to start, he found himself with one of the coach leaders, though he did not at that time know it. The horse, as it afterwards turned out, had an objection to single harness, and "flared up" at starting; the commercial traveller drew the whip smartly across it, and the horse bolted, kicked the trap to pieces, and so injured its unlucky occupant that his life was despaired of.

Page 286.—Pomegranate, leader in the Exeter mail when the coach was attacked by a lioness. The event took place on the 20th October 1816. The Exeter mail, when on her way to London, was attacked, at Winterslow Hut, seven miles from Salisbury, by a lioness which had escaped from a travelling menagerie. The lioness was seen to be approaching the coach, and presently sprang at the leaders. These naturally became so restive that the coachman, whose name, I think, was Olliver, had the utmost difficulty in keeping his horses in the road. Two inside passengers, on finding the coach come to a standstill, hurriedly jumped out, and took refuge in a neighbouring cottage. The coachman, who was by no means deficient in courage, proposed to get down and try to kill the lioness with his knife; but the guard very wisely protested against his doing anything of the kind, pointing out that a hand-to-hand conflict with the animal would probably lead to his own death. At a very critical moment one of the menagerie keepers and a couple of mastiffs appeared upon the scene, and, according to one account, a shepherd and his collie also arrived. One of the dogs—it does not clearly appear which—attacked the lioness, who promptly left the horse and turned on the dog. On hearing her keeper's voice, however, she crawled under a granary, where the attendant managed to secure her.

INDEX

Fares in 1838, 225.
—— between Portsmouth and Bath and Bristol, 280.
—— cheap, between Brighton and Southampton, 289.
Farmers aiding smugglers, 257.
Farnham Protector coach, 298.
Fast coach between Brighton, Bath, and Bristol, 289.
—— —— wear and tear of horse flesh in, 308.
—— driving, "Dashwood" on, 178, 179.
Fee system, 136, 137.
"Field, The," Soft Soap's letter to, 310.
First coach on Brighton road after collapse of old coaches, 247.
Fisher (mail-guard), fatal accident to, 230.
Fitzherbert, Mrs., her house, 9; birth and parentage, ib.; her history, 10; first seen by Prince of Wales at Richmond, ib.; her marriage with Prince of Wales, 11; her death, 12.
Fleet (coachman), his dread of accident from badness of Tunbridge Wells road, 272, 273; accidents to, 273; his death, 274.
Fleet Prison, the, 100.
Floods, 81, 156, 262, 281.
Flying Dutchman (train), the, 145.
Flying machine (stage), from Brighton to London, 33.
Flying Scotchman (train), the, 145.
Folding whip, 304.
Forage, contract prices for, in 1893, 97; rise in price of, 61.
Four Horse Driving Club, 82, 302; founded, 247; its break-down, 302.
Foxhounds used for draught, 169.
France, conveyance of mails in, 185.
Freeman, Mr. Stewart, first takes Brighton road, 249; buys his horses instead of contracting, 251.
French Government desire to buy English mail-coaches, 106.
Frosts, 81, 278.

Full hand, driving with a, explained, 303.
Fuller's Lewes and Eastbourne coach, 255.
Furious driving, penalty for, 151, 190, 223.

Galloping, 179.
Gammon, Mr., his Bill for limiting number of outside passengers, 24, 26.
General Stage-Coach Company, 134, 135, 136, 137, 138, 146.
Genn's coaches managed by Newman, 123; his coaches in 1821, 124.
"Gentleman's Magazine" and Brighton, 2.
"Gentlemen coachmen," 81, 245; "Nimrod" on, 201.
Gentry, the, aiding smugglers, 257.
George III. visits Weymouth, 10.
George and Blue Boar, coaches from, 130; its accommodation, 131; to be let, ib.
German coaches, 149.
German Legion, 81.
Gig-horse, frightened by steam-coach, 186.
"Gin and bitters," the drink of coachmen in last century, 48.
Glasgow, coaches to, from London, 132.
Gloucester mail put on, 290.
"God permits," meaning of, 41.
Going down-hill with short wheel-rein, 302, 303.
Good coachmen, do they depend upon bad roads? 309.
Goodman and Marquis of Worcester, 190.
Great Western Railway, 299.
Green peas, price of, in 1814, 94.
Gronow, Captain, on Prince of Wales (George IV.), 15.
Growth of coachmanship, 300 et seq.
Guards seldom carried by old coaches, 53; not carried by ordinary coaches, 163; mail-coach, salaries of, raised, 238.

Y

THE END

PRINTED BY BALLANTYNE, HANSON, AND CO.
EDINBURGH AND LONDON.

Lightning Source UK Ltd.
Milton Keynes UK
176598UK00001B/132/P